AWAKE, O CHRISTIANS, and SERVE THE LORD IN TRUTH

Vol. III

Marriage and the Family

SECOND EDITION

Joseph N. Mfonyam

Uriel Press

Copyright © 2024 Joseph N. Mfonyam.

All rights reserved. No part of this book may be used or reproduced by any means, graphic, electronic, or mechanical, including photocopying, recording, taping or by any information storage retrieval system without the written permission of the author except in the case of brief quotations embodied in critical articles and reviews.

Uriel Press books may be ordered through booksellers or by contacting:

Uriel Press
1663 Liberty Drive
Bloomington, IN 47403
www.urielpress.com
844-752-3114

Because of the dynamic nature of the Internet, any web addresses or links contained in this book may have changed since publication and may no longer be valid. The views expressed in this work are solely those of the author and do not necessarily reflect the views of the publisher, and the publisher hereby disclaims any responsibility for them.

Any people depicted in stock imagery provided by Getty Images are models, and such images are being used for illustrative purposes only. Certain stock imagery © Getty Images.

The Holy Bible, English Standard Version. ESV® Text Edition: 2016. Copyright © 2001 by Crossway Bibles, a publishing ministry of Good News Publishers.

ISBN: 979-8-8861-2031-8 (sc)
ISBN: 979-8-8861-2032-5 (hc)
ISBN: 979-8-8861-2033-2 (e)

Library of Congress Control Number: 2024905667

Print information available on the last page.

Uriel Press rev. date: 10/25/2024

This book is dedicated to God the Father and to Jesus Christ, the Son, the Bridegroom of the Church, His bride.

Now to him who is able to keep you from stumbling and to present you blameless before the presence of his glory with great joy, to the only God, our Saviour, through Jesus Christ our Lord, be glory, majesty, dominion, and authority, before all time and now and forever. Amen. —Jude 1:24–25

WHAT PEOPLE SAY ABOUT THIS BOOK

The author, in this treatise, touches on almost all the issues connected with marriage and the family in a fascinating and challenging way. He goes deep in describing what marriage and the family mean theologically and practically. First he looks at the institution of marriage and the family in the Creation story, and then he looks at marriage and family in ancient Israel and in the traditional society of Bafut in the Northwest Region of Cameroon. He brings out what God had put in these communities to testify to His revelation in their culture. From his comparisons and contrasts, one is reminded that there is a lot in our traditional cultures to enable us know God and to make Him known to the world (Acts 17:26–28).

God revealed His whole purpose for creating mankind right at the beginning of the Creation story. In creating them male and female, (man and woman) (Genesis 1:27), His purpose included marriage, a union in matrimony. The author makes the point very succinctly that God's mission for the world and purpose for creating a man and a woman are effectively carried out when the man and the woman enjoy their unity and work in unity with their Creator and with each other. Marriage thus becomes the ideal context where the mission of God begins and is effectively carried out. It is in this light that the family is the foundation of both the church and the society. A good marriage, one that has its foundation in the Lord, gives hope for a just society and a better world.

Joseph Mfonyam, in the treatment of marriage and the family, points out what God teaches about the role of each member of the family. He brings out the virtues that make marriage and the family to be bonded together and functional. Today we have many dysfunctional families, and the rate of divorce in the world, and even in the church, is alarming. Reading and applying the message, truths, and virtues in this book on marriage and the family should help couples and families to begin enjoying their lives together, growing stronger and becoming more passionate in fulfilling the mission of God in this world. This book is a must-read for Christians, as well as marriage and family therapists.

Rev Dr Donald Ndichafah,
Executive President (Emeritus)
General Secretary, Cameroon Baptist Convention
Chair of Theological & Christian Board,
Associate General Secretary of All Africa Baptist Fellowship
Lecturer, International Leadership University–Yaounde,
Executive Director of Hope Services Group Ltd.
Conference Speaker

Mrs Esther Ndichafah, CEO of Hope Services
Marriage Counsellor
Conference Speaker

Our God is love, and He is full of grace and mercy to show us what that love truly means. One of the clearest pictures of His love is seen through godly marriage and Christian families. This book is a study of Christian marriage as seen through different cultural lenses. It is a signpost pointing us back to the truth of the Bible and forward to the joy of the Marriage of the Lamb. The book is a timely word for all believers.

Mrs Elizabeth Roettele
Teacher and Literacy Coordinator
SIL, Cameroon

Ever since Eve sinned and Adam implicitly faulted God for giving her to him, marriage has been under attack. It is clear that Satan attacks marriage because it, as instituted by God, bears witness to his own nature.

This book's author explains, among other things

- how our commitment in love and faithfulness to our spouses and our children should be like God's commitment to us;
- –how we are to honour and love every family member just as our Heavenly Father; his Son, Jesus Christ; and the Holy Spirit honour and love one another; and
- –how our loved ones are to draw strength and direction from God through our mutual family life.

It is striking that among the world's major religions, one has the dominant metaphor of slavery, another has the dominant metaphor of nothingness, and in a third its devotees strive to lose their own selfhood in what they regard as the great universal "Oneness."

Only those who worship the God and Father of our Lord Jesus Christ experience the dominant spiritual theme of family. Rather than losing our independence to slavery that grinds us down, or to nothingness in which we become lost, or to "Oneness" that obliterates our own individuality, we, the followers of Christ, experience in him the fulfilment of all that he means each of us to be. That is what this book is about.

James N. Pohlig
PhD in Biblical Languages, University of Stellenbosch
Adjunct Professor at Wingate University (retired)
Adjunct Professor at the University of South Carolina at Lancaster in Religion and Philosophy (retired)
Author of *Introduction to Biblical Themes in Cultural Context* (Cognella, 2020).

Marriage and the family constitute the nucleus of society, and the author has addressed the subject very adequately. In doing so, he has communicated in a language that is accessible to all readers.

The practical examples from the Bible and from contemporary society give credence to the subject and prove that the matter is real and current. With what we experience today, marriages are severely threatened. This book is therefore a wake-up call which must not be taken lightly.

We strongly recommend this work to both the married and the unmarried. It promises to be a reference source that will benefit many by rescuing some current and future marriages from collapse. God is indeed at the centre of any successful marriage and any truly thriving society. We can testify this from practical experience.

Very Rev. Dr Festus
Moderator Emeritus, Presbyterian Church in Cameroon
Marriage Counsellor

Mrs Jenny Asana
Teacher and Educator
Marriage Counsellor

Dr Mfonyam's new book is a wonderful resource to understand the Bible's teaching on marriage and the family. He clearly presents God's creative structure and intention for marriage, family roles, and relationships. The book effectively compares marriage in ancient Israel with his Bafut (Cameroon) tradition. He notes some similarities in marriage and family practices in these communities, showing how God's purposes have been revealed even in pagan cultures. Dr Mfonyam clearly explains that marriage is central to God's creation structure and redemptive plan for people on earth. Also, when marriage practices differ from God's intention, social chaos will result. The book comprehensively explains how human marriage is a symbol of the marriage of Jesus Christ with His redeemed company of believers and followers, the church. Dr Mfonyam emphasizes the importance of God's agape love being expressed in marriage and family relationships. He gives practical examples for parents on the training of children in biblical knowledge and faith. He shares the ways his own family has applied biblical teaching. There is a touching testimony near the book's end from his daughter and son-in-law. The book includes a detailed table of contents and study questions and notes for use with readers and groups. I highly recommend this book to church leaders and counsellors as a helpful resource for their ministry and teaching. God has used this book personally to help me review and evaluate my own marriage and parenting, for which I am thankful.

Rev. Philip H. Muir
Retired Pastor and Missionary
Conference Speaker
Marriage Counsellor

I totally endorse this book as an important contribution to the realm of knowledge, and particularly the knowledge of God and His will for mankind and the knowledge of His purposes regarding Marriage and the family.

Prof Paul Nkwi
Former Deputy Vice Chancellor of Academic Affairs,
Catholic University of Bamenda
Member of the Constitutional Council of Cameroon

This book, *Marriage and the Family,* is a comprehensive, fundamental biblical classic on marital processes and the marriage life, written from a culturally sensitive worldview, by a married intellectual African. Dr Mfonyam is a servant of God who has lived and experienced in depth the joys and difficulties of marriage in our local setting for scores of years. The book is a concise and compact teaching, and at the same time a panoramic view on marriage processes, the life in a marital home, the responsibilities of the actors, and the dangers of not adhering to divine principles. It is highly recommendable, first of all, for those who desire to know God's requirements for a fulfilling marriage, and, secondly, for institutes of theological training and marriage counselling. This book breaks the paradigm of non-contextualized, culturally insensitive writings from non-African backgrounds.

Marriage and the Family is biblically sound and gives elaborate and good contemporary illustrations and testimonies, which are culturally relevant and well researched, giving us a flare of living a fulfilled marital life within our African environment. It comes with the experience of a Christian who has lived a successful marital relationship, given his children into marriage, and experienced grandparenthood. He is more than worth the content and teaching in this book, from which I believe all its readers would benefit.

Dr Mfonyam has given us a wealth of divine family recipes for a successful family life, and graceful warnings against marriage failure, including divorce, polygamy, and postmodernist threats. Read it, digest it, and live it for your good.

Rev. SHU Daniel, MD
University Professor of Leadership
Marriage Counsellor
President and Founder of LEAD Higher Institute, Yaounde, Cameroon

This book is a work that, as a matter of fact, touches on many issues of marriage and the family. It takes a straightforward approach of tackling the journey of coming together in marriage and creating a family. It makes a study of the questions raised in marriage life and the family, and insightfully digs deep into the Word of God to offer answers to the questions that are raised, and goes further to propose practical guidelines for applying the lessons learnt. Truly, this book is not only a roadmap for the married or families; it is also a beacon beckoning all those aspiring to this state. The book is a beacon of hope in a time of troubled marriages. Joe, as I affectionately call him, does not simply pass on theory and principles on the subject of marriage and family; he is an example in this enterprise, for he admirably succeeds in this life with his wife, Reverend Becky Mfonyam. It is in this respect that he provides us a model of marriage and the family—one which is real, one that braves all the odds of these two fundamental God-given institutions and rejoices in the blessings therein. This is a book to be read regularly as a model for churches and schools alike. I strongly recommend the reading of this work and, of course, putting into practice the recipe that emerges from it.

Rev Dr Jean Libom Li Likeng
President of the Cameroon National Prayer Breakfast
President of the Alliance of Evangelicals of Cameroon
Vice President of the Association of Evangelicals in Africa

This book on marriage is worth reading because it offers practical advice that all of us, even the more experienced couples, can find useful. Marriage is not an event or a ceremony; it is an experience to be lived and nurtured as a process. Marriage is not something you find; it is something you make and keep making. A happy marriage begins when we marry the one we love but blossoms and endures when we love the one we marry. And that is the secret! For the rest of the time, the love for the one we marry will determine how long that marriage lasts. It will enable us to go through all of the challenges and difficulties we face with determination and optimism.

Professor Beban Sammy Chumbow
Emeritus Professor, University of Yaounde 1
Pro Chancellor University of Bamenda
President Cameroon Academy of Sciences
President of the Assembly of Academicians, African Academy of Languages (ACALAN - African Union) ICT University USA, Cameroon Campus

Then God said, "Let us make man in our image, after our likeness. And let them have dominion over the fish of the sea and over the birds of the heavens and over the livestock and over all the earth and over every creeping thing that creeps on the earth." (Gen 1:26)

Therefore a man shall leave his father and his mother and hold fast to his wife, and they shall become one flesh. (Gen 2:24)

And God blessed them. And God said to them, "Be fruitful and multiply and fill the earth and subdue it, and have dominion over the fish of the sea and over the birds of the heavens and over every living thing that moves on the earth."

And God said to Abraham, "As for Sarai your wife I will bless her, and moreover, I will give you a son by her. I will bless her, and she shall become nations; kings of peoples shall come from her." (Gen 17:15–16)

This mystery is profound, and I am saying that it refers to Christ and the church. (Eph 5:32)

Husbands, love your wives, as Christ loved the church and gave himself up for her, that he might sanctify her, having cleansed her by the washing of water with the word, so that he might present the church to himself in splendour, without spot or wrinkle or any such thing, that she might be holy and without blemish (Eph 5:25–27)

And you, who once were alienated and hostile in mind, doing evil deeds, he has now reconciled in his body of flesh by his death, in order to present you holy and blameless and above reproach before him. (Col 1:21–22)

Let us rejoice and exult and give him the glory, for the marriage of the Lamb has come, and his Bride has made herself ready; it was granted her to clothe herself with fine linen, bright and pure." (Rev 19:7–8)

CONTENTS

What People Say about This Book	vii
Foreword	xxi
Acknowledgements	xxv
Introduction	xxvii

1. Divine Institution — 1
   1.1. God's Purpose for Man in Creation — 1
   1.2. The Nature and Character of Man — 2
   1.3. Blessing in Creation — 4
   1.4. The Need to be Equipped — 12
   1.5. Man and the Woman Made One — 18
   1.6. It Is Not Good for the Man to Be Alone — 22
   1.7. One Flesh — 25
   1.8. Marriage as a Covenant — 27
   1.9. Marriage and the Mission of God — 28
      1.9.1. The Regal Aspect of Man's Duties — 30
      1.9.2. The Priestly Duties of Man — 39
   1.10. Blessed to be Fruitful — 56

2. Marriage in Ancient Israel — 61
   2.1. Marriage within the Group — 61
   2.2. Intermarriage — 62
   2.3. The Importance of Having an Heir — 69
   2.4. Virgin and Virginity — 71
   2.5. Betrothal — 75
      2.5.1. Engagement — 75
      2.5.2. Bride Price — 76
      2.5.3. Dowry — 77
      2.5.4. The Betrothed of God — 78
   2.6. Marriage Arrangement — 78

	2.7. Marriage Ceremony, Rite, and Consummation	79
	2.8. Forms of Marriage	82
	2.8.1. Monogamy and Polygamy	82
	2.8.2. Levirate Marriage	83
	2.8.3. Celibacy	84
	2.9. Roles and Relationships in the Family	89
	2.9.1. The Husband	89
	2.9.2. The Father	90
	2.9.3. The Woman	96
	2.9.4. Parents	98
	2.9.5. Children	103
	2.10. Divorce	104
3.	**Bafut Traditional Marriage**	**110**
	3.1. Definition of Terms (yɔ'ɔ̂/nìyɔ̀'ɔ̂, sà'â/nìsà'â)	111
	3.2. The Betrothal (ŋ̀kòsə màŋgyè)	112
	3.3. Soft Wine (mìlù'ù mî bɔrə̀)	113
	3.4. Big Wine (mìlù'ù mî wè)	114
	3.5. Duties of the Young Man to His Father-in-Law	115
	3.5.1. Clearing the Farm (m̀bù'û ǹsòo ighòrə̀)	115
	3.5.2. Splitting Wood (ǹsàâ ŋ̀kwee ighòrə̀)	115
	3.5.3. Roofing Grass (bwii ighòrə̀)	115
	3.6. Sauces and Food for the Women (ǹnù'û ǹjyà)	116
	3.6.1. First Marriage Sauce	
	(ǹnù'û ǹjyǎ atu yì m̀bɔrə̀)	116
	3.6.2. Oil of Mothers-in-Law	
	(mìghurə mi nswoŋ bìnɔ̂ ŋsə̀)	116
	3.7. The Marriage Sauce (ǹnù'û ǹjyà yî ŋwè[ǹjya nìyɔ'ɔ̂])	117
	3.8. The Marriage (nìyɔ'ɔ̂)	118
	3.8.1. Solemnization of the Marriage	118
	3.8.2. Bridal Procession	119
	3.9. Form of Marriage	121
	3.10. Roles and Relationships in the Family	121
	3.10.1. Father	121
	3.10.2. Wife and Mother	122
	3.10.3. Children	122
	3.11. The Need to Have Children	122

		3.11.1. Boys and Girls	123
		3.11.2. The Need to Have a Boy	123
	3.12.	Levirate Marriage	123
	3.13.	Divorce (*ǹsà'â nìyɔ'ɔ̀*)	124

4. **Ancient Israel and Traditional Bafut Marriage: Cultural and Religious Import** — **126**
   - 4.1. Similarities and Differences — 126
   - 4.2. Redemptive Analogies — 127
     - 4.2.1. The Family — 127
   - 4.3. Husband, Betrothed, Wife, Bridegroom, and Bride — 134
     - 4.3.1. Yahweh, the Bridegroom and Husband — 135
     - 4.3.2. Jesus Christ, the Bridegroom — 136
   - 4.4. Virtues — 143
     - 4.4.1. Purity — 143
     - 4.4.2. Love, Obedience, and Trust — 144
     - 4.4.3. Love Means Caring for One Another — 147
     - 4.4.4. Erotic Love — 148
   - 4.5. Authority, Submission, and Head — 152
   - 4.6. Unity — 152
   - 4.7. Light — 153
     - 4.7.1. God Is Light — 155
     - 4.7.2. Jesus Is Light — 157
     - 4.7.3. The Word of God Is Light — 160
     - 4.7.4. Believers Are Light — 161
   - 4.8. Oil and Anointing — 162
     - 4.8.1. Functions of Oil — 164
     - 4.8.2. Anointing of the First Kings of Israel — 165
     - 4.8.3. Anointing of the Monarch of the United Kingdom — 180
     - 4.8.4. The Anointing of Queen Elizabeth II — 186
     - 4.8.5. The Anointing of King Charles III — 193
     - 4.8.6. Biblical Symbolism of Anointing, Kingship, and Servanthood — 206
   - 4.9. Summary — 211
   - 4.10. Marriage and the Family in Salvation History — 213

  4.10.1. Symbolism and the Import of the
     Familial Terms   214
  4.10.2. The Family of God   225
  4.10.3. Marriage and the Family and God's Purposes 226
  4.10.4. The Family Line of Jesus Christ the Saviour 227
  4.10.5. Priesthood and the Family   228
  4.10.6. God's Revelation as King: Ancient
     Israel and Traditional Bafut   246

5. Marriage in the New Testament   251
 5.1. Foundation of Marriage and Family in the
    New Testament   251
 5.2. The Family of Jesus   253
   5.2.1. The Birth of Jesus   254
   5.2.2. The Siblings of Jesus   257
   5.2.3. The Family in the New Testament 259
 5.3. Reaffirmation and Consolidation of Marriage
    and the Family   263
   5.3.1. Jesus' Affirmation   263
   5.3.2. Paul's Affirmation   264
 5.4. Roles and Relations in Marriage and the Family 284
   5.4.1. Husband and Wife   286
   5.4.2. Parents and Children   302
   5.4.3. Marriage Boundaries   317
 5.5. The Corporate Family   324
   5.5.1. Becoming Members   324
   5.5.2. Working as a Family   324
   5.5.3. The Role of the CEO and the
      Leadership Team   326

Conclusion   329
Appendix I   331
Appendix II: Testimonies   335
Study Questions and Notes   343
References   355
About the Author   359

FOREWORD

Awake, O Christians, and Serve the Lord in Truth, vol. III, is a masterpiece of biblical and pastoral reflection on Marriage and Family in the Bible and in the Bafut culture. It shows a broad and deep knowledge of the biblical texts on the subject. This is the fruit of many years of the translation of the Bible into various languages and of the constant reading, meditation on, and praying of the Word of God. Mfonyam cites frequently, freely, and profusely from both the Old and New Testaments and applies the texts with dexterity to life situations. It is amazing how he brings together and applies texts from different contexts both from the Old and New Testaments to the events of modern history, such as the recent coronation of King Charles of England, to serve his purpose. This is because, as he says, "Marriage and the family are the institutions and frames best suited for the mission of God on earth. God created man and woman in his image, so that they would effectively carry out His purposes for mankind."

The author has a good mastery of the Bafut tradition and culture concerning marriage and family. He has succeeded in bringing out the similarities and differences between the biblical understanding of marriage and the Bafut traditional understanding of marriage and family, without falling prey to the generalizations which are often made by some authors. He has avoided this trap by the introduction of what he calls "Redemptive analogies," highlighting "those values and symbols in Bafut culture and traditional religion (BTR) that God has placed there as redemptive analogies. These are concepts in the tradition and customs of the people that serve as beachheads for the gospel, the good news of salvation." In this regard, the Second Vatican Council, in the Decree on Non-Christian Religions (Nostra Aetate, n. 2), says that nothing of what is true and holy in non-Christian religions should be rejected. On the contrary, we should have high regard for the manner of life and conduct, the precepts, and the doctrines which, although differing in many ways from the Christian teaching, often reflect a ray of that truth which enlightens all men and women.

God's blessing on marriage begins with the family. God blessed the couple and said, "Be fruitful and multiply and fill the earth." This in and of itself is a profound theological statement which can be ignored, abused, or distorted to violate God's design in marriage and the family, as we see in the world today. Marriage and the family, as treated in this book, are all-inclusive, because whether you are married or not, you have a family. The family is where our identities begin and get grounded. The family begins with God, and our true identity is in God, through our Saviour Jesus Christ. The author clearly brings out the blessings and obligations that are ours when we are adopted into God's family. We have an inheritance, which is the kingdom of God. And mysteriously, God Himself is our inheritance, and we are His inheritance. Both marriage and the family are God's revealed mysteries into which the author has delved deep to reveal their hidden meanings. The family of God, the family of Christ, the priestly family, the royal family, the corporate family—these are manifestations of the family motif that the author treats to bring out clearly their implications in the design of God concerning humans and their lives in the mission of God. The world will be a better place if the concept of the family is rightly understood, owned and appropriately applied. Marriage is also all-inclusive in that it begins in Eden and ends in heaven with the marriage of the Lamb, the Bridegroom of the church. Both the married and the celibate, by design or vocation, find their fulfilment in Christ, their Bridegroom, and this bridges the gap between the married and celibate. By making us see marriage and celibacy from the biblical perspective, Mfonyam brings out the blessings of both states and highlights the special blessings of those called to be single, as well as those who have been called for the sake of the gospel of Christ to take the vow of celibacy. The author, a practical theologian, carefully makes us see not only the family and marriage but also the Christian life from the perspective of practice (i.e., experientially).

This book is a timely publication. In the present society, marriage and the family are increasingly under attack by anti-life philosophies and are going through a lot of challenges. There is an urgent need to reaffirm the traditional and orthodox Christian concept of marriage and family, which has its foundation on natural and divine law. This book gives a wide spectrum of the different ways in which the Sacred Scriptures—that is, the inspired Word of God—can be applied to almost every situation of marriage and the family life. As the apostle Paul puts it, "All Scripture is inspired by God and can profitably be used for teaching, for refuting error, for guiding people's lives and teaching them to be holy" (2 Tim 3:16). I highly recommend *Awake, O Christians, and Serve the Lord in Truth*, vol. III, to everyone who wants to know why God created the human person, male and female, in his own image. I recommend it, in particular, to every family, to pastors, to youth and marriage counsellors, and also to seminaries and Bible institutes.

Cornelius Fontem Esua
Archbishop Emeritus of Bamenda

ACKNOWLEDGEMENTS

Many people contributed to the making of this book. I am very grateful to Mr Matthew Lee, who helped me in formatting the book, making it presentable and easy to read. I am very thankful for his willingness to take time out of his busy schedule to answer my questions. Mr Chenwi Tamando Mfonyam designed the cover of the book and and also helped in formatting it. I am very grateful to him for the many hours he put into designing the cover, working sometimes into the wee hours of the morning. I want specially to thank Dr Z. F. Ntumngia, whom I consulted when I was writing the chapter on Bafut traditional marriage customs and rites. He went through the whole process when he married.

Mrs Elizabeth Roettele took time to read and edit the manuscript of this book. I am very grateful for the many hours she spent reading, correcting, and making useful comments. Sr Rosmarie Hilfiker and Miss Rachel Robinson encouraged and supported me in various ways while I wrote this book. They read sections of the book and made helpful comments, for which I am very grateful.

I am thankful to God for Ruth and Val Exis, who gave me the occasion to write this book on marriage and the family. It was when we were planning the blessing of their marriage that I decided to write it. I appreciate the fact that they agreed to write out their testimonies, which are included in the appendix of the book. I am grateful to God who has given us, my wife, Becky, and me, a very loving, caring and understanding family. I am grateful that Becky was at home with the children when they were growing, taking care of them when I often travelled for work. As a family, we have had our struggles and joys, which have enabled me to write this book from a practical perspective.

I am thankful to my faithful supporters and prayer partners, who prayed me through this book. Without their prayers and support I wouldn't have been able to write and finish it.

I am, most of all, thankful to God, the giver of all wisdom and understanding, the God of all creation, who inspired me and gave me the stamina to write this book. I praise Him for creating both the man and woman, instituting, right from the beginning, both marriage and the family. I pray that He will bless this book and use it to His glory. To Him be glory and honour forever and ever.

INTRODUCTION

This book is the third in the series of the Awake books. The Awake series is meant to address practical needs of the church, allowing the Scriptures to speak anew to the heart and arouse Christians to wake up and serve the Lord in truth as the Spirit moves in a new way in the life of the church. The first in the series was *Awake O Christians and Serve the Lord in Truth*. The second was *Awake O Christians and Serve the Lord in Truth*, vol. II: *Teacher's Manual*. These two books are linked although they can be read independently; but it will be good to read the first before the second because the teaching tool uses the first volume in the application part.

This is the second edition of *Marriage and the Family*. This edition has been expanded, and I have elaborated on the core truths of the first edition, making clearer some of the points that were not so clear and highlighting some of the values concerning marriage and family life, showing how these tie in with the purposes of God and His mission.

The book has as its primary aim to address the purposes of God in creation with regard to marriage and the family. What is the purpose of marriage, as we can read in the Creation story narrated in the first three chapters of Genesis? What is the true picture of marriage? The foundation of marriage is found in this narrative. Allender and Longman III (1995:13) underline this for us:

> The first three chapters of Genesis provide the picture [of marriage]. They offer not only a perspective on the problem but also the cure. If I want to know God's design for my marriage, I must begin at the ground floor of the Bible to understand the foundational perspectives that guide my passage through life.

Why did God make Adam and Eve? What is the purpose of man's life? This book has been written to remind us of what our purpose in life is. It is our prayer that we discover the will of God concerning our lives as we read the pages of this book. It is important for the believer to discover the will of God for his or her life. The will of God for our lives is within the covers of the Bible. God has also revealed His will in nature, in all of His creation. This being the case, our duty should be to discover it. Most of the time, it is not the case that we do not know the will of God. His general will is no matter of speculation. Micah, the prophet, emphatically tells us that God has revealed it to us:

> He has told you, O man, what is good; what the LORD requires of you. (Mic 6:8)

Given this, our prayer should be that He guide us into doing His will. However, there may be times when His will, in specific situations, is not clear, and so we are confused. In such a case, this should be the time to pray more and to listen, for He has promised that even when we are at a crossroads, He will be there to help us choose the right path (Isa 30:21; Ps 32:8). The Lord does not only teach us His will and His way; He also makes us willing and able to do what He wants (Phil2:13). The whole purpose of the family prayer which Jesus taught His disciples was to guide them and us into the Father's will so that in the end it will be done on earth as it is in heaven to His glory. And God, being the good Shepherd that He is, will always be there to lead us in paths of righteousness (Ps 23:1–3).

The will of God for our lives should be a moment-by-moment and day-by-day experience. This calls for an open ear and a total surrender of ourselves and our wills to Him. This means offering our lives to God so that He will mould us, enabling us to do what is acceptable and pleasing to Him. And all this boils down to what Paul calls the "good, acceptable, and perfect will" of God for our lives (Rom 12:1–2). To put this in other words, We need to place all that is happening in our lives, what we feel or do, into the hands of our wise and loving Father, who weaves all together into a redemptive whole, a tapestry that will in the end be good and beautiful to behold, and, above all, pleasing to Him. The end result is that we become vessels of glory, wonderfully made to display His glory. And at this point it will be in our nature to glorify the Lord in all we do, as Paul exhorts the believers in Corinth and Colossae to do (1 Cor 10:31; Col 3:17). The will of God is, in effect, a way of life. And what Gerald Sittser (2000:29) says in the following quote affirms it:

> It deals with our motives as well as our actions. It focuses on the little decisions we make every day even more than the big decisions we make about the future. The only time we really have to know and do God's will is the *present moment.*

Discovering the will of God for our lives is so important that Paul exhorts believers to be mindful of this:

> Do not be foolish, but understand what the will of the Lord is. (Eph 5:17).

God equips and empowers us in order to do His will (Heb 13:20–21).

While it is clear that the will of God is found within the pages of the Bible—that is, the inspired and authoritative Word of God—it is not always clear what it is in some circumstances. In this situation we learn it by experience as we move forward in faith and love. And so when it comes to making choices in the grey areas, God will guide us and show us the way to go, as we read in Isaiah 30:21. We will be encouraged and happy when in the end we discover that what we chose to do was inspired and guided by the Holy Spirit. Jennifer Benson Schuldt (20:23) describes the process of getting to know the perfect will of God in terms of the transforming work of the Spirit in our lives as He transforms our minds to conform to His character, thus enabling us to know His will (Rom 12:2). She writes,

> As we allow the Holy Spirit to uncouple us from the world and its ways, our thoughts and attitudes begin to change. We become more loving, more

hopeful, and filled with inner peace. Although this transformation process is ongoing, and often has more stops and starts than a train ride, the process helps us understand what God wants for our lives. It takes us to a place where we "will learn to know God's will." Learning his will may or may not involve specifics, but it always involves aligning ourselves with His character and His work in the world.

God wants the family to be the cradle and veritable vehicle of His will, fulfilling His purposes in everything "for His good pleasure." The sum of God's will for us all is that we know Him and be saved and bring others to discover the good news of our salvation, which is the Word of Truth, and proclaim it. This is the ultimate purpose of this book. The family, the basic unit of Christ's body, the church, should be the embodiment of the whole counsel of God. Jesus came to reveal God the Father, and His Word, which contains His will for us. He summarized the will of God in the two love commands: to love God wholeheartedly and to love one another as we love ourselves (Luke 10:27). Paul echoes this in his epistles (Rom 13:8; Gal 5:14). These two commands are best learned and exercised in marriage and the family. Gary Thomas (2000:40) puts it this way:

> Marriage can be the gym in which our capacity to experience and express God's love is strengthened and further developed.

It is my hope that through this study of marriage and the family, all members of families, parents and children, will grow to love God, themselves, and others more. Gary Thomas (2000:13) further says that the purpose of marriage is "to equip you to love your God more and to help you reflect the character of His Son more precisely."

Jesus tells us very clearly in the gospels what the purpose of God for His life is. What He did and said underpinned the truth that He came not to do His own will but the will of the Father. He came to serve and to give His life in order to redeem the lost and give them abundant life, making sure that none is lost but that all who come to Him would be raised to glory to be with Him and the Father in the end-time resurrection (John 6:37–39; 10:10; Mark 10:45). And Paul tells us that even at the time we are saved, while still here on earth, we are raised to sit with the Father in Christ in heaven above and that when Christ returns, we shall appear with Him in glory (Eph 2:5–6; Col 3:1, 3–4). The will of God for Jesus Christ, His purpose for sending Him on earth, runs through the Bible, in all of Scripture from Genesis to Revelation (Gen 3:15; Ps 40:8–10; Is 53; Heb 10:4–7; Rev 5:10, 12).

Love is the cardinal virtue, for it is the very nature of God. St John, who experienced the love of God personally through Christ, later writes,"God is love" and He "so loved the world" that He gave Jesus to show us the ultimate and sacrificial love on the cross. And finally and emphatically, he challenges us:

> See what kind of love the Father has given to us, that we should be called children of God. (1 John 3:1)

And as Paul says, the love of Christ, in all its dimensions, is unfathomable (Eph 3:17–19).

Given the importance of love in life, both in relating to God and to one another, I have paid particular attention to the concept of love, as viewed first in ancient Israel, then in Bafut traditional society, and finally in Scripture. God's command, which is also His ultimate will for us, is summarized in the one word "love." Christ's command to us is to love one another as He loved His disciples. And this in turn is based on the fact that He loved the same way that God the Father loved. And James comes to characterize the second great commandment as 'the royal law' (i.e., the law of the kingdom [James 2:8]). Obeying God's commandments means loving God and loving one another (John 13:34; 15:12). So if God's commandments are rightly understood and followed, they will bring believers great joy and freedom and so will no longer be a burden. The Bible says that love is a fulfilment of the law (Rom 13:9).

Paul exhorted husbands to love their wives as Christ loved the church and gave His life for her. As the Scriptures teach us, the duty of parents is to bring up their children in the Lord such that they will love and fear Him. And in this way, the family will love the Lord wholeheartedly and serve Him passionately and sacrificially, just as Christ and Paul did. The soul and heartbeat of every member of the family should be like that which moved Paul, who, in his testimony to the elders of Ephesus, said,

> I did not shrink from declaring to you the whole counsel of God. I do not account my life of any value nor as precious to myself, if only I may finish my course and the ministry that I received from the Lord Jesus, to testify to the gospel of the grace of God. (Acts 20:27, 24)

Paul, following the example of our Lord and Master Jesus Christ, lived passionately and sacrificially, and was prepared to pay the ultimate price. This is what makes the difference in the world. If we want to make a difference in the world, if we want to transform the world, this should be our aim in life. We must be prepared to suffer and even die, just as Christ and the early apostles did. Paul brings this out as a challenge to us, the children of God:

> Therefore be imitators of God, as beloved children.
> And walk in love, as Christ loved us and gave himself up for us, a fragrant offering and sacrifice to God.
> (Eph 5:1–2)

Brother Andrew, founder of Open Door Ministries, has said that we are not able to make inroads into the Muslim world, and evidently into the hardened world at large, because we are not willing to pay the ultimate price.

Bringing up our children to know God and to passionately carry out the purposes of God is the best way to make sure that the message and mission of God is passed down from one generation to the next. So if a godly father wants to leave a God-fearing legacy to his children, his last word to his children should echo the charge of King David to Solomon his son:

> My son, know the God of your father and serve
> him with a whole heart and with a willing mind.
> (1 Chron 28:9)

And it is encouraging to see that Isaac Watts' father gave his son a similar charge:

> Keep perpetually in mind that God is our Creator,
> and serve him with a willing mind.

And because of the godly guidance and influence of Isaac senior on his son, Isaac Watts was inspired to serve God faithfully by doing what he knew how to do very well through the inspiration of God: he wrote hundreds of hymns, some of which we still love to sing today—for example, "O God Our Help in Ages Past" and "Joy to the World." Isaac Watts' songs had such a spiritual impact that he was called the "Father of English hymns."

The powerful impact of a good legacy is depicted in a country music song by Randy Travis—"Three Wooden Crosses." In the song, Travis says that what one leaves behind at death is of utmost importance: the blood-stained Bible that a faithful preacher left with a prostitute who was in the same accident that killed him and two of his companions led to the conversion of the woman and her son. The son of this woman became a pastor and gave a testimony of the legacy of the preacher, showing the blood-stained Bible to his congregation.

Given the impact that a godly family can make in the world, I have therefore sought to show that the redemptive plan of God is carried out through the family, as we see it in the Bible from Genesis to Revelation. The motif of family runs throughout the Scriptures.

Abraham and his family line and the line of King David stand out in Scriptures as chosen by God to carry out His redemptive plan, the plan of salvation. Kings, kingship, and kingdom are highlighted in the history of salvation. Kings, kingdoms, and anointing are symbols that foreshadow the promised Messiah-King, His person (nature and character), and His mission as the suffering Servant and sin-bearer (equipped for service, serving the people and ministering to God the Father). The Messiah is literally the anointed one of God.

Right at the time when God made His covenant with Abraham, He said, "I will make you into nations, and kings shall come from you" (Gen 17:6). And walking down memory lane, we see that God chose David and had him anointed as king. He also made a covenant with him regarding his house (i.e., his family line (2 Sam 7:14]) and promised that He would "raise up for David a righteous Branch, and he shall reign as king" (Jer 23:5). The above promises constitute key texts in the history of salvation, for it is in them that the Lord promises to raise the Messiah, "a son" from the line of David, who, as the son of David, inherited David's role as representative of God's people. And so the Lord promised to make one from the family of David His servant, whose throne He would establish forever.

Since kings were chosen as servants of God to rule His people in righteousness and justice, I have made a study of the anointing of kings and their role in the history of salvation to show that God, as King, intended for kings to rule for Him in order to point His people to the kingdom of God. So in Ancient Israel and traditional Bafut, God set up kings to represent Him and to lead the people to Him. And in the New Testament, Paul says that rulers are God's servants, set up to rule for the good of the people (Rom 13:1, 4). I have also made a study of the anointing of British monarchs to show the link between them and the biblical kings. They, like the anointed of the Lord, wanted to serve as God's representatives before their people. Consequently, they swore an oath to uphold the Church and rule with honour, wisdom, justice, and mercy. Thus kings, and all those in positions of authority, are there to do the will of God. If they are made aware of their God-given responsibilities and challenged to carry these out, the world will be a different place than what we see it to be today. So there is a need to awaken rulers and to point out to them their role in bringing about the kingdom of God on earth as it is in heaven.

The Levitical priesthood and the high priesthood of Jesus are highlighted to explain the change of order from Levi to Judah that opened the way for all believers to serve as priests, thus establishing the universal priesthood of believers.

Throughout the book, I have allowed the truth of the Word to speak, rather than myself. Our thoughts and words have no power, no authority, and no wisdom unless they are backed by the truths of the Scriptures. When the Scriptures speak, they have power and are authoritative and effective because it is the Almighty Himself speaking. This is why I have made extensive use of the Word of God, both quoting it directly and paraphrasing it. I have sought to let the Word of God inspire and inform me. I have sought in the end to make this book a reflection of the will and the whole counsel of God so that the reader is brought to reflect on the whole counsel of God. Every idea and all that is written herein has been prayerfully thought through so that, as much as possible, it reflects what God says in His Word.

We learn from what is around us, in our environment and culture, going from the concrete (what we see) to the abstract (what we cannot literally see or touch). And it is from these that we build the basic principles, theory, theology, or doctrine of life. Also, we are familiar with what is in our cultures, and often we apprehend what is in other cultures through the lenses of our own cultures. But it is when we put the two together and compare them that we see their realities and what is same and what is different. What is the same reinforces what we have in our cultures and lives. And often it is when two realities or cultures come together that they yield the best in life. And it is that which has stood the test of time that becomes a constant—that which lasts. God has put in all cultures things, including institutions and cultural values, that reflect His values, and it is these that stand out for us to see and follow. This is why, in my description of marriage and the family, I have looked at what these institutions are and how they were viewed in both ancient Israel and traditional Bafut. Whatever is in any culture was put there by God, since He is the Creator of all things. These things were all affected by the Fall and were misused and either directed to serve man or other forces of nature—"cosmic powers [of] darkness, [and] spiritual forces of evil in the heavenly places" (Eph 6:12). And so, Jesus came not only to redeem humanity but also to redeem our cultures (1 Peter 1:18–19). These things, known as redemptive analogies, point us back to God the Creator (Ps 19:1–6; Rom 1:19–20; 2:14–15).

Marriage was instituted at Creation. The purpose of marriage and the family, and the values therein, were given by God. The institution of marriage evolved and took on the colourings of different ethnic groups, cultures, and subcultures. And so, among a given people, the marriage contract, rites, and celebrations differ according to families and their social classes or statuses in society. Jesus came either to affirm them or to redeem what had been lost, misinterpreted, or misused. These values—whether in ancient Israel, in Bafut traditional society, or in any other culture—have converged to form a pool of values that Jesus has redeemed, restored, and made new in the new covenant, the New Testament Scriptures. And these are interpreted in the epistles by the apostles, particularly by Paul and Peter.

My study of marriage and family will turn mainly on two axes: the vertical axis, which views marriage from the biblical perspective; and the horizontal axis, which will look at marriage in the context of the family and society. Despite the cultural and social implications of the marriage contract, I view marriage from the biblical perspective, and so the bottom line will be the biblical world view of marriage. In order to establish a closer and more limited and narrower context, I will be asking or answering basic questions about the Christian view of marriage. This means that I am not just going to talk broadly about the biblical theology of marriage. The discussion will be underpinned by what I consider the Christian biblical theology of marriage. I am aware of the debate among Bible scholars about this assertion. While there is a school that will argue that Christian theology is biblical, there are others who will say that not all that is subsumed under Christian theology is biblical. However, I am not going to be weighed down by these details in a book like this, because of its limited scope. What I am concerned about is what is practised, as sanctioned by Scripture. Thus, this book deals with life and practice—that is, the subject of practical theology. So while what we believe and teach is important, it is more realistic and helpful to look at the teaching of the Bible from a practical point of view.

The view of Christianity as a way of life will be the basis of my discussion. Our Christianity should be integrated into all aspects of our lives. It is this conviction that prompted my writing of this book, the first edition of which was presented during a marriage celebration. The book was occasioned by the questions I faced when our daughter, Ruth, and her husband, Val, discussed the blessing of their marriage with me. Looking beyond our discussion, I also thought of the problems young people face in choosing marriage partners. Also, parents face the same issues when their children present to them the ones they think are the right ones to marry. How are we guided when faced with these practical problems?

It was in view of all these questions that I decided to look at marriage from the time of the Creation, determined to find out the purpose of God regarding marriage and the family. Studying marriage in ancient Israel and in Bafut traditional society will enable us to see how marriage and family were viewed and lived there and then. The Word of God and history should inform us in the understanding of these basic but fundamental institutions. Issues addressed in marriage and the family are the subject of practical theology. Today, people are coming up with different definitions of marriage and the family. The fundamental values of marriage and the family are seriously being threatened. This book will remind us that the truths of the Bible alone should serve as the basis of our choices and our views of marriage and the family.

I also believe that theology should be practical and all-pervasive. The desire of every parent is to see his or her son or daughter married. Marriage is often, and naturally, seen as a joyful event. It is a state into which people aspire to enter, and so they eagerly look forward to it. At the same time, it is often the case that there is a bitter side to it. While a couple can be giving themselves to each other and feeling the joy and hope of a happily-ever-after life, there will be some within the families of the couple who will be agonizing and fearful because of the concerns they have about the union. Also, in the case of an arranged marriage, a couple, especially the bride, might not be happy going into the marriage.

Marriage and the family are the basic institutions for training the people of God to be their utmost in order to do their utmost for the Lord. The ultimate purpose of marriage is to present the people of God as the bride that is perfect and blameless before the Lord (Eph 5:25–27; Jude 24–25). In other words, marriage is a school where a man and woman grow in love and develop the discipline of patient endurance through the grace of God in Christ and the Spirit, and the result is perfection and joy in the Lord. The man and woman, as godly parents, will be in a position to grow children who are prepared to do the will of God. This way, the family—parents and children—become the ideal church and missionary unit through whom the purposes of God are carried out.

It must be understood right from the beginning that this book is not a book on marriage counselling, but rather a study of what marriage is. While this study will hinge on practical biblical theology, it will also touch on issues of pastoral theology. It is my view that all theology must be pastoral, because theology should lead people to the knowledge of God and from thereon guide them in living godly lives. This will, in turn, lead them into an increasing knowledge of God and a closer walk with Him. It therefore follows that, since the Incarnation was the most concrete form of theology, bringing God Himself and His life into human life, our theology in a real sense should be Christian—that is, Christ-centred. And so marriage and the family should be Christ-centred.

Before examining the practice of marriage in our cultural context, so to speak, I will describe briefly how marriage was viewed in ancient Israel. This, of course, will be based on the fact that marriage began at Creation and was sanctioned by God. In doing this, I will provide Scripture to show how marriage was done in ancient Israel. We can never really have a full picture of how marriage was conducted then, but we can glean from the Old Testament and even from the New Testament to piece together what the practice was. I will then go on to describe marriage from the perspective of Bafut traditional culture. I will describe how it is viewed and what happens in a Bafut traditional marriage, which will also be a reflection of marriage in the Grassfields regions of Cameroon.

After looking at marriage in Ancient Israel and in the Bafut community, I will focus on what the Christian view and practice of marriage is. I will also examine how Jesus Christ viewed the institution of marriage. The writings of Paul say quite a bit about marriage and family. What he said even in passing will inform my examination.

I stress the fact that marriage is a family institution primarily because the first instruction concerning marriage was to the end of reproduction (i.e., procreation). The secondary implication is that marriage is not a matter of two people deciding to form a union of two individuals, but it is rather a matter of two families coming into union. This point should be emphasized strongly in the present context of a cultural revolution that goes counter to established values and established institutions. Since marriage and family were the primary institutions established by God, rejecting the values that are their core values will mean disregarding God's Word and His values. As a result of the present counter cultural revolution, more and more young people are defying the concept of a family as a communion, united and working together for the good of all. They are clamouring for freedom of choice and thus opting for individualism. As individuals, they think that freedom of thought and action is the most important quality of a society, rather than shared effort and responsibility. Individualism goes against the grain of Christianity, the heart and calling of Christ and the gospel, which preaches death to the self and death to a self-centred life. Orthodox Christianity fosters a Christo-centric form of life, which is presented as a blueprint by Paul in his epistles, as we read in the following Scriptures:

> Do nothing from selfish ambition or conceit, but in humility count others more significant than yourselves. Let each of you look not only to his own interests, but also to the interests of others ... Have this mind among yourselves, which is yours in Christ Jesus, who, though he was in the form of God, did not count equality with God a thing to be grasped, but emptied himself, by taking the form of a servant, being born in the likeness of men. And being found in human form, he humbled himself by becoming obedient to the point of death, even death on a cross. - I try to please everyone in everything I

do, not seeking my own advantage, but that of many, that they may be saved. (Phil 2:3–8; 1 Cor 10:33)

Although the family—church or corporate—is made up of individual members, these members form one union or body, and each member supports the others. And everybody takes care of everybody. And so in the family each person works for the good of the others and for the good of all. This image of the family unit is also the picture of the body of Christ—that is, the church.

Young people have asked me whether traditional African institutions and values are still relevant in their lives as Christians, especially given their exposure to Western cultures. What they should ask themselves is whether the Old Testament is relevant to their lives. What God has put in our cultures, so long as it does not conflict with God's moral law and honour, is not to be rejected. Jesus came into the Jewish culture, lived in it, and ministered in it. Paul followed in step with Him, as his testimony and ministry showed. He lived as a Jew in his culture, and as a Gentile among Gentiles, to win all to Christ (1 Cor 9:19–23). This means that we should respect peoples and their cultures. We are called to live with people in their cultures, paying attention to what Christ taught His followers; and as such, we are to be in their cultures without being of them (John 17:14–16). We are to be in the world to influence it for good. Christ does not call us out of our cultures to leave them or reject them, but on the contrary, He has called us in our cultures to serve there as witnesses for Him by letting what He has done in us reflect His light and glory.

My aim has been to teach, and so I have, as much as possible, tried to make things simple and understandable. I have repeated main ideas for emphasis, and consequently my teaching points are the strands woven throughout the book. Love (the love of God and our love for God and for one another) is the main strand that runs through the book, for love is the fulfilment of the law and the will of God (Rom 13:8; Gal 5:14; John 15:12; Mark 12:30–31). The key themes are repeated to make sure they are well understood. Zig Ziglar underpinned this truth by saying:

> Repetition is the mother of learning, which makes it the architect of accomplishment.[1]

Also, Plato remarked way back in history, "The greater part of instruction is being reminded of things you already know." And the apostles, who were all great teachers, said the same thing. For example, Paul said to the Philippians, "To write the same things to you is no trouble to me and is safe for you" (Phil 3:1). Another translation of this verse is even more explicit, as we can read here:

> Therefore I will always remind you of these things, even though you know them and are established in the truth **you** now have.[2]

At the end of the book, I have asked questions for reflection and further study. It is my hope that these questions will help people to understand, and I am trusting that they will also be moved to practise the truths learned. I believe that what is taught is effective only when people start to apply what they have learned in their lives. And this is when we see change in the transformed lives of people and in our communities. I do not consider that I have truly learned something until I have put it into practice. And as the adage goes, "Practice makes perfect." The questions can be studied in groups, by couples, or by families.

---

[1] https://www.google.com/search?client=firefox-b-d&q=who+said+%22repetition+is+the+mother+of+learning%22

[2] *The Treasury of Scripture Knowledge* is a study tool useful for devotional study and teaching of the Scriptures. It has five hundred thousand Scripture references and parallel passages.

1

DIVINE INSTITUTION

1.1. God's Purpose for Man in Creation

God is omniscient, so even before creating mankind, He had already known the whole purpose of man.[3] This purpose included marriage. And that is why it is stated, "Male and female he created them" (Gen 1:27). So creating them male and female (man and woman) suggests that at some point there will be a union in matrimony. And as we will see, marriage will be for the purpose of procreation or reproduction and production in view of personal subsistence and sustenance. This, in a nutshell, was the purpose of God at Creation. What is called "the creative will and wise purposes of God" boils down to the knowledge of God; His glory, holiness, righteousness, and suffering; and the blessings following faithfulness to the covenant.[4] This is what we read in the prophecy of Isaiah:

> I form light and create darkness, I make well-being and create calamity, I am the LORD, who does all these things. "Shower, O heavens, from above, and let the clouds rain down righteousness; let the earth open, that salvation and righteousness may bear

---

[3] The Hebrew word for "man" is transliterated as *"Adam,"* and "Adam" is the generic word for "mankind." It also became the name "Adam."

[4] The ESV Study Bible—notes on Isaiah 45:7–8.

fruit; let the earth cause them both to sprout; I the LORD have created it. (Isa 45:7–8)

I will elaborate on the purposes of God for man in 1.9, when I discuss marriage and the mission of God. Before I undertake to describe marriage and the purposes of God in marriage, I will look at the foundational perspective of marriage. As we will discover, Genesis 1–3 gives us the principles that are to guide and shape our marriages. We are relational beings; these chapters also tell us how we are to relate to God and to one another. Our marriage relationships can be very complex. Allender and Longman III (1995:14) give us what they call the five Creation Foundations:

1. Who are we as husbands and wives?
2. What are our roles as husbands and wives?
3. How will we work together as husbands and wives?
4. How do we experience the deepest, most profound intimacy of body and soul?
5. How do we, two sinners, learn to live with each other?

All these questions will be addressed in the study of the first three chapters of Genesis, and I will further address them as we look at marriage in ancient Israel and in traditional Bafut society, and especially when we look at the mystery of Christian marriage in the New Testament from the perspectives of Paul and Christ.

1.2. The Nature and Character of Man

At the moment when God created man, He had a purpose concerning both the nature and the primary function of man, as we read in the following verse:

> Then God said, "Let us make man in our image, after our likeness. And let them have dominion over the fish of the sea and over the birds of the heavens and over the livestock and over all the earth and over

every creeping thing that creeps on the earth." (Gen 1:26)

God defined the nature and character of man before creating him. He was to bear *the image of God* since the man would be His regent, performing the duties He would assign him.[5] So the importance of man was spelled out very clearly even before he came into being: he was to have *dominion* "over the earth," which means that he was to rule over the rest of God's creation.[6] So the first task of man was to rule, which entails taking care of God's creation. This also means that he was to keep, watch over, and manage it. Thus, all of creation was to be under his stewardship. And this entails taking care of the environment, for God had created everything good, pure, and clean. So man's stewardship begins with the environment.

As an administrator or manager, he would have more than property to manage. He would need a team under him with whom to work. We can begin to read in this the need of partnership. And thus, the reason why God created not only the man but also the woman is that the man would have her as a human partner. And, of course, being God's regent, he would bear in mind the fact that God is his first and more important partner.

---

[5] The image of God in man speaks of His righteousness, His holiness, and His other character traits, as Paul exhorts the Colossians to put on "the new self, created after the likeness of God in true righteousness and holiness" (Eph 4:24). And as Peter and John affirm, God did not only create man in His image, but He made sure that, through His Word, promises, and the help of the Spirit, man would grow in character and would be increasingly sanctified, to share in the very nature and glory of God (Eph 4:13; 2 Cor 3:18; 2 Pet 1:4). John tells us that in the end we shall be like Him (1 John 3:2). So the image of God in us began at Creation and will be complete at the return of Christ. Man therefore finds his identity in God because, in Christ and through Christ, he is marked by the very character of God.

[6] The word "dominion" as used here does not mean coercion and subjugation or rule by force as used by autocrats. Man was given control over all creation, which included taking care of God's creation. This means that he was given authority to act according to the nature and rule of God.

The next purpose of God at Creation was procreation, as is made clear in the following quote:

> And God blessed them. And God said to them, "Be fruitful and multiply and fill the earth and subdue it, and have dominion over the fish of the sea and over the birds of the heavens and over every living thing that moves on the earth." (Gen 1:28)

The above verse states the second purpose of God for man (i.e., the role he was going to play), and He also reinforces the first duty, which is dominion. So God wanted the man to be fruitful. The fact that he was to be fruitful presupposed marriage. In the nature of things, as it will be seen below, reproduction can take place only when the male and female come together. So the creation of man and woman was in view of marriage.

1.3. Blessing in Creation

The blessing of God occurs before man ever engages in any meaningful and fruitful endeavour. There is no way man was going to dominate God's creation without His blessing. The grace and presence of God were evident in all creation—especially in the creation and defining of the duties of the man. The grace of God was in action from the creation of the world, and man was the object of God's special blessing. And so we find it in focus:

> And God blessed them.

Blessings were bestowed on the man and woman before they ever started to do anything. They had not done anything to deserve the blessing. This is grace demonstrated from the very beginning, and it would continue as the lodestar illuminating the goodness that underlies the action of God to man. The goodness in the nature of our God and Father is what distinguishes Him from the gods of other religions. The sovereign Lord God does not only create His people; He blesses them. This will be seen later on when He calls

Abraham and makes a covenant with him. Divine blessing was the fundamental and key element of the call and mission of Abraham, as we read here:

> And I will make of you a great nation, and I will bless you and make your name great, so that you will be a blessing. I will bless those who bless you, and him who dishonours you I will curse, and in you all the families of the earth shall be blessed. (Gen 12:2–3)

Abraham was called and blessed so that he would be a blessing to his offspring and to the nations. Nations would come to know God as a result of his testimony and instruction (Gen 18:19). And nations will be blessed with the knowledge of the Lord.

The immediate blessing of Abraham would be in terms of fruitfulness, which consisted of the fruit of the womb. Adam and Eve had children, and Abraham was promised a seed, Isaac. And the seed of Abraham would yield peoples that would fill the whole earth. God made this clear in the covenant:

> And God said to Abraham, "As for Sarai your wife I will bless her, and moreover, I will give you a son by her. I will bless her, and she shall become nations; kings of peoples shall come from her." (Gen 17:15–16)

The covenant with Abraham was a promise of blessing, an embodiment of divine favour. First of all, he would be in a special relationship with God, and from this relationship would flow blessings.[7] The divine blessing would be children, land, the nation

---

[7] Of all men, it was Abraham who was called God's friend (Isa 41:8). He trusted God and obeyed Him unconditionally, as testified by James:

> Was not Abraham our father justified by works when he offered up his son Isaac on the altar? You see that faith was active along with his works, and faith was completed by his works; and the Scripture was fulfilled that says, 'Abraham believed God, and it was counted to him as righteousness'—and he was called a friend of God. (James 2:22–23)

of Israel, and gentile nations that would eventually join themselves to the people of God to form a new and holy people, the new Israel of God.[8] Abraham would be exceedingly fruitful:

> I have made you the father of a multitude of nations. I will make you exceedingly fruitful, and I will make you into nations, and kings shall come from you ... will surely bless you, and I will surely multiply your offspring as the stars of heaven and as the sand that is on the seashore. (Gen 17:5–6; 22:17)

The blessing and multiplying of the seed of Abraham came true even while they were in captivity. This covenant promise was repeated to Jacob, who testified it to his son, Joseph, when he followed him to Egypt, as follows:

> God Almighty appeared to me at Luz in the land of Canaan and blessed me, and said to me, 'Behold, I will make you fruitful and multiply you, and I will make of you a company of peoples and will give this land to your offspring after you for an everlasting possession.(Gen 48:3–4)

Moses saw the fulfilment of the covenant promise and testified it to the children of Israel, as we read in the following statement about the faithfulness of the Lord:

---

[8] In 1 Peter 2:9, the apostle Peter sees the church as the new Israel and takes what is said in Exodus 19:5–6 about Israel and applies it to the church. Peter was writing to Gentile believers in the other nations: "To those who are elect exiles of the Dispersion in Pontus, Galatia, Cappadocia, Asia, and Bithynia" (1 Pet. 1:1). John, in Revelation 1:6, sees the churches in the Dispersion as "a kingdom" made up of "priests" to God. Israel's roles and duties are now being carried out by those in the nations who have been freed from their sins by the blood of Jesus. The message of Revelation, destined to comfort the suffering church, is centered on the death of Christ and the redemption, which brings freedom from sin and physical, social, and political domination.

> Your fathers went down to Egypt seventy persons, and now the LORD your God has made you as numerous as the stars of heaven. (Deut 10:22)

Our God is faithful in His promises, and we can trust Him, knowing that what He promises, He will do.

Jesus Christ was the ultimate seed of Abraham, as interpreted by Paul in the following verse of Scripture:

> Now the promises were made to Abraham and to his offspring. It does not say, "And to offsprings," referring to many, but referring to one, "And to your offspring," who is Christ. (Gal 3:16)

Jesus Christ, the ultimate blessing, was announced in Genesis, predicting the redemption declared at the Fall, prophesied in the prophets, effected in the gospel, and explained in the epistles.(Gen 3:15; 2 Cor 9:15). Isaiah predicted this in the following terms:

> For to us a child is born, to us a son is given; and the government shall be upon his shoulder, and his name shall be called Wonderful Counsellor, Mighty God, Everlasting Father, Prince of Peace.(Isaiah 9:6)

And Luke reports the birth of the Christ, the ultimate seed, as follows:

> And the angel said to them, "Fear not, for behold, I bring you good news of great joy that will be for all the people. For unto you is born this day in the city of David a Saviour, who is Christ the Lord. (Luke 2:10–11)

And through His witness and instruction while on earth, God would give the Christ children of His own, which He will in turn present before the Father (Isaiah 8:1), as the writer to the Hebrews testifies here:

And again, "I will put my trust in him." And again, "Behold, I and the children God has given me." (Heb 2:13)

Indeed, those who come to believe in Christ are children won to the Father. In fact, in the Bafut language, believers in Christ are called *"bɔɔ bɨ Kristo"*—that is, "children of Christ."

So we see that the coming of Christ brings a lot of blessings to the world. His coming will give us the opportunity of becoming the children of God (John 1:12–13) and then will enable us to enjoy the fuller measure of the *grace* of God, as we read from the gospel of John:[9]

> For from his fullness we have all received, grace upon grace. (John 1:17)

We will continue to enjoy this grace after the glorification of Christ, as the writer of Hebrews exhorts believers:

> Let us then with confidence draw near to the throne of grace, that we may receive mercy and find grace to help in time of need. (Heb 4:16)

Just as in Abraham the people of Israel became sons (children) of God through the seed of promise, Isaac, Gentile believers, such as we are, become the offspring Abraham (the new Israel of God) through the ultimate Seed. And so, in Christ we become children of Abraham, according to the apostle Paul:

> In Christ Jesus you are all sons of God, through faith ... For as many of you as were baptized into

---

[9] Grace is God's unmerited favour, which brings blessings and joy that comes from a special relationship that grows from the blessing. It is the source of godly living: "His divine power has granted to us all things that pertain to life and godliness" (2 Peter 1:3). God's grace in Christ results in a godly life, as we are by faith imputed the righteousness of Christ and enabled, by the power of the Holy Spirit, to lead lives characterized by the virtues that reflect the divine nature (Gal 5:22–23; 2 Peter 1:3–11).

Christ have put on Christ ... And if you are Christ's,
then you are Abraham's offspring, heirs according to
promise. (Gal 3:26–27, 29)

Paul has a characteristic and gripping way of describing our coming into a personal relationship and union with Christ, following the view and descriptions of Christ in John's gospel, which we can read in John chapters 14 to 17. Christ teaches His followers how close they can be to Himself and the Father and makes this clear in His prayer when He prays, saying, "That they may all be one, just as you, Father, are in me, and I in you, that they also may be in us" (John 17:21). Paul sees the Christian as being in Christ and also being able to put on Christ, using the language of clothing, which is also used both in the Old Testament and the New Testament. Paul sees a close relationship of the believer with Christ as the transforming work of the incarnation and redemption, which brings the life and workings of Christ into the life of the Christian. He is speaking from personal experience, since in the later part of his life He would testify as follows:

> I have been crucified with Christ. It is no longer I
> who live, but Christ who lives in me. And the life I
> now live in the flesh I live by faith in the Son of God,
> who loved me and gave himself for me. (Gal 2:20)

The Creation story begins with the creation of man, followed by the covenant with Abraham—that is, the old covenant. The old covenant stated: "I will bless those who bless you, and him who dishonours you I will curse" (Gen 12:3).

The coming of Christ initiates a new covenant, which makes us a new creation, as Paul says:

> Therefore, if anyone is in Christ, he is a new creation.
> The old has passed away; behold, the new has come.
> (2 Cor 5:17)

With this new covenant, we enter into the blessings of Abraham, as his offspring, and so we are blessed to become a blessing. It is on the basis of this covenant relationship that Christ, in the Sermon on the Mount, calls us to bless:

> But I say to you who hear, love your enemies, do good to those who hate you, bless those who curse you, pray for those who abuse you. (Luke 6:27–28)

Peter reminds believers in the Dispersion that, as the seed of Abraham and the new Israel of God, they have been called to bless, as we read in his first epistle:

> Do not repay evil for evil or reviling for reviling, but on the contrary, bless, for to this you were called, that you may obtain a blessing.(1 Peter 3:9)

Paul, in light of the teaching of Christ, exhorts believers in Rome as follows:

> Bless those who persecute you; bless and do not curse them. (Rom 12:14)

We notice a significant difference between the old covenant and the new covenant: Whereas in the old covenant those who dishonoured Abraham were cursed, Christ in the new covenant asked believers, members of the new covenant, to bless even those who persecute or curse them. Peter reminded believers of the "Dispersion" that they were called to bless, even those who insulted or did them evil.

God blesses us not only spiritually but also materially, as we read in the following verse:

> The blessing of the LORD makes rich, and he adds no sorrow with it. (Prov 10:22)

And so we see that the Bible does not call us to bless people only with our words. Our blessings should also be expressed in our actions. We must do something to meet the needs of our brothers and sisters, as James tell us in the following Scriptures:

> If a brother or sister is poorly clothed and lacking in daily food, and one of you says to them, "Go in peace, be warmed and filled," without giving them the things needed for the body, what good is that? (James 2:15–16)

And so John tells us that blessing and love must be expressed in deeds, as we read in his epistle:

> But if anyone has the world's goods and sees his brother in need, yet closes his heart against him, how does God's love abide in him? Little children, let us not love in word or talk but in deed and in truth. (1 John 3:17–18)

So we see that the grace of God underlies everything that He does to His people, grace is a package which flows from the love of God for us and it overflows with blessings expressed by the action of giving: God so loved the world that He gave His one and only Son, and the Son would give Himself and all that He has for our benefit. Paul expresses these truths in His epistles, as follows:

> For you know the grace of our Lord Jesus Christ, that though he was rich, yet for your sake he became poor, so that you by his poverty might become rich. (2 Cor 8:9)

> He who did not spare his own Son but gave him up for us all, how will he not also with him graciously give us all things? (Rom 8:32)

The love and blessings of God should be the motivating factor in our relationships with one another and in our service to God. God extends His grace, His blessings, to us to make us be blessings to others, as Paul tells the Corinthian Christians who had been blessed by the Macedonian brethren. He told them the following:

> And God is able to make all grace abound to you, so that having all sufficiency in all things at all times, you may abound in every good word. (2 Cor 9:8)

The Christians in Macedonia, though poor, had given sacrificially for the relief of the churches in Judea, and these very brethren had, through their giving, supported Paul so that he preached the gospel to the Corinthians free of charge (2 Cor 11:7–9; Phil 4:15–18). Paul was thus encouraging the Christians in Corinth to follow the examples of Christ and the Macedonian churches and give generously, for those who give will themselves be blessed.

Paul goes on to describe what motivates us in our Christian lives and ministries:

> For the love of Christ controls us, because we have concluded this: that one has died for all, therefore all have died; and he died for all, that those who live might no longer live for themselves but for him who for their sake died and was raised. (2 Cor 5:14–15)

So far, all that we have seen tells us that the tone of godly living was set right at Creation. The creation of man was an act of grace by which God blessed the man. Thus the grace of God and His blessings will characterize this kind of life. Godly living would be established by the covenants He would make with the patriarchs, and the covenant promises repeatedly underlined the life that would be passed to succeeding generations and to the nations.

1.4. The Need to be Equipped

As stated previously, at Creation, God gave Adam and Eve work to do. He blessed them in view of the mission they were assigned. So we, too, are on God's mission, engaged in His work. As we are engaged in God's work, we should be aware of the fact that we need not only be called to do the work, we also need to be blessed. We need God's blessing because without this we will be neither equipped nor motivated for the task. So right at Creation we are taught practically that we need God's blessing and help to be fruitful and effective. As previously stated, God blessed the man and woman before commissioning them. His blessing was upon them even before bringing them into union (i.e., before making them husband and wife). This is in the nature of God that He prepares and equips His special instruments, those He has a special plan for, even before they are born. This was the case for Jeremiah and John the Baptist, and even Samson. John the Baptist was filled with the Spirit right from the womb, while Samson was called before he was conceived in the womb. He was blessed before he ever started his mission, and he was moved by the Spirit of the Lord:

> And the LORD blessed him. And the Spirit of the LORD began to stir him. (Judges 13:24–25)

Jeremiah was called and consecrated while still in the womb, as declared by the Lord Himself:

> Before I formed you in the womb I knew you, and before you were born I consecrated you; I appointed you a prophet to the nations. (Jer 1:5)

The Lord wants His servants to be purified and prepared so they can serve effectively and so their service will be acceptable before God. He had to purify them, as stated in the following text:

> But who can endure the day of his coming, and who can stand when he appears? For he is like a refiner's fire and like fullers' soap. He will sit as a refiner and purifier of silver, and he will purify the sons of Levi and refine them like gold and silver, and they will bring offerings in righteousness to the LORD. (Mal 3:2–3)

The Lord prepares His servants by making them go through the discipline of suffering. This is underlined by the apostles Peter, James, and Paul in their epistles. James says this to us:

> Count it all joy, my brothers, when you meet trials of various kinds, for you know that the testing of your faith produces steadfastness. And let steadfastness have its full effect, that you may be perfect and complete, lacking in nothing. (James 1:2–4)

Peter teaches that suffering is willed by God. Suffering is a school that trains and purifies believers. Suffering proves the genuineness of their tried faith and makes them grow to be established, standing firm, and thus better prepared for ministry and for the end time, when they inherit their future salvation, guarded in heaven for them (1 Peter 1:6–7). And so the process of perfection goes through the school of suffering, which has proved for all time to be the best preparation for a fruitful ministry here on earth while we wait for our inheritance in the presence of our Father and His Christ, our Lord and Saviour. Trials and suffering make us humble and weak, making room for God to come and strengthen us. This is what He reminded Paul when he asked to be spared the suffering that he had borne all the time since his dramatic conversion on the road to Damascus. It was God's grace that he needed in the trying moments of suffering, for His "power is made perfect in weakness" (2 Cor 12:9–10). And God was faithful to His promise to be with Paul and to strengthen him (Acts 18:9–10; 2 Tim 4:17). Yes, God's power is greatly seen when we are at our weakest point—that is, when we have reached our limits. Everything that happens to us is engineered by God working everything out towards the goal of perfecting us to be our utmost for Him (Rom 8:28). Morgan (1997) gives us a testimony about the commitment of Isaac Watts (the father of Isaac Watts the hymn writer), who was repeatedly imprisoned and persecuted for his Nonconformist beliefs, on 21 May 1685. While in prison, Isaac wrote the following to his family, particularly addressing his eleven-year-old son, Isaac, cited by Morgan (1997):

> We must endeavour by patient waiting to submit to His will without murmuring; and not to think amiss of His chastening us, knowing that all His works are the products of infinite wisdom.

The life of Isaac Watts senior was an illustration of a life totally surrendered to God. Isaac Watts was suffering for the truth of the gospel and did not complain but followed the example of Christ and the apostles. He believed that God was using the trials to perfect him, just as James says in his epistle (James 1:2–4). The impact of this life that was prepared by suffering was felt down through history, beginning with his family, seeing as how much his life shaped that of his son, Isaac. The books he wrote and the classic songs that are still sung in the church show the spiritual impact of a life that has been trained and formed in the school of suffering.

Even Christ had to be prepared through suffering for doing the will of God, the ultimate act of obedience, to redeem us, as we read here in this quote:

> Although he was a son, he learned obedience through what he suffered. And being made perfect, he became the source of eternal salvation to all who obey him. (Heb 5:8–9)

And so it was because Christ obeyed the Father in suffering and dying on the cross that He was able to do the perfect will of God: dying in order to save us. It is to this kind of obedience that He calls us, to follow in His footsteps, as Peter tells us in his epistle (1 Peter 2:21). And John also calls us to the same commitment and says that if Christ suffered and died for us, we ought to be prepared to lay down our lives for our brothers and sisters (1 John 3:16).

The Holy Spirit's gifts and fruit (Eph 4:7–16; Gal 5:22–23) are given to leaders of the church to prepare and equip believers for ministry:

> And he gave the apostles, the prophets, the evangelists, the shepherds and teachers, to equip the saints for the work of ministry, for building up the body of Christ, until we all attain to the unity of the faith and of the knowledge of the Son of God, to mature manhood, to the measure of the stature of the fullness of Christ. (Eph 4:11–13)

As it was with the prophets, Jesus Christ needed to be equipped for ministry, and this was predicted by Isaiah in the following text:

> The Spirit of the Lord GOD is upon me, because the LORD has anointed me to bring good news to the poor; he has sent me to bind up the brokenhearted, to proclaim liberty to the captives, and the opening of the prison to those who are bound. (Isaiah 61:1)

In the above text, if it is the Messiah speaking, it means that even before the Incarnation, the anointing, and, thus, the equipping of the Christ had already been done or assuredly foreseen. And so it is that Christ will quote this passage at the beginning of His ministry in Galilee and say, "Today this Scripture has been fulfilled in your hearing" (Luke 4:21). At this point, Jesus had already been baptized and had been in the desert and fasted for forty days and nights to be equipped. And so it is that at the start of His ministry in Nazareth, Luke reports the following:

> And Jesus returned in the power of the Spirit to Galilee, and a report about him went out through all the surrounding country. And he taught in their synagogues, being glorified by all. (Luke 4:14–15)

We thus see that even Jesus Christ, though He was God, while He was in the form of man, needed to be equipped before His public ministry, both at Baptism and in the desert. This was so not necessarily because He was lacking in any way, but because He needed to show us the example. When John questioned why He needed to be baptized, His response was revealing:

> But Jesus answered him, "Let it be so now, for thus it is fitting for us to fulfil all righteousness." Then he consented. (Matt 3:16)

Jesus was the servant par excellence and was exemplary in His life and ministry. He did everything before His disciples and the public so His followers would have a blueprint to follow. After washing the feet of His disciples, He said to them,

> If I then, your Lord and Teacher, have washed your feet, you also ought to wash one another's feet. For I have given you an example, that you also should do just as I have done to you. (John 13:14–15)

Jesus Himself knew the power of the Holy Spirit. He was baptized and Spirit-filled and so instructed the apostles not to depart from Jerusalem or attempt anything until they themselves were filled with power from on high. The power of example is an important leadership principle. Paul the apostle knew the power of example, and so He was keen to look at Christ and to imitate His example. He was so successful and effective in his life and ministry because Christ was His master, and he followed His example faithfully, even unto death. He confidently asked those he mentored to watch him and follow his example:

> Be imitators of me as I am of Christ. (1 Cor 11:1)

And he was able to tell the believers in Philippi,

> What you have learned and received and heard and seen in me—practice these things, and the God of peace will be with you (Phil 4:9)

The world needs people who can lead by example. It is very rare to have leaders who confidently tell those they lead to watch them and follow their examples. Even in families, it is difficult for parents to tell their children to watch them and follow their example. My mother, who lived to a ripe old age, was one of the few who would tell people openly and without question to follow her example. She and my father served the Lord together for fifty-two years before my father died at the age of ninety-six. She walked so closely with the Lord that she was visibly an example to both younger and elderly women. When we had a thanksgiving service, organized to thank God for her life, she stood in front of the congregation and told people that God had impressed on her and enabled her to walk before all as an example for them to follow. And the impact of her life on the congregation was evident. At her funeral several years later, people testified, saying how much they had been impacted by her example. The writer of Hebrews knew the importance of faithful and exemplary leaders, and so he urged his readers in the following words:

> Remember your leaders, those who spoke to you the word of God. Consider the outcome of their way of life, and imitate their faith. (Heb 13:7)

God, who is perfect and good, doing all things well, after seeing that all He had created was good, was determined to see that those He had created would be effective in the mission He was assigning them. God is committed to seeing us do a good job as we continue with Him the work of creation. It is also man's responsibility to maintain the world in as good a state as it was in at Creation. This is why he started by equipping the man and woman for that task. And as we have seen above, this became important and necessary to give value to man by equipping him for the task. Blessing and equipping those that are called into any ministry or job is what anyone called into a leadership position should pay attention to. Whether in the family, in the church, or in Christian organizations, it is important to give value to those within our sphere of influence so they will be equipped for their work and ministry.

1.5. Man and the Woman Made One

Now we come to the point where God creates the man, Adam. When God had created all the other things, He could not just stop there, for the man who would rule over the animals and other creatures and work the land had not been created, as affirmed here:

> No bush of the field was yet in the land and no small plant of the field had yet sprung up—for the LORD

God had not caused it to rain on the land, and there
was no man to work the ground. (Gen 2:5)

So God created the man, but not by speaking him into being, as He had done in the creation of all that was created already. Because man was special and was to be in His image and to exercise regal duties, He took time to make him, as we read:

Then the LORD God formed the man of dust from the
ground and breathed into his nostrils the breath of
life, and the man became a living creature. (Gen 2:7)

It is said above that "the Lord ... formed the man." This signifies that He took time to shape and form the man as a potter would fashion a vessel, using all his skills. Isaiah uses this image of God being the potter and man being the clay. Man is the crown of God's creation, and because He took the time to create him, it is obvious that this will be His masterpiece. The Psalmist uses the word "knit," which tells of the intricacy and beauty of God's creation—that is, man. And he exclaims at the thought of it as follows:

For you formed my inward parts; you knitted me
together in my mother's womb. I praise you, for I am
fearfully and wonderfully made. Wonderful are your
works; my soul knows it very well. (Ps 139:13–14)

After creating each set of beings, God made an evaluation of each piece of His work. On six occasions, He affirmed that what He had made was good ("And God saw that it was good"). But after the creation of the man and woman, the crown of His creation, He stood back, as it were, and appraised all that He had made; and so it is reported:

And God saw everything that he had made, and
behold, it was very good. (Gen 1:31)

So the value and beauty of man completed and graced all of creation. And to this fact the wise Preacher testifies:

> He has made everything beautiful in its time. (Eccl 3:11)

So the creation of man was the capstone of His handiwork. This was the quintessence and hallmark of His glorious creation order. Again, it is the poet and songwriter David, the psalmist, who paints an even brighter picture of God's created order in the following verses:

> When I look at your heavens, the work of your fingers, the moon and the stars, which you have set in place,
>
> What is man that you are mindful of him, and the son of man that you care for him?
>
> Yet you have made him a little lower than the heavenly beings and crowned him with glory and honour. (Ps 8:3–5)

We see here that David, after marvelling at the beauty of God's created order, focuses on man and zooms in on both his beauty and on the power bestowed on man over other created beings.

The other thing to be noted concerning the Creation story is that prior to the creation of man, the generic word for God was used, indicating that the deity was the transcendent Creator. However, from the point when He created man, we are introduced to God's personal name, Yahweh, translated as "LORD," following the Jewish tradition which substituted it with the term "Adonai," which means "Lord." "Yahweh" is also the covenantal name of God. The significance of the use of the name "Yahweh here is that it underlines the personal and relational nature of God. This will naturally create a personal relation with the man. Right at Creation, we see that the Lord God is the one who initiates any relation that man will have with Him. So the narrative gives us a true and balanced picture of God. And so we see that although God is sovereign and transcendent, He is a God who is both immanent and personal.

The Lord did not only touch and craft the man; He put something of Himself, His own life, into the man. A comprehensive view of the action of breathing life into the man captures what life in man means. This means that God breathed physical, mental, and spiritual life into man, the only creature that will bear His image. The term "living creature" in the Creation narrative includes land and sea creatures (Gen 1:20, 24).

God breathed life into the man so that he became a living being, and Paul affirms this, saying, "The first man Adam became a living being" (1 Cor 15:45). And the fact that God breathes the spirit of life into Adam further stresses the personal relation between God and the man. It is from this perspective that stems the spiritual nature of this relationship, and this will be the fact that also explains the existence of the character traits of God in man. It will also explain the longing for worship. James comments about this link when he writes,

> Or do you suppose it is to no purpose that the Scripture says, "He yearns jealously over the spirit that he has made to dwell in us?" (James 4:5)

God created man and put in him a spirit. And it is for this reason that He deeply desires that our spirits would worship Him. Yes, it is the spirit which God has placed in man that makes Him jealously desire that we worship Him. This is the basis of true worship, as Christ told the Samaritan woman that He met at the well:

> God is spirit, and those who worship him must worship in spirit and truth. (John 4:24)

Just as God longs for the spirit that He makes to dwell in us, the spirit that He put in man makes man seek to find Him and to worship Him. Man is restless until his spirit finds God, His Creator, and finding Him brings joy—joy in worship. Because of this, St Augustine declared in his *Confessions* that "You have made us for yourself, O Lord, and our hearts are *restless until* they rest in You."

And so, as a mark of our gratitude to God for what He has done in us and for us, we should seek Him and rejoice in Him. This is what the psalmist exhorts us to do:

> Glory in his holy name; let the hearts of those who seek the LORD rejoice!
>
> Seek the LORD and his strength; seek his presence continually! (Ps 105:3–4)

1.6. It Is Not Good for the Man to Be Alone

What God put in man by fashioning him as the crown of his creation (i.e., the beauty and wonder of man's form, and the beauty of character), speaks for the value of man. The value that God gave to man explains the special relation that exists between Him and man, His creation. God could not have the relation that He has with man with the other creatures, the things He created, including the animals. It also follows that the man could not have a relationship with the rest of the created things. God Himself saw that none of them was "found a helper fit for him" (Gen 2:20). The animals were not fit for him; they would also not be suitable companions.

Since God had put in man the need to relate to Him, man then became a relational being. And being a relational being, He did not want the man to be alone. Therefore, God decided to create the woman to be his companion. God knew the needs and longing of man's heart and knew what is good for him, as we read in his next step:

> Then the LORD God said, "It is not good that the man should be alone; I will make him a helper fit for him." (Gen 2:18)

God, being a personal and relational being, wanted to institute and formalize the state that would bring order and harmony and the most satisfaction in life. He created a spouse for the man.

The character and role of the spouse would be determined by

the responsibility that God had purposed for the man. It is clear that God had not caused plants to grow, because "there was no man to work the ground" (Gen 2:5). And so, after creating him, He would put him in the garden "to work it and keep it" (v. 15). This tells us that since the man would work and keep the garden, the creature who would be created and given him should be one who would partner with him in his work. This is why God created for Adam "a helper fit for him." A helper is one who supplies what is lacking, either strength or wisdom, thus enabling the one helped to accomplish the task or responsibility that falls to him or her. This by no means implies that the helper is stronger or weaker than the one helped. "Fit for him" means the woman should be suitable for the man. The way the Lord formed the woman spoke to the other aspect of fitness: the relational nature in marriage and the family:

> So the LORD God caused a deep sleep to fall upon the man, and while he slept took one of his ribs and closed up its place with flesh. And the rib that the LORD God had taken from the man he made into a woman.[10] (Gen 2:21–22)

The Lord knew that the woman, to be a fit partner, must be closest to the man and be of the same form and nature. The rib is a delicate part of the body, but it protects the heart and other vital organs of the body. It is closest to the heart, and the heart is the centre of the thoughts, emotions, and will of man. From there flow the thinking, feeling, and actions of a person; it represents the person. So the rib of the man brings all of the man into the woman, and this formed the basis of the closeness that existed between them. This is probably why God had to take this part of the man to form the woman. In this case, since the woman was from the body of the man, she was literally one with the man. This act gives a picture of marriage, as will be spelt out and explained later.

---

[10] It will be good to note here that God created only one woman for Adam. He could have created two or more women for Adam. He did create only one man for the woman. So God's original plan at Creation was one man and one wife, one wife and one husband.

Furthermore, when the Lord brought the woman to the man, it did not take a minute for him to recognize himself in the woman, and so we see how excited he is in the following exclamation:

> This at last is bone of my bones
> and flesh of my flesh;
> she shall be called Woman,
> because she was taken out of Man. (Gen 2:23)

So Adam saw his newly created bride not as part of himself but as the best of himself, his quintessential self, which is what he means by "flesh of my flesh" and "bone of my bones." The man calls her "woman" because she was taken out of man. Again, this emphasizes the fact of being the same nature and form. The similarity is further highlighted by the fact that the Hebrew words for woman ("*ishshah*") and man ("*ish*") sound alike. And all this put together gives the best picture of the relation that can exist between a man and a woman. In other words, the closest relation between two persons can be found in marriage.[11] It shows what one should be looking for in a woman or man when one sets out to look for a spouse. This means that a young man or woman, when looking for a life partner, should pray and depend on God to find the right person, because He only is the best matchmaker. It is a blessing to find a person who will fit one's expectations, "the dream spouse." This is why the Bible stresses that only God can give us the right spouse, as we read in the following Scripture:

> House and wealth are inherited from fathers, but a
> prudent wife is from the LORD. (Prov 19:14)

---

[11] Although the relation between Jonathan and David is one of the closest that links any two people as friends, where, as it is described, "the soul of Jonathan was knit to the soul of David" in love (1 Sam 18:1), it is all the same different from the relationship in marriage. In marriage, the two spouses are one flesh (intimating sexual intercourse). Just as the friendship between Jonathan and David made Jonathan more loyal and obligated to David, so also in a marriage relationship does loyalty to one's spouse override loyalty to parents. This, however, does not absolve the wife or husband from their responsibility towards their parents.

One should note that since the purpose of God for life and ministry is to serve and to minister to Him and his people in a way that glorifies Him, young people should take time and seek counsel from their parents and spiritual leaders. It is important that parents should be praying for their children and guiding them, to know God's will as concerns marriage and family. A spouse is a ministry partner, as we have seen so far. God created the woman to be a partner in the work that He had made them to do, and so, having the wrong spouse can frustrate one in ministry and make life miserable for both the man and woman. This thus calls for wisdom and care.

1.7. One Flesh

We have come to the point in the narrative where God shows us what marriage should be: a union of two persons, the man and woman, who are closely related in the most intimate of all human relationships.

In order to fulfil their calling as husband and wife, they have to live together, reason together, and act together. And so, the Lord declares,

> Therefore a man shall leave his father and his mother[12] and hold fast to his wife, and they shall become one flesh. (Gen 2:24)

The motif of "flesh" and "one flesh" is seen in its sublime usage when God uses it to portray the union in matrimony. That the two "shall become one flesh" means perfect oneness in nature, body, and action, the two working in tandem. This also implies the idea

---

[12] As we shall see later in this study, in ancient Israel, sons did not move away from their fathers' homes when they got married; instead they stayed close to their parents because they would inherit the family land upon the deaths of their fathers. As we will see later (2.7), the woman leaves the parental home to go with her husband. And in Bafut it is the woman who leaves her mother and father to go to the man she marries (3.8.2).

of consummation of the marriage when the man and woman meet in the act of sexual intercourse.

The expression "Hold fast," as used in the above quotation, reinforces the idea of closeness and sticking together as a team in partnership and fellowship. It is used elsewhere in the Old Testament to show covenantal faithfulness (i.e., faithfulness to the covenant and faithfulness to God), as we read here:

> You shall fear the LORD your God. You shall serve him and hold fast to him, and by his name you shall swear. (Deut 10:20)

Just as "holding fast to the Lord" refers to faithfulness to the Lord God, in the same way, holding fast to one's wife signifies faithfulness to one's spouse.

Paul pulls these two texts (Gen 2:24 and Deut 10:20) and brings them together in His first epistle to the Corinthians as follows:

> Or do you not know that he who is joined to a prostitute becomes one body with her? For, as it is written, "The two will become one flesh." But he who is joined to the Lord becomes one spirit with him. (1 Cor 6:16–17)

The idea of bringing two people together as one foreshadows what God was going to do in Jesus, bringing Jews and Gentiles into the body of Christ. Paul describes this truth in his letter to the Ephesians, as we read in the following text:

> But now in Christ Jesus you who once were far off have been brought near by the blood of Christ. For he himself is our peace, who has made us both one and has broken down in his flesh the dividing wall of hostility by abolishing the law of commandments expressed in ordinances, that he might create in himself one new man in place of the two, so making peace. (Eph 2:13–15)

Again we see how, right at the beginning of Creation, God tells the whole salvation story, and all of this He places within the context of marriage and the family.

1.8. Marriage as a Covenant

Marriage between a man and woman is a covenant made before God. This is especially so when the vows are taken in a ceremony in a worship service and are witnessed by the congregation of God's people, the church. Malachi brings this out clearly in his diatribe against the people because of their violation of the covenant that they made with God, as we read in the following text:

> Have we not all one Father? Has not one God created us? Why then are we faithless to one another, profaning the covenant of our fathers? Judah has been faithless, and abomination has been committed in Israel and in Jerusalem. For Judah has profaned the sanctuary of the LORD, which he loves, and has married the daughter of a foreign god. (Mal 2:10–11)

Malachi, treating idolatry as spiritual adultery, links idolatry to unfaithfulness in marriage. This is described by Hosea as follows:

> My people inquire of a piece of wood, and their walking staff gives them oracles. For a spirit of whoredom has led them astray, and they have left their God to play the whore. They sacrifice on the tops of the mountains and burn offerings on the hills, under oak, poplar, and terebinth, because their shade is good. Therefore your daughters play the whore, and your brides commit adultery. (Hos 4:12–13)

Hosea here describes unfaithfulness to God and the covenant, which is idolatry, and calls it whoredom. Turning away from God and his covenant is therefore spiritual adultery. The consequence of the parents turning away from God is seen in their children, their *brides*, straying into sexual immorality.

Malachi also regards marriage as a covenant made before God, as we read in the following verse:

> But you say, "Why does he not?" Because the LORD was witness between you and the wife of your youth, to whom you have been faithless, though she is your companion and your wife by covenant. (Malachi 2:14)

We see that marriage is an institution of God and established at Creation, and so this should be taken seriously and not entered into lightly. Marriage seen from this perspective mirrors the relation that exists between God and His people. The faithfulness of God to His covenant people should guide our marriage and family relationships.

1.9. Marriage and the Mission of God

God revealed His mission in the Creation story both when he created man and at the point when He instituted marriage. He gave His purpose in creating man and His purpose in marriage. His mission and purposes are effectively carried out when the man and woman work in unity with Him, their Creator, and in unity with each other as partners in mission. Marriage thus becomes the ideal context where the mission of God begins and is effectively carried out. It is in this light that the family is the foundation of both the church and the society. A good marriage, which has its foundation in the Lord, gives hope for a just society and a better world.

It is very important for us to know the purpose of God for our lives. Knowing the will of God and doing it will lead to the welfare of the family, the church, the community, and the world. This is summed up in the key verse of the book of Romans:

> And we know that for those who love God all things work together for good, for those who are called according to his purpose. (Romans 8:28)

God created and called us according to His purpose, and He works all things according to His plan and purpose (Eph 1:9–11). God had a plan for man in Creation and has called us to fit into that plan so that through us He will carry out His purpose. Whatever happens in the world, good or bad, is according to that plan and purpose, and all things will work out together to that end. Paul urges the Christians in Ephesus to seek a close relation with God in order to be wise enough to know His will. This call is all the more urgent given the confusion, chaos, and evil—especially the evil that has risen to the degree of violence and cruelty that we see today. And thus he advises,

> Look carefully then how you walk, not as unwise but as wise, making the best use of the time, because the days are evil. Therefore do not be foolish, but understand what the will of the Lord is. (Eph 5:15–17)

I want to stress that it is important to know the will of God and the purpose for which He made us and which he called us to, so as not to repeat the failures of the first humans, Adam and Eve. The purpose and call of God was to be faithful to Him, living in obedience to Him in order to spread the blessings of Eden to the whole earth. Adam and Eve betrayed the purpose of God and so occasioned the Fall of man, which has affected the world, leading to wickedness, violence, ruthlessness, and chaos. And now it is only God's grace that can redeem and restore things to where they were when He created everything very good. Thankfully, God sent His Son, the Christ, to show us the way. This is why we are going to look to Jesus as our example when we discuss the mission of God.

1.9.1. The Regal Aspect of Man's Duties

God said, before He had created the man and the woman, that they would subdue the earth and have dominion over fish, birds, and livestock, and over all the earth (Gen 1:26). The fact that man was created in the image of God prepared him for the duties he would carry out as God's vice regent. God is the sovereign Ruler of the earth, and the man (and the woman) would be called to rule as God's representatives and so would rule wisely and justly. The term "to subdue" in the present context means that the man and woman would make earth's resources beneficial to themselves and to others. And this also means that they would develop and manage the resources of the earth, making these useful to all of humanity.

Their careful and wise exploitation would then be the basis of scientific, technological, and economic development. So the command to subdue and rule the earth that God gave the man certainly points to the fact that God ordained development for the welfare of peoples and societies.

So we see that God commanded man to work at the time of Creation. "Work," in this case, meant doing productive activity to meet his needs: agricultural exploitation, producing food, tending livestock, nursing plants for vegetables and for fruits, and so forth. Everyone is therefore to work and not to be lazy. And Paul gave this advice to the believers in Thessalonica:

> For even when we were with you, we would give you this command: If anyone is not willing to work, let him not eat. For we hear that some among you walk in idleness, not busy at work, but busybodies. Now such persons we command and encourage in the Lord Jesus Christ to do their work quietly and to earn their own living. (2 Thess 3:10–12)

God set us the example by His work of creation. When He sent Jesus Christ on earth, He gave Jesus work to do following the Father's example. And Jesus Himself testifies in the following verses:

> The works that the Father has given me to accomplish, the very works that I am doing, bear witness about me that the Father has sent me. - My Father is working until now, and I am working. - Truly, truly, I say to you, the Son can do nothing of his own accord, but only what he sees the Father doing. For whatever the Father does, that the Son does likewise. (John 5:36, 17, 19)

Jesus did what His Father did and so was an example for us to follow. He exemplified work by what He did and said about work and took joy in accomplishing the work that the Father gave him to do. And so He told His disciples:

> My food is to do the will of him who sent me and to accomplish his work. (John 4:34)

Paul also showed the believers an example of how they ought to work and gave them this order:

> With toil and labour we worked night and day, that we might not be a burden to any of you. (2 Thess 3:8)

So how should we work in a way to be doing the will of God, carrying out His purposes? We should follow the example set by God, Jesus, and the apostles. This will result in the well-being of all living in a healthy environment. So we have come to understand that the evil exploitation and the resulting pollution of modern technological development is the consequence of a fallen world—a world that is greedy and is turning its back on God and His values. Bad governance results in oppression, injustice, violence, or even wars, and consequently misery in the life of the people governed. But good governance results in the just management and distribution of resources, both material and human, so that there is well-being, peace, and joy.

The regal responsibility of man was recognized by David the psalmist, who, picturing the order of Creation as it unfolded in Genesis 1 and 2, carefully describes it in the following words:

> What is man that you are mindful of him, and the son of man that you care for him? Yet you have made him a little lower than the heavenly beings and crowned him with glory and honour. You have given him dominion over the works of your hands; you have put all things under his feet. (Ps 8:4–6)

Psalm 8 is a hymn that praises the glorious Creator and celebrates the glory and privileged position of man in the creation order. Man, Adam and Eve, the pinnacle of God's creation, was crowned with glory and made ruler of all of God's creation. Indeed, Honor Books (2003:7) rightly says that "man is heaven's masterpiece."

The psalm is covenantal and speaks of man in general terms and depicts Israel as the called-out servant to live worthily before the Lord. In verses 4–6, the psalm looks beyond Israel, to Jesus, the Davidic king, th eideal Israel, and the ideal man, the Son of Man, being crowned with glory. The reign of Christ will be the culmination of His ministry and the consummation of all things, when there will be no pain and tears, but rather joy and peace, because God Himself will rule perfectly.

The psalmist's use of the phrase "the work of your hand" to describe all that God has made, including man, the pinnacle of His creation, which He skilfully formed, is meaningful and revealing.[13] This motif is picked up and used in several other places in the Scriptures. As we have seen before, man is the primary work of God's hands. This is expressed by David in the following psalm:

> The LORD will fulfill his purpose for me; your steadfast love, O LORD, endures forever. Do not forsake the work of your hands. (Ps 138:8)

---

[13] The skilful masterpiece of God's handiwork, which was the creation of man, still continues, and it is now done beginning in the womb and continues when, through the Spirit, in Christ and by the Word, one is born again, rightly called the new creation (Ps 139:14–16; Titus 3:5–6; 2 Cor 5:17; 1 Peter 1:18).

Yes, David sees himself as the special work of God's hand, His creation, as he very well expresses in Psalm 139:14.

So the man, as the design and creation of God's hand, will reflect God, his maker, for several reasons—not only because of the image of God in him, but also because God's work will be his blueprint. He is going to imitate God in the work of his own hands.

God created the man for a purpose, and so David prays and trusts that God will accomplish the specific plan He has for him. And so it is that when God has done his work in a man, he is able to do what God created him to do. We see this in the affirmation of David in the following psalm:

> Let the favour of the Lord our God be upon us,
> and establish the work of our hands upon us; yes,
> establish the work of our hands! (Psalm 90:17)

As previously stated, the grace of God was at work at Creation. The grace of God is what moves Him. And man is the object of His grace and love, from the beginning to the end. David is well aware of this. He knows that without the grace and blessing of God, he cannot succeed or be effective in life. It is only that which is done with the help and blessing of the Lord that has eternal value. And how did God effectively prepare man so that he would effectively carry out the work of his hands, which will be His glory and praise? This foundation and the means of achieving His purpose in us and through us was accomplished in the art of creation beginning in the womb, which is described as "fearfully and wonderfully made" (Ps 139:14). Bible scholars' interpretation of this piece of Scripture, which describes God's creation, is revealing, for it connects it with the rest of the Bible passages that speak to God's covenantal love. The ESV Study Bible (2008) footnote favours the text that reads, "I am fearfully set apart." This makes us appreciate what God does in creating us even more when we marvel over the skilful work that He does on us as we see the mysterious process of a baby's development. We find it even more striking when we realize that we are "fearfully set apart" even from the womb. This, then, corresponds to the meaning of the word as used when God sets

His people apart, as in Exodus 8:22. When God set apart the land of Goshen, where His people were, He distinguished them from the Egyptians by showing them favour in that none of the plagues that He visited on the Egyptians affected the Israelites. And He added that the Egyptians and Pharaoh "may know that I am the LORD in the midst of the earth." This recognition formula is used repeatedly by God to highlight the purpose of His actions, especially His mighty acts of judgment or His gracious acts, to show His favour and steadfast love towards His covenant people. This means that God sets us apart to display His glory and to make people know Him and recognize that He is God of the whole world. So there is a missiological purpose that underlies God's setting us apart. It has rightly been said that God loves us for the world, and that is why we are called to be missionaries. God calls us and positions us to win the world to Him. All the blessings of His favour, including His provision, equipping and protection, are to enable us to be, and to do His will. In other words, this is a call to an inner transformation in us and in our mission and ministry. God transforms us into His image in order that we may be agents of transformation so that Christ's person and character are formed in those we minister to. It is this that Paul is in anguish to bring forth when he addresses the Galatians, saying, "... my little children, for whom I am again in the anguish of childbirth until Christ is formed in you" (Gal 4:19). And when this is fully accomplished, for those won to Christ and brought up to fully reflect His image, His glory and the glory of God will be seen in the world, because God in Christ has come to dwell in them. And this is the truth he points out regarding his ministry among the Colossians, as we read in Colossians 1:27–29. And so he brings out the crux and hallmark of the covenant revealed to the saints, as we read in this important verse:

> To them God chose to make known how great among
> the Gentiles are the riches of the glory of this mystery,
> which is Christ in you, the hope of glory. (Col 1:27)

The blessings of God, first to the Jews and now mediated by Paul to the gentiles, were embodied in the mystery which is being revealed and working in the Colossians and in the rest of the Gentile believers, to which we also now belong.[14] Our recreation, through which we are called to an ever-increasing inner transformation, is the grace and love of God, doing its work in us, for His sake. Paul describes how the work of creation in the beginning is continued when the gospel of truth is proclaimed and it meets with faith:

> Put off your old self, which belongs to your former manner of life and is corrupt through deceitful desires, and to be renewed in the spirit of your minds, and to put on the new self, created after the likeness of God in true righteousness and holiness. (Eph 4:22–24)

The total inner transformation of a person begins with the mind, and the person begins to think in new and right wayswhen he or she meditates on the truth of God's Word and old habits are put away. The heart of the believer is transformed, and he becomes a new man, "the new self." The believer is therefore recreated in Christ after "the likeness of God," which connects this process with the original creation of God in Genesis when "God created man in His own image" (Gen 1:27). New life in Christ happens at conversion, but the building up and sanctification is a process that continues throughout the Christian life until the believer attains mature manhood and the fullness of Christ. This being the case,

---

[14] Paul explains the grace of God, seen in His blessings to the Jews in Romans 9:4–5. He lists eight blessings: adoption (as sons), the glory, the covenants (that God made with their forefathers [the patriarchs], the law which was given to them through Moses, the worship [of God], the promises that God made them, the patriarchs [Abraham, Isaac, and Jacob], and, above all, the Christ (the Messiah), who is God. The new covenant mediated by Christ and ratified through His blood (death and resurrection) have now accrued to the Gentiles, culminating in Christ and God coming to dwell in the Gentile saints, as Paul describes his ministry to the Christians in Colossae (Col 1:24–29).

all Christian believers should aspire to grow "to the measure of the stature of the fullness of Christ" (Eph 4:13).[15]

This is the very truth that Paul describes in his epistle to the Colossians. He begins with the divine nature, God's very nature, being full and complete in Christ the Son. He then extends that to the Christians, who in Christ—that is, in union with Christ, and having become sons (daughters) of God—are full and complete:

> And you have been filled in him, who is the head of all rule and authority. (Col 2:10)

This is indeed a remarkable statement, because this implies that we share in Christ's authority since we are in union with Him. Through the grace of God, we have come to share His glory and excellence (2 Peter 1:3), as we are called to live in harmony with and reflect God's own moral character. And though we have become "partakers of the divine nature" (2 Peter 1:4), we do not become part of God, or divine in the same way as Jesus Christ is, but amazingly, we share in His nature, as we become increasingly like him (2 Cor 3:18).

Christ is not only the means and mediator of the riches of the grace of God; He is the example every Christian should seek to pursue, such that the world looking at us would see Christ. And the purpose of God for us is that we become like Christ. And given that He is working in us to make us both willing and able (Phil 2:13), He will continue to work this out in our lives. C. S. Lewis, in his book *Mere Christianity*, says that this process of growth that Christ gradually works in the believer turns him into a new little Christ who shares His joys and power.

The work of God in us through Christ is ongoing, and since He is faithful we can trust Him that He will bring this work to completion, as Paul affirms here:

---

[15] The fullness of Christ is the full expression of both His divine and human nature in perfection. The fullness of God is in Christ, and He is "the exact imprint of God's nature" (Heb 1:2) and the image of the invisible God (Col 1:15). And as Paul says elsewhere, "In him the whole fullness of deity dwells bodily" (Col 2:9).

> And I am sure of this, that he who began a good work in you will bring it to completion at the day of Jesus Christ. (Phil 1:6)

This work will be completed when Christ returns and glorifies us by giving us new bodies in the resurrection:

> But our citizenship is in heaven, and from it we await a Saviour, the Lord Jesus Christ, who will transform our lowly body to be like his glorious body, by the power that enables him even to subject all things to himself. (Phil 3:20–21)

All that we need to do is unconditionally surrender ourselves to Him so that He will have free reign to do His work in us. He often accomplishes this work in the crucible or furnace of great trials and all that He engineers in our lives to finally perfect His work in us, such that, in the end, the whole tapestry is done for all to see, as Paul succinctly describes in Romans 8:28–30. This process of spiritual transformation is best defined by Barton (2008:15–16) as follows:

> Spiritual transformation is the process by which Christ is formed in us for the glory of God, for the abundance of our lives and for the sake of others.

The biblical metaphor of the process of the transformation of the embryo in the womb (into the child that is brought forth in the pangs of child birth), which Paul uses in Galatians 4:19, had already been used by David in Psalm 139:13–16, as quoted previously. So our call is to be part of the revival that God is poised to see break out as His Spirit moves in His church. God is continuing the work of creation nowadays through us, as He uses us in Christ for the new creation as we faithfully give the world the gospel of truth for the salvation of mankind (Rom 1:16). The history of the church has been punctuated by revivals, characterized by the ebb and flow of the Spirit in the church. When the church has been at low ebb, the Lord has moved and touched people to pray and bring about a revival from on high. The more people have surrendered themselves to the Lord and His service, the more the Spirit has moved to revive the church.

We could give the phrase "fearfully set apart" (Ps 139:14) another sense, the objective sense, as we see in Genesis 35:5, where "a terror from God fell upon the people of the cities" through which Jacob and his sons travelled, and so the people became afraid and did not attack them. This fear also seized the servants of Abimelech, king of Gerar, when he had told them of the warning of God to punish him because he had taken Sarah, the wife of Abraham (Gen 20:8). So when God chooses people to fulfil His purposes, they become special, because they are set apart. And because they bear the image of God and the fear of God is in them, people will be afraid to touch them, because God berates people who speak against his anointed, as it was in the case of Miriam and Aaron (Num 12:7–8). He also said, "Touch not my anointed ones" (Ps 105:15), for, as He later warned, whoever touches His people Israel, "touches the apple of his eye" (Zech 2:8).

In the above section, we have looked at the regal duties of man. And we have seen that God gave the first man the responsibility of working the land, taking care of it and the animals (livestock, the birds, fish, and so on [i.e., the living things]). His work included stewardship, management, and governance, which means ruling over these. This part of man's duty focuses primarily on man and his material needs and all that belongs to him and comes to his benefit and for his well-being. We have also seen the work of God in the process of renewal and transformation, when God works on people after they have heard the gospel and believed in Christ and the Holy Spirit transforms and builds them up.

However, when the focus shifts, and is on God, His service, and his glory, as well as taking care of the spiritual needs of God's people, this is where the priestly work of man begins. This I will examine in the following section. We have already seen above that God sets people apart to fulfil His purposes.

1.9.2. The Priestly Duties of Man

Chapter 1 of Genesis highlights the regal duties and character of man (the human being)—how he was given command to govern (that is, to have dominion over the other created beings) and to manage the land and its resources. The second phase of Creation, narrated in Genesis 2, focuses on the priestly status and functions of the man (Adam and Eve, representing the human being). Of all the created living beings, it is to man alone that God gave a royal and priestly status, because he was made in His image.

As we will see later, it will not be necessary or easy to draw the line between the regal and priestly functions of man, because the work that God's people do in pursuit of their calling should be for the glory of God, as Paul says:[16]

> whatever you do, do all to the glory of God. (1 Cor 10:31)

And Paul tells the Christians in Colossae that whatever task or work they are doing, they are doing it for the Lord; and so they "are serving the Lord Christ" (Col 3:23–24). Peter, in the same line, says that we are the called, the chosen, and that we are a holy priesthood whose purpose is to proclaim and reflect the excellencies—that is, the glory and marvellous light of God in a dark and fallen world (1 Peter 2:9). And Jesus said that we are the light of the world, called to work in such a way as to glorify God (Matt 5:14, 16), and that whatever we do to His people, (i.e., those who believe in Him), we do it for Him (Matt 25:40).

This therefore means that all the work we do is to the end of

---

[16] The aim or purpose of God for man, right from the Creation, is to glorify Him, and thus we are to live for the sole goal of glorifying Him (Eph 3:3–6). This is what God said through His prophet: "Bring my sons from afar and my daughters from the end of the earth, everyone who is called by my name, whom I created for my glory, whom I formed and made" (Isaiah 43:6–7). God created man to work, but work was meant to be a means of glorifying God, not an end in itself; neither should we make what we get from our work an end in itself, as Solomon cautions here in his wisdom: "Do not toil to acquire wealth; be discerning enough to desist" (Prov 23:4).

ministering to God the Father, to Jesus Christ, and to His people. So even civil leaders and governing authorities not only exercise their regal functions but are also called to carry out priestly functions, shepherding God's people. The tone was set by God Himself when He chose and anointed David to rule His people, Israel, as He says here, in His indictment against the wayward prophets and priests of Israel:

> Thus says the Lord GOD: Ah, shepherds of Israel who have been feeding yourselves! Should not shepherds feed the sheep? I myself will be the shepherd of my sheep, and I myself will make them lie down, declares the Lord GOD ... And I will set up over them one shepherd, my servant David, and he shall feed them: he shall feed them and be their shepherd. And I, the LORD, will be their God, and my servant David shall be prince among them. I am the LORD; I have spoken. (Eze 34:2, 15, 23–24)

David was appointed to govern the people of Israel. However, he would be required also to exercise priestly functions. When the leaders of Judah—the judges, priests, and prophets—failed in their work, God took over to shepherd and to restore the scattered, hurting, and exploited sheep, as a good shepherd would do. God will in time send Jesus to shepherd His people. Jesus picked this shepherd motif up, reflecting what God specified in the prophecy of Ezekiel, and echoed it in the good shepherd passages in the gospel of John, as we read, for example, in the following verses:

> I am the good shepherd. I know my own and my own know me. And I have other sheep that are not of this fold. I must bring them also, and they will listen to my voice. So there will be one flock, one shepherd. (John 10:14, 16)

What we see God and Jesus doing is the work of the priest and the prophets. And so we see that the governing or regal duties of David blended into the priestly functions. And so we can see that this was a precursor to the kingly and priestly functions of the Davidic Messiah, Jesus Christ. The prophets therefore foresaw the coming of the Messiah who would be both king and priest, as predicted in the following Scripture:

> Behold, the days are coming, declares the LORD, when I will raise up for David a righteous Branch, and he shall reign as king and deal wisely, and shall execute justice and righteousness in the land. (Jer 23:5)

And indeed, when Jesus came, people realized that He was the Messiah and King of Israel, as we read in the following Scriptures:

> Now after Jesus was born in Bethlehem of Judea in the days of Herod the king, behold, wise men from the east came to Jerusalem, saying, "Where is he who has been born king of the Jews? For we saw his star when it rose and have come to worship him." (Matt 2:1–2)

> Nathanael answered him, "Rabbi, you are the Son of God! You are the King of Israel!" Jesus answered him, "You will see greater things than these." And he said to him, "Truly, truly, I say to you, you will see heaven opened, and the angels of God ascending and descending on the Son of Man." (John 1:49–51)

The Wise men from the East recognized Jesus as the king of the Jews. Nathanael saw in Jesus not only the king of Israel but also the Son of God—that is, the Messiah—which is what both appellations signified in the Old Testament. And Jesus communicated to him and to us that He, the Son of Man, the Messiah, would do greater things than any yet seen, even in the Old Testament, because He was not only the greater Adam but was also greater than Solomon because He was the Promised One in the Davidic line. When Jesus calls Himself the Son of Man, He means that he is not just a son of *a* man, an ordinary human being, but the greatest man of all time.

"Son of Man" is a messianic title that refers back to the human–divine figure described in Isaiah as "one like a son of man"—the one who will be given dominion over all, the one whom all peoples and nations will serve (Dan 7:13–14). And Jesus echoes this when He declares to the Jews the purpose of His coming into the world:

> And I, when I am lifted up from the earth, will draw all people to myself. (John 12:32)

On his way to Paddan-ram, Jacob had a vision of the heavens opening and a ladder with angels descending and ascending on it (Gen 28:12). When Jacob became aware of the presence of God, he exclaimed, "How awesome is this place! This is none other than the house of God, and this is the gate of heaven" (Gen 28:17). Jacob's vision prefigured Jesus and His redemption and mediation work. We see Jesus interpreting it in John 1:51. Jesus is the greater way or access to God, greater than the ladder on which angels moved between Jacob and God. Bethel foreshadowed Jesus, the new temple of God, (as He Himself intimated in John 2:19). Jesus is the way to God and His presence mediates the presence of God (John 14:6, 9–10). And so wherever Jesus is, God is. He is thus the "new Bethel", God's sanctuary, the house of God (the temple). As Bethel was where God was revealed to Jacob, so is Jesus the revelation of God to us.

The words *"Messiah"* (Hebrew) and *"Christ"* (Greek) both mean "The anointed of God." In the Old Testament and Judaism, "Messiah" summed up a number of expectations about the coming "anointed one:" He would save, teach and lead God's people. He is the great King and Saviour in the line of David (predicted, for example in 2 Samuel 7:13–14). So Jesus, the Davidic King, is a fulfilment of prophecy and as such links the Old Testament and the New Testament, mediating the new covenant. His death on the cross already opened the way for God's people, believers, to approach God (Heb 10:19). This affirmed the new covenant established by Christ during the Last Supper and sanctioned the universal priesthood of believers. This will be further discussed later in this study.

After God had created the man, He put him in the garden. The description of the Garden of Eden paints the picture of a garden that resembles a park. The location of the garden is not specified, so it would be plausible to think, as some biblical scholars have said, that this was intended to be part of the divine sanctuary.[17] The reason why God asked Moses and the children of Israel to construct the tabernacle was because He wanted to come and meet with His people there:

> The LORD said to Moses, "Speak to the people of Israel, that they take for me a contribution. And let them make me a sanctuary, that I may dwell in their midst. Exactly as I show you concerning the pattern of the tabernacle, and of all its furniture, so you shall make it." (Exod 25:1–2, 8–9)

So originally God wanted the Garden of Eden to be the place where He would come and meet the man and woman He had created in His own image and fellowship with them. This will be evident in Genesis 3, where we read that God comes taking a walk in the garden in the cool of the day (Gen 3:8). If things had worked for the man and woman as God had planned, then we would see that during His meetings with them, He would talk with them, giving them more instructions concerning their work. And the man and women would in turn give Him an account of their work. This would be a time of joyful communion, when the man and woman would enjoy the presence of God and relish in His presence. The Lord God our Father is seeking the presence of His own, who are His joy. This is well expressed by Johnson (1996:14) in this quote:

---

[17] Bible scholars see heaven, God's dwelling, as the temple or sanctuary, as we can read from these Scriptures: "In my distress I called upon the LORD; to my God I cried for help. From his temple he heard my voice, and my cry to him reached his ears" (Ps 18:6). "The LORD is in his holy temple; the LORD's throne is in heaven; his eyes see, his eyelids test the children of man" (Ps 11:4). The same idea is found in other Scriptures, such as Micah 1:2 and Habakkuk 3:20. This supports the idea that Eden was intended to be the sanctuary of God, where His will is done. This will be in line with perception of Jesus. He taught His disciples to pray, "Your will be done on earth, as it is in heaven" (Matt 6:10). Adam and Eve were driven out of Eden because they disobeyed and therefore failed to do God's will.

God created us out of love and stamped us with His image. He chose for Himself the role of parent, relishing human companionship as pictured by His walking in the cool of the day with Adam and Eve in a young creation. God delights in us and wants us to connect with Him.

The sisters of the Evangelical Sisters of Darmstadt, Germany, fellowship with God even when they work in their garden, planting seeds or harvesting crops: vegetables, fruits, and suchlike. They sense the presence of God with them and testify that they find joy and satisfaction in their work because at this point the garden becomes a sanctuary where they sing and worship God, who gives rain and causes the garden to produce and yield a good harvest. This fits with what Helen Steiner Rice (1992) says in the following poem:

> My Garden beautifies my yard
> And adds fragrance to the air …
> But it is also my cathedral
> And my quiet place of prayer.

So the above poem is in line with the notion that Eden, "the Garden of the Lord" (Isaiah 51:3), was meant to be His sanctuary on His virgin created earth.

Though Adam and Eve failed to make the Garden of Eden, and subsequently the whole earth, the temple of God, a sanctuary where God's presence would be felt, seen, worshipped, and glorified, He was determined to see that His purposes would be accomplished. His plan will never be thwarted (Job 42:2). So He declared to the people of Israel, who, after the rebellion of Adam and Eve, had also rebelled against Him:

> But truly, as I live, and as all the earth shall be filled with the glory of the LORD, none of the men who have seen my glory and my signs that I did in Egypt and in the wilderness shall see the land that I swore to give to their fathers. (Num 14:21–23)

The glory of the Lord is the special presence of the Lord God with His people, especially at the sanctuary. The glory of God filled the tabernacle and the temple (Exod 40:34–35; 1 Samuel 8:11). Habakkuk affirmed and echoed what the Lord declared to rebellious Israel, as he and other prophets strongly believed and longed for the day when the glory and light of God would fill the whole earth, including the pagan nations. Even though the Children of Israel disobeyed and rebelled against the Lord, and even though wicked nations oppressed and mistreated Judah and Israel, He will come to His people and the nations will see His presence:

> For the earth will be filled with the knowledge of
> the glory of the LORD as the waters cover the sea.
> (Hab 2:14)

David, who was earnestly seeking the presence of the Lord, earnest prayed:

> Blessed be the LORD, the God of Israel, who alone
> does wondrous things. Blessed be his glorious name
> forever; may the whole earth be filled with his glory!
> Amen and Amen! (Ps 72:18–19)

God's purposes can never be defeated by human failure. Despite the sin of Adam, which led to the Fall and the rebellion of all people, He will fulfill His plans for the world.

God wanted to stay connected to Adam and Eve and work with them. But, as stated above, it did not quite work out that way because of the Fall! And as Paul said, Adam "was a type of the one who was to come" (Rom 5:14). Jesus, the second Adam and the ideal man, would perfectly exemplify the kind of fellowship that God wanted His people to have with Him in accomplishing His mission. Jesus started His day by communing with the Father so they could plan the day together, as Mark tells us:

> And rising very early in the morning, while it was
> still dark, he departed and went out to a desolate
> place, and there he prayed. (Mark 1:35)

He also ended the day with the Father (i.e., after the day's work, He went to the Father to give Him a report), as Matthew tells us:

> And after he had dismissed the crowds, he went up on the mountain by himself to pray. When evening came, he was there alone. (Matt 14:23)

Although the above text says Jesus was alone, it is to be understood that He was with the Father, and even with the Holy Spirit at this point. Matthew meant that no human was with Him, since He had dismissed the crowd.

And when Jesus had an important decision to make, He would spend even more time with the Father to discuss and agree on the best choices and the best way to go. He strategized together with the His Father. This we see in the following report by Luke:

> In these days he went out to the mountain to pray, and all night he continued in prayer to God. And when day came, he called his disciples and chose from them twelve, whom he named apostles. (Luke 6:12–13)

Choosing the right partners or followers, those who would later continue the work after His departure, was crucial for the accomplishment of the messianic mission, or the Great Commission. We measure the importance of this task by how much time Jesus spent with the Father praying (talking and discussing with Him): *all night*. The Lord and God held an all-night prayer meeting! This is challenging! The church, as Paul rightly said, was going to be built on the foundation of the apostles (and the prophets), and this is why Jesus had to think hard and spend that much time in prayer before acting. This teaches us that we need to take time in prayer in order to choose those to be involved with us in the mission of God.

How much time do we spend praying when we choose leaders in our churches or groups? The apostles had learned this very well, as we see in the early church: it was when the believers were in the presence of God, fasting and worshipping Him, that the Holy Spirit revealed to them the choice of Barnabas and Saul, to set them apart as missionaries (Acts 13:2). And so it was reported:

> Then after fasting and praying they laid their hands on them and sent them off.(Acts 13:3)

In the same light, it is also needful for young people to spend time praying, as they look for the right spouse. For, as stated previously, our spouses are our ministry or mission partners. This does not only speak to young people, for marriage can take place at any age. Although John Wesley got married in his late forties, he unfortunately made a wrong choice after failing twice to marry the ladies he fell in love with. In the end, he made a hasty decision, getting married to Marry Vazeille, the nurse who took care of him in her home when he suffered a fall. It had been just one week after meeting her! And this wrong choice made life very difficult for him. In Robert Morgan (1997), we read the following account of one of the unhappy moments of their marriage, given by John Hampson, one of John Wesley's friends:

> Once I went into a room and found Mrs. Wesley foaming with fury. Her husband was on the floor, where she had been trailing him by the hair of his head; and she was still holding in her hand venerable locks which she had plucked by the roots. I felt as though I could have knocked the soul out of her.

The marriage of John and Mary was a disaster. The two spent little time together, such that when Mary died, John was not informed, and he found out only after she had been buried. Again this example of a failed marriage tells us how much we need to pray and plead before God and seek wise counsel before getting locked in marriage. Therefore, we see from Jesus' example, and from the example of the believers in the early church, that working with God is a must in our mission strategy. Jesus said this to His disciples, just as He is reminding us today:

> Abide in me, and I in you. As the branch cannot bear fruit by itself, unless it abides in the vine, neither can you, unless you abide in me. I am the vine; you are the branches. Whoever abides in me and I in him, he it is that bears much fruit, for apart from me you can do nothing. (John 15:4–5)

Even after communing with the Father before and after His day's work to strategize, He stayed in contact with Him all the time; and the Father accompanied Him as He worked away. And so while at work He would raise His head and hands up to consult with the Father or ask Him for His blessing. Much more importantly, closeness and oneness with the Father are things that Jesus demonstrated in His work strategy and life. He Himself tells Philip, one of the disciples, the following:

> Do you not believe that I am in the Father and the Father is in me? The words that I say to you I do not speak on my own authority, but the Father who dwells in me does his works. Believe me that I am in the Father and the Father is in me, or else believe on account of the works themselves. (John 14:10–11)

God's design for work was reflected and modelled by Jesus, the second Adam. He saw the work His Father did at Creation, since He was with Him and participated in the Creation Himself, as John tells us:

> In the beginning was the Word, and the Word was with God, and the Word was God. He was in the beginning with God. All things were made through him, and without him was not anything made that was made. (John 1:1–3)

In the Creation story, God is the Creator doing the work and bringing all that was created into being. Jesus accompanies Him in this work. After this, there is the work of governing and caring for all of creation, including humans. Whatever God does and whatever Jesus does becomes spiritual because it is done with the Spirit; it lasts and therefore is eternal. After God created the world, His daily and ongoing work has consisted in ruling and maintaining the created world, saving and protecting His people—those who believe in His Son, Jesus Christ.

And Jesus is sent down to earth by the Father with a mission: to save the world and draw all who believe in Him to God the Father. And so He said,

> And I, when I am lifted up from the earth, will draw
> all people to myself. (John 12:32)

Jesus came into the world in human form (John 1:14; Phil 2:7–8). And since humans "shared in flesh and blood, Jesus himself likewise partook of the same things" (Heb 2:14), this means that Jesus became truly human, sharing the feelings and responsibilities of humans. He, from childhood, did the chores that children do at home and helped His father in his carpenter's shop. And He was obedient to His parents Luke 2:51). And so He had an ordinary life until He started His public ministry.

It was when Jesus started His public ministry that He focused on the priestly ministry. And He worked with the Father in tandem, as we have already seen above. And when we look closely and follow His movements, we will see that He worked closely with the Father, whether it concerned teaching, saving people, healing them, raising some from the dead, performing all the signs and wonders, feeding the crowd, or other such acts. God was working with Him. And so, at one point when He saw a blind man needing healing, He told His disciples that the condition of the man was there for a purpose:

> that the works of God might be displayed in him.
> We must work the works of him who sent me while
> it is day; night is coming, when no one can work.
> (John 9:4)

And when He is confronted by the Jews who persecuted Him because He healed a man on the Sabbath, He answered them:

> My Father is working until now, and I am working. (John 5:17)

Having seen the work of the Father and the Son from Creation and having seen the nature of their work, I will now look at the priestly function of man. We will see that this reflects the ministry of Jesus and the work of God.

God put the man "in the garden of Eden to work it and keep it" (2:15).

The term "work" (Hebrew [Hb] "*abad*") denotes preparing and tending the ground. And the word "keep" (Hb "*shamar*") adds to it the idea of preparing and tending it. Since the command to work (verses 5 and 15) was given before man sinned, work would not be punishment or something to be avoided. It follows that productive work is part of God's purpose for man in creation.

Later on in the Bible, the same verbs are used together to portray the work carried out by the priests and Levites in the tabernacle, meaning "minister" or "serve" (Hb "*abad*") and "guard" (Hb "*shamar*"). These words are used in the following Scriptures in regard to the work of the Levites in the tabernacle in the service of God:

> Bring the tribe of Levi near, and set them before Aaron the priest, that they may minister to him. They shall keep guard over him and over the whole congregation before the tent of meeting, as they minister at the tabernacle. They shall guard all the furnishings of the tent of meeting, and keep guard over the people of Israel as they minister at the tabernacle. (Num 3:6–8)

These very words are also used with regard to the work of the priests, as we read in the following text:

> So the LORD said to Aaron, you and your sons with you shall guard your priesthood for all that concerns the altar and that is within the veil; and you shall serve. I give your priesthood as a gift. (Num 18:1, 7)

So the same words used to describe the regal functions of the man are also used to describe his priestly duties. The sense of each word changes according to the context. When it concerns meeting the needs of the man, especially His spiritual and bodily needs, keeping the whole person—body, soul, and spirit—in good health, this parallels what God does for His people. He saves and keeps both man and all of creation. These words with their specific meanings are used, for example, in the following Scriptures:

> My help comes from the LORD, who made heaven and earth. The LORD is your keeper; the LORD is your shade on your right hand. (Ps 121:2 & 5)

> Bless the LORD, O my soul, and forget not all his benefits, who forgives all your iniquity, who heals all your diseases, who redeems your life from the pit, who crowns you with steadfast love and mercy. (Ps 103:2–5)

> After two days he will revive us; on the third day he will raise us up, that we may live before him. (Hos 6:2)

> Now may the God of peace himself sanctify you completely, and may your whole spirit and soul and body be kept blameless at the coming of our Lord Jesus Christ (1 Thess 5:3)

> Are they not all ministering spirits sent out to serve for the sake of those who are to inherit salvation? (Heb 1:14)

The verses quoted above describe what God does for His people. The priests in the Old Testament served as the representatives of God among the people and served the people by enabling them to be in a position where they would effectively receive their covenant blessings.

The key word that best expresses the priestly duties of man is "serve," along with its derivative, "service," which translates into "minister" and "ministry," respectively. And again taking our cue from Jesus, we can see how He tells us about His ministry:

> The Son of Man came not to be served but to serve, and to give his life as a ransom for many. (Mark 10:45)

Moses and Jesus are called servants of God in the Old Testament, and the writer of Hebrews characterizes their ministry in the following way:

> Therefore, holy brothers, you who share in a heavenly calling, consider Jesus, the apostle and high priest of our confession, who was faithful to him who appointed him, just as Moses also was faithful in all God's house. (Heb 3:1–2)

The above text describes the roles of God's most faithful servants, both messengers of God. Jesus is called "the apostle" (i.e., "the sent one," or "one who is sent"). A faithful servant is one who serves wholeheartedly. The Bafut translation of verse 2 brings out the point clearly:

> He [Jesus] was working for God who appointed him with all his heart, just as Moses was also working with all his heart in the house of God.

So again, here the word that characterizes the ministry of both Moses and Jesus is "serve" (and its derivative "servant," which occurs in verse 5: "Now Moses was faithful in all God's house as a servant.") It is to be noted that the word "servant" is translated into Bafut as "person who works" or "worker."

Talking about the purpose of the gifts of the Spirit, Paul says that these spiritual gifts were given to equip the Christians for the work of ministry, as we read here in the following verse:

> And he gave the apostles, the prophets, the evangelists, the shepherds and teachers, to equip the saints for the work of ministry, for building up the body of Christ. (Eph 4:11–12)

Paul describes the effort of building up and equipping the saints and strengthening the church for work in ministry, pinpointing the priestly work of the priests (pastors or ministers).

Peter gives a more explicit and elaborate description of what the work of ministry in the church consists of and how and to what purpose it should be done:

> As each has received a gift, use it to serve one another, as good stewards of God's varied grace: whoever speaks, as one who speaks oracles of God; whoever serves, as one who serves by the strength that God supplies—in order that in everything God may be glorified through Jesus Christ. To him belong glory and dominion forever and ever. Amen. (1 Peter 4:10–11)

Through His work on the cross, Christ opened the way for us to approach God by grace, without an intermediary (except Christ). He made us nations of priests (Rev 1:6; Exod 19: 5–6; 1 Peter 2:9). And so the work of Jesus on the cross opened the way to God for all believers to be able to perform the priestly work, so doing away with the Levitical priesthood and passing their function onto the individual believer (Heb 10:19–22). And so, because of the universal priesthood of believers, we can perform the work of priests. This is affirmed by Peter in the following quote:

> As you come to him, a living stone rejected by men but in the sight of God chosen and precious, you yourselves like living stones are being built up as a spiritual house, to be a holy priesthood, to offer spiritual sacrifices acceptable to God through Jesus Christ. (1 Peter 2:4–5)

Therefore, in the new covenant, there is a new dispensation which now enables us to offer spiritual sacrifices, no longer blood and animal sacrifices of the old order. The writer of Hebrews gives us examples of spiritual sacrifices, as we read in the following verses:

> Through him then let us continually offer up a sacrifice of praise to God, that is, the fruit of lips that acknowledge his name. Do not neglect to do good and to share what you have, for such sacrifices are pleasing to God. (Heb 13:15–16)

So our songs of worship, our prayers, and all that we give to help people in need and to advance the work of the ministry and the kingdom of God, are now the sacrifices we offer. And such gifts Paul calls "a fragrant offering, a sacrifice acceptable and pleasing to God" (Phil 4:8). Of course, Paul exhorts us to first of all offer ourselves to God as living sacrifices (Rom 12:1; 2 Cor 8:5).

In this section we have carefully described the mission of God in marriage and thus in the family. God created man for a purpose, and the purposes of God, as stated previously, are best and most effectively carried out within the family. The family has been widened to include the people of God, which becomes the family of God. In the context of the New Testament, the family of God is the church. And the church begins in the family. Therefore, worship and ministry should begin in the family. Godly and strong Christian families will form the basis of the church. This is why in the Old Testament God laid emphasis on teaching the children, making sure the Word of God was visible in the family in the sense that it was lived and shared. This policy should characterize the family in our day and age.

We have also seen that at the beginning, God specified two functions of man: the regal and priestly duties. In the Old Testament the priestly duties were carried out mainly by one group of people, the Levitical priests, while the rest of the people, including the elders and judges (and kings), carried out the regal duties. However, Israel as a people are in the Prophets regarded as the embodiment of the servant of God and therefore were to carry out the priestly functions of reaching the nations for God. It is in the New Testament that believers are given the priestly functions. And so all that believers do will be seen as serving the Lord as they reach out with the gospel, establish churches, and build them up. And all practical work done, including works of mercy and care, can be seen as godly, because it is motivated by what the Christian faith or religion teaches, and so James reiterates:

> Religion that is pure and undefiled before God, the Father, is this: to visit orphans and widows in their affliction, and to keep oneself unstained from the world. (James 1:27)

This concept of ministry is brought home by this story of a child: A child who was very sick was painstakingly being cared for by his loving and compassionate mother. At the point where the mother became tired and discouraged, the child asked her, "As you are caring for me, you are serving God. Isn't it so, Mother?" This question by the child reminded the mother that it was God who had placed her in this difficult situation to show God's compassion. The mother was doing what God would do, as Isaiah says:

> Can a woman forget her nursing child, that she should have no compassion on the son of her womb? Even these may forget, yet I will not forget you. (Isa 49:15)

So we see that God's compassionate heart and care are embodied by the caring mother. Paul compared the caring and compassionate character of the pastoral work to that of a mother or a nurse (1 Thess 2:7–8). He is thus echoing what God says to Israel in Isaiah 66:13.

We have also seen how Jesus carried out His ministry. He worked with the Father, and wherever He was, the Father was. Working like the Christ, bringing God into all we do, we can make the world a sanctuary, making ourselves and all our work an offering unto the Lord, since all that we do in that case will be for the service of the Lord, as Paul tells us in Rom 12:1 and Col 3:23–24. Just as God intended the Garden of Eden to be a sanctuary, we can make the world a sanctuary of the Lord by our devotion and service to Him.

1.10. Blessed to be Fruitful

The motif "be fruitful and multiply" is recurrent in Genesis. It occurs in Genesis 1:22 when God blesses the sea and sky creatures. When God created the man and woman, He blessed them and said, "Be fruitful and multiply and fill the earth" (1:28). This motif is associated with God's blessing, for example, in Genesis 9:1, 7.

> And God blessed Noah and his sons and said to them, "Be fruitful and multiply and fill the earth. (Gen 9:1)

The motif tells us two things. Firstly, it tells us that being fruitful is a result of effective service. Man's hard and faithful work—that is, any kind of hard and faithful work or labour—will yield results. The farmer works hard to produce a good crop. This is related to what has been stated above about the regal aspect of man's work. At the same time, bearing fruit has also to do with the priestly aspect of man's work.

Jesus called His disciples to bear fruit for His Kingdom, as we read in the following text:

> I chose you and appointed you that you should go and bear fruit and that your fruit should abide, so that whatever you ask the Father in my name, he may give it to you. (John 15:16)

God is glorified when we do what He calls us to do. When Jesus was about to leave this world, He gave His report to the Father and said, "I glorified you on earth, having accomplished the work that you gave me to do (John 17:4). God's will for us is that we bear fruit. And so Jesus wanted His disciples also to glorify the Father as He did, by doing what He had called them to do, and so He told them the following:

> By this my Father is glorified, that you bear much fruit and so prove to be my disciples. (John 15:8)

Our joy in ministry comes from knowing that we are doing what God has called us to. And since we know that He has blessed us so we can serve Him, we will seek to surrender ourselves more to Him so He can work through us. Henry Nouwen (2011:56) tells us how we can position ourselves for effective fruit-bearing if we ask the following question:

> The question is not, "How much can I still do in the years that are left to me?" The question is, "How can I prepare myself for total surrender so my life can be fruitful?"

If we align ourselves with the movement of the Holy Spirit, He will empower us and make us able. The Holy Spirit produces fruit in our lives:

> The fruit of the Spirit is love, joy, peace, patience, kindness, goodness, faithfulness, gentleness, self-control; against such things there is no law. (Gal 5:22–23)

We are able to develop character and be effective in ministry because the Holy Spirit produces fruits in us, making us reflect the character of Christ. The beauty of Christ, reflected in our lives, enables us to attract and influence lives for Him. The good lives of believers who are witnesses for Christ make the gospel beautiful, as Paul tells Titus (Titus 2:10). Paul, who was always guided by the Holy Spirit, was very fruitful in his ministry, as we can see from what he says here:

> But on some points I have written to you very boldly by way of reminder, because of the grace given me by God to be a minister of Christ Jesus to the Gentiles in the priestly service of the gospel of God, so that the

offering of the Gentiles may be acceptable, sanctified
by the Holy Spirit. (Rom 15:15–16)

What Paul offers to God as an offering or sacrifice is the fruit of his ministry—that is, the Gentile Christians who believed in God as a result of his hard work.

The second thing about the motif of being fruitful has to do with bearing biological children.[18] This duty can be fulfilled only in marriage. So God's purpose in marriage is to produce children and form a family.[19] God here defines marriage as a union between a man and woman who will bear children in order to perpetuate the human race.[20] When God blesses and commands the first couple saying, "Be fruitful and multiply and fill the earth," He wants them to give birth and increase in number so as to populate the earth. This forms the basis of the biblical view that part of God's creation plan for mankind is to raise faithful children so that the whole earth may be populated by people who know Him and serve Him faithfully and wisely as vice regents. The children of Israel were required to teach their children the Word, statutes, and commands of the Lord so that, growing in the Lord, they would learn to walk by them and pass this on to succeeding generations:

---

[18] This motif is placed second because the more important thing about man is his being—that is, his character. That is why God created man in His image, as emphasized earlier in this chapter. Producing children and rearing them demands character, because who people are influences their children, hence the adage "Like father, like son."

[19] In God's redemption history, it is God that gives children, apart from the fact that the process of creation and recreation starts from the womb. He can give or withhold the gift of children, just as Jacob reminded Rachel: "When Rachel saw that she bore Jacob no children, she envied her sister. She said to Jacob, 'Give me children, or I shall die!' Jacob's anger was kindled against Rachel, and he said, 'Am I in the place of God, who has withheld from you the fruit of the womb?'" (Gen 30:1–2)

[20] This clearly says that God's plan for marriage is between a man and a woman, and so same-sex marriage is a travesty. It is on this basis that homosexuality is seen as an abomination in the Bible. And it is because of this grievous sin that Sodom and Gomorrah were destroyed (Gen 19).

> And these words that I command you today shall be on your heart. You shall teach them diligently to your children, and shall talk of them when you sit in your house, and when you walk by the way, and when you lie down, and when you rise. You shall bind them as a sign on your hand, and they shall be as frontlets between your eyes. You shall write them on the doorposts of your house and on your gates. (Deut 6:7–9)

Parents were to teach their children to love the Lord with all their hearts and to make the children memorize the Scriptures so as to have them on their hearts. Having the Word of the Lord on their hearts was done in anticipation of the new covenant, wherein the Lord Himself would write His laws on their hearts and cause them to walk in them, as we read in Jeremiah and Ezekiel:

> Behold, the days are coming, declares the LORD, when I will make a new covenant. I will put my law within them, and I will write it on their hearts. And I will be their God, and they shall be my people.
>
> And I will give you a new heart, and a new spirit. And I will put my Spirit within you, and cause you to walk in my statutes and be careful to obey my rules. (Jer 31:31, 33; Ezek 36:26–27)

As we read in the psalms, children are a heritage from the Lord; the fruit of the womb a reward (Ps 127:3). This calls to mind the motif of blessing and fruitfulness. The covenant that God made with Abraham did not limit God's commitment and blessing to Abraham and his children only. It was to the effect that they would bless the world, making them also become the children and people of God. This is what motivated the following prayer of Moses, the man of God:

> Let your work be shown to your servants, and your glorious power to their children. Let the favour of

> the Lord our God be upon us, and establish the work
> of our hands upon us; yes, establish the work of our
> hands! (Ps 90:16–17)

What Moses is praying for is the favour of the Lord—that is, in essence, the grace of God. This is the very grace that was working at Creation: God's blessing on Adam and Eve, the favour which bestowed the image of God on them—the image of God that would enable them to have the virtues that give them character, their moral qualities. It is by the same grace that God also equipped the man and woman for the work they were created to do. And this is what Paul sought to bring home to the believers in Ephesus:

> For we are his workmanship, created in Christ Jesus
> for good works, which God prepared beforehand,
> that we should walk in them. (Eph 2:10)

All this defines essentially the work of God in the life of man. The goodness of the Lord to His people is seen in the glorious things He does to show His power to save, protect, and keep them. These things that God does in the lives of His people enable them to serve Him and thus to accomplish His good purposes. As they raise their children, training them in the ways of the Lord, they are at the same time extending the kingdom of God to the next generation, which also sees God's work manifested. And as previously stated, God made His covenant with Abraham and his children, who themselves must embrace the covenant. The Old Testament faithful sought to pass on their godly heritage to their children and to the nations.

The blessings of God come through marriage and the family. So, as we have seen in our study, God created man to fulfil His purposes, and these purposes are effectively and fully carried out in the context of the family. The bottom line is that the world will be better off when we carry out the Great Commission, the mission of God, making everybody children of God. And so the new world order is one wherein we all are in the family of God.

2

MARRIAGE IN ANCIENT ISRAEL

It is obvious that marriage in ancient Israel was very different from marriage today. Although there is a lot that we do not know about it, there are biblical texts that speak about it and thus enable us to piece together ancient Israeli marriage customs. Economic motivation was more important in marriage than romantic motivation, and marriage was meant for procreation.

2.1. Marriage within the Group

Among pastoral nomadic groups, marriage customs were often designed to foster social continuity and to perpetuate their communities. Endogamy, marriage within the group, was practised, rather than exogamy, marriage outside the kinship or social group.

The first instance of marriage within the group is seen when Abraham insists (in Genesis 24:2–9) that his servant should go back to Haran, to his own people, and get a wife for his son Isaac.

> And Abraham said to his servant, the oldest of his household, who had charge of all that he had, "Put your hand under my thigh, that I may make you swear by the LORD, the God of heaven and God of the earth, that you will not take a wife for my son

> from the daughters of the Canaanites, among whom I dwell, but will go to my country and to my kindred, and take a wife for my son Isaac. (Gen 24:2–4)

Isaac also asked Jacob to go back to his own kinsmen to take a wife for himself, as we read:

> You must not take a wife from the Canaanite women. Arise, go to Paddan-aram to the house of Bethuel your mother's father, and take as your wife from there one of the daughters of Laban your mother's brother. (Gen 28:1–2)

Jacob was obedient to his father and went back to Haran to marry the daughters of his uncle Laban. The high value that was placed on endogamy motivated Jacob to marry within his kinship. This also ensured his staying within the ancestral lineage.

2.2. Intermarriage

It is understood that before the choice of Abraham and his siblings, and prior to the call of Moses and the giving of the law, people followed their cultural customs and lived according to the context within which they found themselves. There was no concern about the commands of God, for the law had not yet been given. And so, in our context, the rule against intermarriage was not yet given. In Egypt, Joseph got married to an Egyptian woman who was given to him as a reward for what He had done for the king and the nation of Egypt. Pharaoh gave him in marriage Asenath, the daughter of Potiphera, a priest of On (Gen 41:45). Moses was married to a Midianite, Zipporah, the daughter of Reul, the priest of Midian (Exod 2:16–21).[21]

---

[21] In Numbers 12:1 it is said that Moses had married a Cushite woman, which caused Miriam and Aaron to complain, speaking against him. Scholars are not sure whether this is the same person as Zipporah or a second wife that Moses had married. Since it is said that this woman was from Cush, which normally refers to ancient Ethiopia, it is reasonable to believe that she was a second wife, since Zipporah is said to be from Midian.

Whereas Jacob, the third patriarch, obeyed his father, Isaac, to marry within the group, his brother Esau, on the contrary, broke the custom and married two Hittite women, and this caused his parents a lot of hurt, as we read in the following passage:

> When Esau was forty years old, he took Judith the daughter of Beeri the Hittite to be his wife, and Basemath the daughter of Elon the Hittite, and they made life bitter for Isaac and Rebekah. (Gen 26:34–35)

Esau's exogamy fits the theological plan designed beforehand and promised by God—that Esau was not the chosen and loved son.

> Two nations are in your womb, and two peoples from within you shall be divided; the one shall be stronger than the other, the older shall serve the younger. (Gen 25:23)

Just as Esau despised and sold his birthright, he further disqualified himself from being Isaac's heir by marrying Hittite women.

Marriage within the group was mandated by God when He gave command through Moses to His chosen people Israel that they should not marry from the uncircumcised people of Gentile nations. Having chosen Abraham and his seed to be His own people, and having made a covenant with Abraham and with subsequent generations, He wanted to keep the people of Israel separate, set apart, so they would faithfully worship Him. He did not want the Israelites to be married to the nations, lest they be tempted and drawn to worship the gods of their lands. He was driving out the occupants of the Promised Land (i.e., the Canaanites, the Hittites, the Amorites, and the other nations) because of their idolatry and grievous and abominable religious practices. And so before they entered the Promised Land, Moses told them the following:

> You shall not intermarry with them, giving your daughters to their sons or taking their daughters for

your sons, for they would turn away your sons from
following me, to serve other gods. Then the anger
of the LORD would be kindled against you, and he
would destroy you quickly. (Deut 7:3–4)

This command was very strictly upheld, such that any violation incurred the anger of the Lord and therefore met with severe punishment. Even while the children of Israel were still on their way to the Promised Land, and when they came to Shittim, the men started to court the daughters of Moab, committing immorality with them. They even sacrificed to their gods, and as a result, God's anger was kindled against Israel and He commanded that those who had committed this abomination should be executed and impaled:

And Moses said to the judges of Israel, "Each of you
kill those of his men who have yoked themselves to
Baal of Peor." (Num 25:5)

The affront was so flagrant that one of the men of Israel brought a Midianite woman to his family in the sight of Moses and the congregation of all the people, while they were still bemoaning the grievous sin they had committed.

When Phinehas the son of Eleazar, son of Aaron the
priest, saw it, he rose and left the congregation and
took a spear in his hand and went after the man of
Israel into the chamber and pierced both of them,
the man of Israel and the woman through her belly.
Thus the plague on the people of Israel was stopped.
(Num 25:7–8)

So we see the serious consequences of breaking the command against intermarriage with the pagan nations. Intermarriage was punished heavily because this was a breach of faith, since mixing with the nations led to the turning away of the people of Israel from the Lord and their worshipping the gods of the nations, which was, in essence, idolatry. This is why the penalty was the death sentence. The defaulters were impaled so that all might see and be warned not to ever imagine committing such a great sin. One would have thought that this exemplary punishment meted out to those who broke this law would deter the children of Israel from committing this act. However, we will see that this sin continued in the history of Israel. The returning Babylonian exile remnants fell into this sin—a good number of them, including their leaders (priests, Levites, and heads of houses), as we read here in the account given by Ezra:

> The officials approached me and said, "The people of Israel and the priests and the Levites have not separated themselves from the peoples of the lands with their abominations, from the Canaanites, the Hittites, the Perizzites, the Jebusites, the Ammonites, the Moabites, the Egyptians, and the Amorites. For they have taken some of their daughters to be wives for themselves and for their sons, so that the holy race has mixed itself with the peoples of the lands. And in this faithlessness the hand of the officials and chief men has been foremost." (Ezra 9:1–2)

Although the exile returnees had acted in breach of faith and thus had broken the covenant of God, there was still hope because Ezra was so disturbed by this grievous sin that he spent the night fasting, neither eating nor drinking, mourning over the faithlessness of the exiles. He and the people were contrite and made a covenant with the Lord and took an oath to put away the foreign women they had married, together with their children (Ezra 10:1–5). And so the guilt of intermarriage was purged, as we read here:

> Now there were found some of the sons of the priests who had married foreign women: Maaseiah, Eliezer, Jarib, and Gedaliah, some of the sons of Jeshua the son of Jozadak and his brothers. They pledged themselves to put away their wives, and their guilt offering was a ram of the flock for their guilt. (Ezra 10:18–19)

Several issues are involved here with regard to this intermarriage and the putting away of the women and children who resulted from the marriage. The severe action of Ezra and the community shows that they all recognized the serious consequences that the whole community could face because of the actions of even just a few: First, it was a case of disobedience, the people going against the law that God had given. They had committed a presumptuous sin. The other thing was that the serious sin was idolatry and amounted to apostasy, which was punishable by death. Mixing with the people entailed Israel being drawn to worship the gods of the land. This was an abomination, a great evil, which needed to be purged from Israel (Deut 17:1–13). Scholars of the Bible have reasoned that although the implication was that adherents of foreign religions were a temptation to the people of Israel, some of the women would have converted to Judaism. Proselytes were allowed in the Old Testament, as we see this in the case of Ruth, who committed herself to Naomi, to her people, and to her God, saying, "Your people shall be my people, and your God my God"(Ruth 1:16). And in the New Testament, we are given the example of the Ethiopian official who had come to worship God in Jerusalem (Acts 8:27). This would therefore mean that not all the women would have been sent away, for there would have been some who accepted leaving their gods to worship the God of Israel. And so these would not have been sent away.

Another issue that the modern reader might raise is the fate of the women and children who were sent away. How right is it to give birth to children and then leave them and their mothers to fend for themselves? In the context of the Old Testament, this question would not be an issue, since people were under the law and so what God said had to be obeyed or else they would face the consequences. However, this problem is being posed today in the context of the African church when polygamous men get converted and are made to send away some of their wives. I shall discuss this later when I address the question of divorce.

Regarding the violation of the rule against intermarriage, we see that Solomon was treated differently. He fell into the trap of his foreign women, and it was disastrous to his spiritual life, as we read in this account:

> Now King Solomon loved many foreign women, along with the daughter of Pharaoh: Moabite, Ammonite, Edomite, Sidonian, and Hittite women, from the nations concerning which the LORD had said to the people of Israel, "You shall not enter into marriage with them, neither shall they with you, for surely they will turn away your heart after their gods." Solomon clung to these in love. For when Solomon was old his wives turned away his heart after other gods, and his heart was not wholly true to the LORD his God, as was the heart of David his father. (1 Kings 11:1, 3–4)

We can ask why Solomon was not immediately punished, as we have seen God's wrath strike often in the cases of others. Here we see the grace of God and His sovereignty at work, for He said He would have mercy on whom He would have mercy (Rom 11:14). Besides this, Solomon benefited from the promise that God had made to David concerning Solomon, his son, saying,

> I will be to him a father, and he shall be to me a son. When he commits iniquity, I will discipline him with the rod of men, with the stripes of the sons of men, but my steadfast love will not depart from him, as I took it from Saul, whom I put away from before you. (2 Samuel 7:14–15)

God promised to punish Solomon in order to discipline him, and we see this play out in his life. So he did not go unpunished. However, Solomon, coming from David, had the special favour of God because he was in the Davidic line, from which the Messiah, the Son of God, would descend. Jesus was seen as the Son of David, and therefore as the Davidic Messiah, by the crowd that followed Him during the Triumphal Entry, and He accepted this truth (Matt 21:9, 16). So the motif of father and son predicted the birth of the Son of Man, the Son of God the Father. So Solomon belongs in the family of God, and so he is disciplined as a son, for correction and for righteousness, so he may share in the honour, righteousness, and glory of the Father. Discipline is a part of parenting, and every child gets corrected through constant discipline, as the writer of Hebrews explains:

> It is for discipline that you have to endure. God is treating you as sons. For what son is there whom his father does not discipline? If you are left without discipline, in which all have participated, then you are illegitimate children and not sons. (Heb 12:7–8)

Solomon made serious mistakes and faltered a lot in his life, but because at heart he loved the Lord and sought his wisdom (1 Kings 3:3–9), he was neither drastically punished nor rejected by the Lord. It was God who appointed Him king (1 Kings 3:7), and he would not have been allowed to go overboard. He started well, asking for wisdom to rule, and God saw in Him a heart that was yielding, and so His eye was ever on him, for the eyes of the Lord are ever on those who mean to serve Him wholeheartedly (2 Chron 16:9; Prov 15:3; Ps 32:8). After all his adventures, Solomon came to realize that the aim of man in life is to fear the Lord and to be faithful to Him:

> The end of the matter; all has been heard. Fear God and keep his commandments, for this is the whole duty of man. For God will bring every deed into judgment, with every secret thing, whether good or evil. (Eccl 12:13–14)

So what we see playing out in the life of Solomon is the same grace that was working in the life of Jacob. God's choice of Solomon made all the difference. The life of the patriarchs was representative of that of Israel, the nation. It should be recalled that the nation of Israel bears the name of Jacob (Gen 32:28). The fact that God, in His grace, chose Israel to be His people, inheritance, and heritage (Deut 4:20) explains His steadfast love for them. When God sets His eye on a person or nation, as was the case with the patriarchs, Jacob, and the people of Israel, He sets the person or nation apart, distinguished from the rest of the people or nations. This person or nation set apart becomes the object of God's attention and affection, and thus his steadfast love becomes the mark of distinction on this person or people. And so God's heart is soft towards the nation of Israel and the people. In the history of Israel, we see the people fall and get punished and then raised up when they cry unto God. The lesson that we learn in the new covenant is that we should by all means accept the invitation and the grace of God to embrace the covenant, and from there we will enjoy the guidance and help of the Lord in Christ. If we accept the Lord and know Him and are willing to serve Him in truth, we will rejoice about the good news enshrined in these promises:

> Cast away from you all the transgressions that you have committed, and make yourselves a new heart and a new spirit! Why will you die, O house of Israel? For I have no pleasure in the death of anyone, declares the Lord GOD; so turn, and live. (Ezek 18:31–32)

> If we confess our sins, he is faithful and just to forgive us our sins and to cleanse us from all unrighteousness. My little children, I am writing these things to you so that you may not sin. But if anyone does sin, we have an advocate with the Father, Jesus Christ the righteous. He is the propitiation for our sins. (1 John 1:9; 2:1–2)

The believer in Christ has all the blessings and righteousness of Christ, who came right to us to redeem us from the law and indeed fulfilled the law in our place by dying on the cross in our place so that by simply believing in Him we have eternal life and are led by His Spirit, who will work in us and make us willing and able to fulfil and accomplish His purposes for our lives.

2.3. The Importance of Having an Heir

It was important in biblical times to be married into a family with material means and of good standing both for the financial gain and for the honour of the family. But beyond this, it was even more important to have an heir. It can be said that the primary purpose of a marriage in biblical times was to have an heir. The motif of inheritance is recurring in the Bible. Abraham was sad because he was childless, most especially because he would not have an heir. He had been chosen by God; he had acquired a lot of wealth and was of high standing in society. And even though the Lord had promised to still bless him, all this was not as important as having an heir. And so he complained:

> "O Lord GOD, what will you give me, for I continue childless, and the heir of my house is Eliezer of Damascus?" Behold, you have given me no offspring, and a member of my household will be my heir. (Gen 15:1–2)

In the Bible, the concept of inheritance is very important. The covenant that God made with Abraham and the people of Israel had two important components: children (particularly an heir [seed]), and land. The land included the notion of a nation and nationhood. Canaan, the Promised Land, was land to be inherited (an inheritance).

As we know, in the Bible, God and Jesus used earthly things as types, to present spiritual things. And so, since our earthly possessions were an invitation to look beyond the transient to everlasting and eternal things, the seed and heir of Abraham pointed to the Davidic heir who would be born—Jesus Christ, the Messiah. And those who were to believe in Jesus and become God's adoptive sons would become heirs, and more so, "fellow heirs with Christ." Paul puts this well in his epistle to the Romans:

> For you did not receive the spirit of slavery to fall back into fear, but you have received the Spirit of adoption as sons, by whom we cry, "Abba! Father!" The Spirit himself bears witness with our spirit that we are children of God, and if children, then heirs—heirs of God and fellow heirs with Christ. (Rom 8:15–17)

In this case, becoming coheirs with Christ is in view of an

inheritance. In this context, as we see with the coming of Christ to institute and inaugurate the new covenant with those who become children of God through faith in Him, we will now inherit the kingdom of God. And so the physical land inherited by the children of Israel, the called and chosen people of God, foreshadowed the heavenly inheritance of the new Israel, the people of God that we, the church, have become. As Paul said, "our citizenship is in heaven" (Phil 3:20), and so we are looking forward to our heavenly inheritance, the kingdom of God, in a totally new world (Rev 21:1–5).

2.4. Virgin and Virginity

In ancient Israel, girls were ready for marriage when they reached puberty. It was important for girls to maintain their virginity, and it was expected that they be virgins when they got married. Paul, in several Scriptures, states his position as the father in the faith to believers, the fruit of his ministry, and so we hear him express his godly jealous towards the Corinthians as follows:

> For I feel a divine jealousy for you, since I betrothed you to one husband, to present you as a pure virgin to Christ. (2 Cor 11:2)

We see in the above verse that Paul, as a rabbi, is speaking from his deep awareness of Jewish culture and tradition. And here, in this text, Christ is the husband, the bridegroom, and the wedding day is on the Last Day, when Christ returns for believers, the people He has redeemed from all the nations through His atoning death. In ancient Israel, it was the father who gave the daughter in marriage. By tradition, an unmarried woman was under the authority of her father. And as it was so important, for the honour of the family and the community, that the girl being given in marriage should be a virgin, it was the duty of the father to guard his daughter and watch over her. And according to Jewish culture, it was the responsibility of the father to vouch at the betrothal of his daughter that he would present her at her wedding as a pure virgin. The father was conscious of the serious consequences that awaited a girl who was found not to be a virgin at marriage. If a girl was found to have lost her virginity, she would be put to death, as we read here in the text:

> But if the thing is true, that evidence of virginity was not found in the young woman, then they shall bring out the young woman to the door of her father's house, and the men of her city shall stone her to death with stones, because she has done an outrageous thing in Israel by whoring in her father's house. So you shall purge the evil from your midst. (Deut 22:20–21)

So we see that for a girl to lose her virginity entailed being wayward, and thus making not only herself impure but also her community. This is why the punishment of this crime was carried out by the community and in public. In some cases, the girl and the man who defiled her virginity were put to death.

The fact that virginity was an important virtue in the community is underscored by the tragic story of Jephthah. She was an only daughter, and because of the tragic vow that her father had made, which inadvertently meant she was to be sacrificed to the Lord, she had to go up to the mountains with her companions for two months to "weep her virginity." This became an institution for young girls, as we see in the following verse:

> She had never known a man, and it became a custom in Israel that the daughters of Israel went year by year to lament the daughter of Jephthah the Gileadite four days in the year. (Judges 11:39–40)

This young girl is not named in the story because she is called by her father's name. This is, in a sense, normal, because someone (boy or girl) found his or her identity in the father. On the other hand, we could say that this young girl represented all the virgins in Gilead. She thus, in a sense, lost her identity in and for the community and became a symbol in Israel, observed by the daughters of Israel.

Virginity was important for the girl because it was a virtue and a mark of character for the girl herself, for her family, and for the community. It was a mark of purity. It guaranteed marriage, in that she would be able to find a husband. This also gave her the hope of having children and perpetuating the name of the father and family. But for the girl, the foolish vow of her father meant that she would neither marry nor have children of her own. It was tragic for her father because his line would come to an end.

The motif of virgin (virginity) would be highlighted by the prophecy that would link this to the birth of Christ, the Messiah:

> Therefore the Lord himself will give you a sign.
> Behold, the virgin shall conceive and bear a son,
> and shall call his name Immanuel. (Isaiah 7:8)

And when the time came for this prophecy to be fulfilled, the Lord indeed chose a virgin to bear the God-child, Jesus Christ, as we see in the nativity story. At the annunciation, the angel Gabriel came to a virgin betrothed to the man Joseph and said to her the following:

> Do not be afraid, Mary, for you have found favour with God. And behold, you will conceive in your womb and bear a son, and you shall call his name Jesus. (Luke 1:30–31)

The gospel writer Matthew, reporting the annunciation, acknowledged this as a fulfilment of prophecy that was foretold in the Old Testament and affirmed the following:

> All this took place to fulfil what the Lord had spoken by the prophet: "Behold, the virgin shall conceive and bear a son, and they shall call his name Immanuel." (Matt 1:22–23)

And so the motif of virgin comes into the limelight when it is a virgin who is chosen to conceive and bear the Christ child. This makes it clear that virginity had become the mark that sets one apart for a special role—that of bearing the Holy Child—for the angel said that the child will be holy, as stated in the following:

> And the angel answered her, "The Holy Spirit will come upon you, and the power of the Most High will overshadow you; therefore the child to be born will be called holy—the Son of God." (Luke 1:35)

When the archangel Gabriel introduced himself by saying, "I am Gabriel, I stand in the presence of God"(Luke 1:19), he gave an astounding job description, which tells us a lot about his character. He must be of utmost faithfulness and holiness.[22] This will be true because only those who are holy dare approach God, the Holy One,"who dwells in unapproachable light." The fact that he came to Mary must also say something about the nature of Mary (something that they had in common), and most likely that they were both set apart for the service of God. Mary was said to have found grace before God in order to be selected to be the mother of the Holy Child. This grace set her apart firstly because of her virginity and secondly, and more importantly, because her womb would become a sanctuary, thus making her whole body a sanctuary because she would be sanctified by the very presence of the Holy Spirit that would overshadow her, just as the cloud of the presence of the Lord had overshadowed the tabernacle. And she would be holy, and more so, because the holy child would come to dwell in her before ever dwelling among men after His birth. This was the significance of the name Immanuel, meaning "God with us."

---

[22] The 144,000 who had been redeemed from the earth are described as virgins. They had "not defiled themselves with women" and so followed the Lamb wherever he went (Rev 14:4). Their virginity signaled their spiritual purity and consecrated life of celibacy, which entailed keeping themselves from women or foregoing marriage. These symbolized the Bride of Christ, the church, which Christ will purify to present to Himself pure, "holy and without blemish" (Eph 5:26–27).

2.5. Betrothal

2.5.1. Engagement

The process of marriage began with betrothal or engagement. The parents of the young man or their representative would come and declare the intention of marrying the young girl. Negotiations would be made, and if the terms were agreeable to the parents of the girl, the engagement would be undertaken. In the case of Rebekah, her parents recognized that God had ordained that this union take place, so they agreed to the request, as we read below:

> Then Laban and Bethuel answered and said, "The thing has come from the LORD; we cannot speak to you bad or good. Behold, Rebekah is before you; take her and go, and let her be the wife of your master's son, as the LORD has spoken." (Gen 24:50–51)

When the negotiations are completed, the girl would then be informed. In the case of Rebekah, she was asked if she would go with the servant of Abraham to the family she would be married into, as we read in the following verses:

> They said, "Let us call the young woman and ask her." And they called Rebekah and said to her, "Will you go with this man?" She said, "I will go." So they sent away Rebekah their sister and her nurse, and Abraham's servant and his men. (Gen 24:58–59)

Engagement was the first stage in forging the marriage relationship. This stage could last several months but could not extend to more than twelve months before marriage in the case of a maiden. The second stage of the betrothal was officially arranged, and a prenuptial agreement was made before witnesses. Betrothal was a promise of marriage, and it was practically as binding as the marriage itself. Edersheim (1971:354) speaks to this fact in the following quote:

At the betrothal, the bridegroom, personally or by deputy, handed to the bride a piece of money or a letter, it being expressly stated in each case that the man thereby espoused the woman. From the moment of betrothal both parties were regarded, and treated in law (as to inheritance, adultery, need of formal divorce), as if they had been actually married.

This is why Joseph, to whom Mary was betrothed, considered breaking with her tantamount to a divorce, as we read in the gospel:

> And her husband Joseph, being a just man and unwilling to put her to shame, resolved to divorce her quietly. (Matt 1:19)

Since it was expected that the bride be a virgin at the time of betrothal, there were no sexual relations before marriage, and the bride was not to be seen by her intended husband until the time they entered the wedding chamber. This explains why Rebekah "took her veil and covered herself" when she inadvertently saw Isaac, her intended husband (Gen 24:65).

2.5.2. Bride Price

The betrothal, which indeed is a marriage agreement, is established and made firm by the payment of a bride price to the bride's father. It is normally paid in cash or kind (jewellery, precious stone, animals, labour, or the like). Jacob paid with many years of service: Seven years for Leah and seven more years of service for Rachel. David paid in a number of people killed.

> Then Saul said, "Thus shall you say to David, 'The king desires no bride-price except a hundred foreskins of the Philistines, that he may be avenged of the king's enemies.'" And David arose and went, along with his men, and killed two hundred of the Philistines. And David brought their foreskins, which

were given in full number to the king, that he might become the king's son-in-law. And Saul gave him his daughter Michal for a wife. (1 Samuel 18:25, 27)

Othniel, the son of Kenaz, Caleb's younger brother, paid as the brideprice for his wife, Achsah, his capture of the enemy people of Kiriath-sepher, as we read in the following Scripture:

> And Caleb said, "He who attacks Kiriath-sepher and captures it, I will give him Achsah my daughter for a wife." And Othniel the son of Kenaz, Caleb's younger brother, captured it. And he gave him Achsah his daughter for a wife. (Judg 1:12–13)

The servant of Abraham had brought a lot of things—"all sorts of choice gifts"— (Gen 24:10) according to the blessings of God on his master Abraham; and all these he gave to the family of Rebekah as the brideprice. He had special gifts for the bride, as we read in the following text:

> And the servant brought out jewellery of silver and of gold, and garments, and gave them to Rebekah. He also gave to her brother and to her mother costly ornaments. (Gen 24:53)

Before this, the servant had already given Rebekah a gold ring weighing half a shekel and two bracelets for her hands weighing ten gold shekels at the spring when he realized that this was the bride God had shown him to be fit for Isaac, the son of his master.

2.5.3. Dowry

The brideprice was different from the dowry, which was brought by both the bride and the groom. A legal document (the Shitre Erusin) fixed the dowry which each party brought, the mutual obligations, and all other legal points.

It was also customary for the family of the bride to give the couple a gift when they married. And so, in the case of Achsah and Othniel, Caleb gave them land, as we read in the follow passage:

> When she came to him, she urged him to ask her father for a field. And she dismounted from her donkey, and Caleb said to her, "What do you want?" She said to him, "Give me a blessing. Since you have set me in the land of the Negeb, give me also springs of water." And Caleb gave her the upper springs and the lower springs. (Judges 1:14–15)

2.5.4. The Betrothed of God

In Scripture, God reveals Himself as the bridegroom, and Israel is regarded as His betrothed, as stated in the following text:

> And I will betroth you to me forever. I will betroth you to me in righteousness and in justice, in steadfast love and in mercy. I will betroth you to me in faithfulness. And you shall know the LORD. (Hosea 2:19–20)

It thus follows that in ancient Israel marriage and all that it entailed reflected the relationship that God had with His people. The husband ideally had to act as the representative of God. And so what God says about Himself in relation to His betrothed should be the blueprint of the bridegroom vis-à-vis his bride.

2.6. Marriage Arrangement

According to Near Eastern custom in biblical times, marriages were arranged by the parents, as we have seen in the case of Isaac and Rebekah. But it would appear that this was not required by biblical law. This is why we find different practices in the biblical texts. However, customarily the parents of a young man chose a young woman to be married to their son. In the case of Ishmael, it was his mother who made the arrangement. Hagar arranged the marriage between him and an Egyptian woman (Gen 21:21). While Jacob obeyed his parents to go and get a wife from among his kinsmen, marrying from the family of his uncle Laban, Esau chose his own wives from among the Canaanite women without the consent of his parents (26:34). But when this displeased his parents, he later decided to go and take another wife from Ishmael (Gen 28:8–9). It should be noted that in general the young people to be married did not take the initiative, because it was not in the custom of Israel to do so. However, Samson took the initiative concerning the choice of the woman to marry, as we read:

> Samson went down to Timnah, and at Timnah he saw one of the daughters of the Philistines. Then he came up and told his father and mother, "I saw one of the daughters of the Philistines at Timnah. Now get her for me as my wife." But his father and mother said to him, "Is there not a woman among the daughters of your relatives, or among all our people, that you must go to take a wife from the uncircumcised Philistines?" But Samson said to his father, "Get her for me, for she is right in my eyes." (Judges 14:1–3)

The case of Samson was not only unique but also tragic. Although Samson acted following his whimsical desires, it was God who had planned it for His own purpose. He wanted to use this marriage to go against the Philistines, who were enemies to Israel. Of course, this marriage did not end well because in the end Samson suffered as a result of his marriage to the girl he had said was the right choice in his eyes.

2.7. Marriage Ceremony, Rite, and Consummation

It has already been stated that the marriage process began with the betrothal, which was binding. Normally the bride remained in her parents' house till solemnization, the marriage ceremony, which was done in the parents' house. During this ceremony, which was performed by the father, the bride would be blessed. In the case of Rebekah, her siblings blessed her, saying,

> Our sister, may you become
> thousands of ten thousands,
> and may your offspring possess
> the gate of those who hate him! (Gen 24:60)

When the marriage ceremony was over, the bride was taken to the husband's home. The bride-price would have been paid at this point.

In ancient Jewish marriage custom, the groom and his friends would leave his home and proceed to the home of the bride, where the marriage ceremony would be conducted. This would take place at night. While waiting, the bride would be veiled and adorned with jewellery and bridal ceremonial attire. From the bride's home, the entire wedding party would return to the groom's home for a celebratory banquet. The bride and her maids, in the bridal procession, are described as follows:

> All glorious is the princess in her chamber, with robes interwoven with gold. In many-coloured robes she is led to the king, with her virgin companions following behind her. With joy and gladness they are led along as they enter the palace of the king. (Ps 45:13–15)

Edersheim (197:354) describes the bridal party in detail as follows:

> On the evening of the actual marriage (Nessuin, Chathanuth), the bride was led from her paternal home to that of her husband. First came the merry sounds of music; then they distributed among the people wine and oil and nuts among the children; next the bride, covered with the bridal veil, her long hair flowing, surrounded by her companions, and led

by the friends of the bridegroom, and the children of the bride-chamber.

The bridal procession was a joyous one, and those in the party were dressed for the occasion. Some in the group carried torches or lamps on poles. Others carried myrtle branches and bouquets of flowers. Those along the route, and everyone, saluted the procession or joined in it; and they would break into praises, shouting of the beauty and virtues of the bride. Arriving at her new home, the bride would be led to her husband.

A ceremony would be performed using a formulaic statement such as, "Take her according to the Law of Moses and of Israel." The bride and bridegroom would be crowned with garlands. At this point, a formal legal document called the Kethubah would be signed. This document stated that the bridegroom would undertake to work for her, honour her, and keep and care for her, as was the manner of the men of Israel. After this there would be the washing of hands and the benediction. The marriage supper would then begin, and the cup would be filled, and a solemn prayer of bridal benediction would be said over it.

The feast lasted days, at the end of which the friends of the bridegroom would lead the bridal couple to the bridal chamber and bed.[23] The bridal chamber would be a tent, since these people were mostly nomadic pastoral groups. With regard to the bridal chamber, King and Stager (2001:56) state the following:

> A special nuptial chamber (huppa) was designated, and the bride was escorted there by her parents. This practice finds its way into the metaphor as we read in the psalms: "In the heavens he [Yahweh] has set a tent for the sun, which comes out like a bridegroom from his wedding canopy (huppa). (Ps 19:4–5)

---

[23] In the ancient Near East, the wedding celebration lasted for seven days. Jacob had to celebrate his marriage with Leah for seven days, after which he would then be given Rachel, the bride he had to work for seven year to marry (Gen 29:27).

Joel, the prophet, also mentions the bridal chamber regarding the bride and bridegroom, saying the following:

> Gather the people. Consecrate the congregation; assemble the elders; gather the children, even nursing infants. Let the bridegroom leave his room, and the bride her chamber. (Joel 2:16)

After the marriage of Jacob, the father of Leah took her to Jacob in the nuptial tent (Gen 29:23).

John, the Gospel writer, was familiar with the varying customs that existed in Galilee and Judah. When he talks of the friends of the bridegroom, he is referring to the bridal custom in Judah, as we read here:

> "I am not the Christ, but I have been sent before him." The one who has the bride is the bridegroom. The friend of the bridegroom, who stands and hears him, rejoices greatly at the bridegroom's voice. Therefore this joy of mine is now complete. (John 3:28–29)

2.8. Forms of Marriage

In ancient Israel, marriage took various forms, and the relationships were different depending upon the roles within the marriage union and within the family unit that resulted from the marriage.

2.8.1. Monogamy and Polygamy

Though from the Creation story, as we have seen earlier, monogamy is presented as the ideal form of marriage, polygamy was practised, especially among the affluent and royalty. The patriarchs, except Isaac, had several wives. Jacob had four wives (Leah, Rachel, and their two servants, Zilpah and Bilhah). It is not clear how many wives David had. All that we know from Scripture is that eight of his wives are named and that he had other wives plus an unknown number of concubines. Solomon had "700 wives, who were princesses, and 300 concubines" (1 Kings 11:3).

2.8.2. Levirate Marriage

The law of levirate marriage was instituted in order to preserve patrimony and ensure that the family line is continued. This custom came from the Latin word "levir," meaning "husband's brother," and the Hebrew word *"yabam."* We read about this law in the following Scripture:

> If brothers dwell together, and one of them dies and has no son, the wife of the dead man shall not be married outside the family to a stranger. Her husband's brother shall go in to her and take her as his wife and perform the duty of a husband's brother to her. And the first son whom she bears shall succeed to the name of his dead brother, that his name may not be blotted out of Israel (Deut 25:5–6)

This law was to be strictly reinforced. And if a brother refused to perform his duty in order to perpetuate his late brother's name, he was shamed by the widow in front of the elders and would be sanctioned by his community. This crime was punishable by death, resulting from divine judgment, as we see in the case of the second son of Judah and Tamar (Gen 38:6–26). Tamar prevailed on her father-in-law to provide a levirate for her when her husband, Er, died without a son. Onan, Judah's second son, was struck dead by the Lord for failing to fulfil the duty of the levir's obligation because when he "went in to his brother's wife he would waste the semen on the ground, so as not to give offspring to his brother" (Gen 38:9). This act of coitus interruptus has come to be known as "onanism." What Onan did was against the order that God gave to the end of propagating human life (in Genesis 1:28) when He said, "be fruitful and multiply."

2.8.3. Celibacy

In Israel, marriage was the normal way of life, for as noted earlier, the chief aim in marriage was to give birth to children and to raise them. And so parents were anxious to see their children married. And each girl very much wanted to be married and have children. To not be married was a humiliation. This is reflected in the attitude of the women described by Isaiah in the following text:

> And seven women shall take hold of one man in that day, saying, "We will eat our own bread and wear our own clothes, only let us be called by your name; take away our reproach." (Isaiah 4:1)

Given this attitude, celibacy was a shameful state, such that the unmarried woman did not have high status in ancient Israel. Apart from the fact that unmarried women were vulnerable and unprotected by a husband, they risked being lumped together with prostitutes.

Men also were expected to marry in order to procreate and have families. In the Bible, the only case of enjoined celibacy is that of Jeremiah. God asked Jeremiah not to marry, as we read in the following text:

> The word of the LORD came to me: "You shall not take a wife, nor shall you have sons or daughters in this place." (Jer 16:1–2)

In biblical history, the Lord often asked His prophets to perform prophetic acts (living messages), foretelling what would happen to the people Israel or symbolizing certain situations of special import. In this case Jeremiah's action was symbolizing the destruction of Jerusalem and the fall of Judah resulting in the death of women and children while the rest of the people of Judah were carried off into exile.

In the New Testament, Jesus recognized celibacy as a virtue and a vocation when He talked about marriage. This is what He said about celibacy:

> The disciples said to him, "If such is the case of a man with his wife, it is better not to marry." But he said to them, "Not everyone can receive this saying, but only those to whom it is given. For there are eunuchs who have been so from birth, and there are eunuchs who have been made eunuchs by men, and there are eunuchs who have made themselves eunuchs for the sake of the kingdom of heaven. Let the one who is able to receive this receive it." (Matt 19:10–12)

Jesus is here speaking to the disciples who had over reacted concerning the risk of a lifelong unhappy marriage if one could not obtain a divorce. Jesus turned to the disciples to talk about voluntary choice of a life of celibacy for the sake of kingdom of God.

Paul was one of the few who, as a religious person, chose not to marry. Barnabas was one of them, and just like Paul, he was not married (1 Cor 9:5). His advice to the unmarried and widows was that they remain single, as he himself was, for that was good for them (1 Cor 7:8). He said that celibacy was a gift of God, which means that the Holy Spirit gives to some the gift of celibacy, just as He gives the other spiritual gifts. And so he says the following:

> Now as a concession, not a command, I say this. I wish that all were as I myself am. But each has his own gift from God, one of one kind and one of another. So then he who marries his betrothed does well, and he who refrains from marriage will do even better. (1 Cor 7:7, 38)

Paul recognizes that one who marries is following the established order of life, because that is why God created man—to marry and propagate humanity, as stated in the preceding section. However, he thinks that if one feels called not to marry but to devote one's life to serve God as a single person, this will even be a better choice, for then he or she will be able to devote his or her life more to the service of God:

> I want you to be free from anxieties. The unmarried man is anxious about the things of the Lord, how to please the Lord. The unmarried or betrothed woman is anxious about the things of the Lord, how to be holy in body and spirit. But the married woman is anxious about worldly things, how to please her husband. (1 Cor 7:32, 34)

Paul chose a life of celibacy because this kind of life not only allowed him to be more focused and single minded, but it also gave him the opportunity to seek to be holy in body and spirit. The four daughters of Philip the Evangelist were celibate, and so they placed themselves in a position to hear directly from the Lord and then prophesy (Acts 21:9).

Institutional celibacy is seen in the monastic life and in the Catholic Church, with regard to priests. They have chosen this path in order for those consecrated or ordained to thoroughly devote themselves to the service of God. The danger is that institutionalized celibacy might no longer be a personal call, motivated from the heart of the individual, but rather a path designated and authorized by the church. This might explain why, over the years, we have seen a lot of abuses and moral scandals among priests and the religious. In the case of priests, it is assumed that all have the discipline of abstinence and the call to be celibate. But from the biblical perspective, the priesthood did not require that priests be celibate. This explains why there have been calls to give the option to marry to priests in the Catholic Church.

Celibacy enables those who have been called to this state to be set apart for the Lord, the bridegroom. And so celibacy is seen as a special state that positions both women and men to be virgins, pure and undefiled for the Lamb. The 144 who had been redeemed and sealed (with the name of the Father) to worship the Lamb, singing and praising Him, who now is glorified and reigning as King, were virgins. Although these are portrayed as celibate males (Rev 14:3) they represent believers of both sexes who die in faith and are gathered as first fruits for God and the Lamb. This is described by John as revealed to him as follows:

> It is these who have not defiled themselves with women, for they are virgins. It is these who follow the Lamb wherever he goes. These have been redeemed from mankind as first fruits for God and the Lamb, and in their mouth no lie was found, for they are blameless. (Rev 14:4–5)

The main motivation of the desert fathers, the first monks, to separate themselves from the society was the seeking of solitude, which enabled them to seek the Lord and to be with Him alone, away from the distractions of the world and its sins. But the only escape from sins and the world is when we are separated unto the Lord and find grace in Him and allow Him to work in us and transform us from within.

From the moment Paul met Jesus, He sought to know nothing more than Jesus Christ (1 Cor 2:2; Phil 3:8, 10) and was single minded in his service for Christ, and this mattered to him more than his own life, as he told the elders of the Ephesian church:

> I do not account my life of any value nor as precious to myself, if only I may finish my course and the ministry that I received from the Lord Jesus, to testify to the gospel of the grace of God. (Acts 20:24)

Paul's life was so focused on Christ that he became one with Him; and this is the raison d'être of the motif "in Christ," which is recurrent in his writings and teaching. He said it was Christ living and working in him (Gal 2:20), and that Christ was his life. And so for him to live was Christ (Phil 1:21). As he said, choosing a life of celibacy allowed him to focus on the things of the Lord—something he could not do if he were a married man. Henri Nouwen (1981:20) calls this kind of consecration of Paul freedom which liberates the children of God from the many things and fears that assail the believers, making them insecure. Instead, focusing their eyes, hearts, and minds on the Saviour will enable them to find their real selves. And so he writes the following:

As we come to realize that it is not we who live, but Christ who lives in us, that he is our true self, we can slowly let our compulsions melt away and begin to experience the freedom of the children of God.

Christ was an example to us in many ways, and here He was also an example to the unmarried, those who had chosen not to be married. He was different from the priests in Israel who, though chosen to minister and focus on the service of the Lord in the temple, could still marry and have families. But as Christ was the best because He obeyed the Father and did the utmost and finally paid the ultimate price, the best is reserved for Him in heaven, from where He came. He will be the Bridegroom of all that He died to redeem. And, amazingly, we, the redeemed, will be at His grand wedding feast, both as the bride and the happy chosen guests—a great multitude from every nation, from all tribes, peoples, and languages, celebrating in joyful songs and praising and worshipping God, saying,

> "Salvation belongs to our God who sits on the throne, and to the Lamb!"
>
> 'And all the angels and the four living creatures worshipped God, saying,' "Amen! Blessing and glory and wisdom and thanksgiving and honour and power and might be to our God forever and ever! Amen." 'Then I heard what seemed to be like the voice of a multitude, crying out,' "Let us rejoice and exult and give him the glory, for the marriage of the Lamb has come, and his Bride has made herself ready." (Rev 7:10, 11, 12; 19:6, 7)

And happy are those who will be invited to the Lamb's wedding feast to rejoice in His presence forever and ever. Amen. And indeed, they will be happy there forever after!

2.9. Roles and Relationships in the Family

As stated in section 1.1, God's purpose for creating man included reproduction: men and women marry to give birth to children and thus form families. We are going to look at the roles of family members and how they relate to one another in the family.

2.9.1. The Husband

In ancient Israel, marriage was patriarchal and authority was in the hand of the husband. Women were subordinate to their husbands. This is partly the result of the Fall and specifically the punishment meted out to Eve because she disobeyed God and listened to the serpent. This is what God said to Eve, the woman:

> To the woman he said, "Your desire shall be for your husband, and he shall rule over you." (Gen 3:16)

However, with the coming of the Christ and the inauguration of the new covenant, the curse of the Fall was removed and a new order began. As Paul explains in his epistle, the relationship between the husband and his wife will take its cue from Christ, the head and the bridegroom of the church. And so he writes the following:

> But I want you to understand that the head of every man is Christ, the head of a wife is her husband, and the head of Christ is God. (1 Cor 11:3)

The question here is one of authority and is not a matter of value or status. Men and woman have equal value because they were created in the image of God. Paul will emphasize this in his teaching when he says,

> In Christ Jesus you are all sons of God, through faith. There is neither Jew nor Greek, there is neither slave

> nor free, there is no male and female, for you are all
> one in Christ Jesus. (Gal 3:26, 28)

The husband has the responsibility to provide for his wife and take care of her needs. And as stated in section 2.6, in the marriage legal document signed when the marriage was solemnized, the husband undertook to work for his wife, to honour her, and to keep and care for her. So we see that part of the responsibility of the man was to provide for and to care for his wife.

2.9.2. The Father

Apart from caring for his wife, the mother of his children, he was to care for the children and provide for their basic needs. He trained his sons to work; this also entailed training them to have trades, preparing them to become fathers in the future. Children followed the trades of their fathers, just like the sons of Zebedee, James, and John, who were fishermen.

The father was the spiritual head of the family and presided over family events and led in the observance of religious feasts. He was God's image, reflecting Him, the Father of Israel, and His work and role. The father embodied the virtues that he commended and so served as the example to his son and expected him to follow his example, as we read in the following verse from the Wisdom of Solomon:

> My son, give me your heart, and let your eyes observe
> my ways. (Prov 23:26)

This verse guides parents in the important task of nurturing their children. They should have as their primary target the children's hearts, the deepest cores of the children's lives. This wise father asked to have his son's heart because it is where all about life begins and develops, and it becomes the home of the Godhead. The other exhortations that this wise father gives his son include a charge to watch his heart, as we read in the following verses:

> My son, be attentive to my words; incline your ear to my sayings. Let them not escape from your sight; keep them within your heart. For they are life to those who find them, and healing to all their flesh. Keep your heart with all vigilance, for from it flow the springs of life. (Prov 4:20–23)

These verses encourage the son to internalize the wisdom of his father, laying it in the heart. According to Jewish thought, the heart is the centre of one's inner life from which he thinks, feels, and acts. As the wisdom from the mouth of the father is laid up in the heart, the wise son should closely guard it. It is in this light that David, in the chapter of the psalms that stresses the paramount position of the Word of God in the life of the godly, poses the key question about worship and answers it. He asks,

> How can a young man keep his way pure? By guarding it according to your word. I have stored up your word in my heart, that I might not sin against you. (Ps 119:9, 11)

The primary target of a father in the task of child rearing should be the heart, because that is what makes people. Jeremiah said the heart is corrupt and sick, desperately wicked (Jer 17:9). And Jesus taught that evil and good come from the heart:

> But what comes out of the mouth proceeds from the heart, and this defiles a person. For out of the heart come evil thoughts, murder, adultery, sexual immorality, theft, false witness, slander. (Matt 15:18–19)

If we want our children to grow up to be godly, we should fill their hearts with godly wisdom, aiming to build godly character in them. When the heart is transformed, it will seek the things of God and so will produce good fruits, as Jesus taught, comparing the fruit borne by a tree to the fruit of the heart—that is, the character qualities that are grown and produced in a person's life—as we read in the following verses:

> For no good tree bears bad fruit, nor again does a bad tree bear good fruit, for each tree is known by its own fruit. For figs are not gathered from thorn bushes, nor are grapes picked from a bramble bush. The good person out of the good treasure of his heart produces good, and the evil person out of his evil treasure produces evil, for out of the abundance of the heart his mouth speaks. (Luke 6:43–45)

Above all, the father was expected to mirror the compassion of God, our Father, exhibiting the fatherly heart in his relation to his son and the rest of the children. David brings out these qualities in Psalm 103:8–14. Our heavenly Father is "merciful and gracious, slow to anger and abounding in steadfast love" (Ps 103:8). David tells us that as a father has compassion on his children, God our Father does the same and even more to those who fear Him. He knows our weaknesses, and so He will be even more merciful to us. Christ teaches the same thing in the parable of the prodigal son (Luke15:11–31). We can see the love of the Father towards the wayward son. This is the same love we should show our children. The parable teaches fathers to be patient, loving, and compassionate, for this is the only way to win back erring children. Regarding stubborn and rebellious children, we see how God shows His love and patience as he patiently waits for them to return. This tells us how He related with rebellious Israel: how a heartbroken, lovesick Father longs for His rebellious children to come back home to Him. He mourns:

> I spread out my hands all the day to a rebellious people, who walk in a way that is not good, following their own devices. (Isa 65:2)

Paul, in Rom 10:21, quotes this verse of prophecy as coming true in the New Testament when the Gentiles receive the gospel whereas the Jews continue in their rebellion.

In the parable in Luke chapter 15, Jesus paints a picture of the father of the Prodigal Son, standing with open arms to catch and embrace his repentant returning son. The father does not chide or even question his son. He simply opens his arms to receive him with joy. That is the Father–heart story, carried over from the Old Testament to the New Testament context. This is the kind of heart all fathers should have. God, our Father, also shows his love for us by disciplining us; so, too, the father should discipline his children in love for their good (Prov 3:12–12; Heb 12:10–11). Disciplining the child is training in righteousness.

Paul, in his relation to those who became his children in the faith, gives us a picture of how a father should treat his children, as can be seen in his epistles (1 Cor 4:14–15; 2 Cor 6:13). He was gentle, loving, and affectionate. He was as caring as a nursing mother, thus taking his cue from the Father, who, like a nursing mother, will never forget His children (Isaiah 49:15). Paul loved just like God the Father and His Son, and he would spend and be spent for the children, ready to give even himself for the children (2 Cor 12:14–15). This, for example, is how he viewed the Thessalonian believers:

> We were gentle among you, like a nursing mother taking care of her own children. So, being affectionately desirous of you, we were ready to share with you not only the gospel of God but also our own selves, because you had become very dear to us. (1 Thess 2:7–8)

In ancient Israel, it was the responsibility of the father to instruct and teach the children, though it was also the responsibility of the mother. This is why in wisdom literature we find in several instances that it is the father who gives instructions to his sons. For example, in the book of Proverbs, chapters 2 to 7 and 23:15–26 the instructions of the father are addressed to the son. And so the chapters begin with the vocative "My son." This is seen in the following Scriptures:

> My son, if you receive my words and treasure up my commandments with you then you will understand

> the fear of the LORD and find the knowledge of God ... My son, do not forget my teaching, but let your heart keep my commandments, for length of days and years of life and peace they will add to you. (Prov 2:1, 5; 3:1–2)

The purpose of the father's teaching and instruction was to lead his son to know God and His Word and to be wise so as to lead a godly life and have success in life:

> Trust in the LORD with all your heart, and do not lean on your own understanding. In all your ways acknowledge him, and he will make straight your paths. (Prov 3:5–6)

Wanting to teach by example, the father looks back to when he was instructed by his own father. And as a result, he tells his son the following:

> When I was a son with my father, tender, the only one in the sight of my mother, he taught me and said to me, "Let your heart hold fast my words; keep my commandments, and live. Get wisdom; get insight; do not forget, and do not turn away from the words of my mouth. My son, give me your heart, and let your eyes observe my ways. (Prov 4:3–5; 23:26)

So we see that the father teaches by example and wants to make the point that wisdom and the heritage of a godly life are passed from generation to generation. So his expectation is that his son will pass what he teaches him to his own children.

In Hebrew religious thought, the child was under the authority and instruction of his father until he turned thirteen, and after this the father released his son to the guardianship and authority of the Lord, as Eli Lizorkin-Eyzenberg explains in the following quote:

> Until the time of becoming a Bar Mitzvah (literally "son of commandment,") the father has responsibility

for his son. He is to offer him close guidance until such time that he will be able to engage with the Torah on his own. It does not mean that the boy is now permitted to desist from honouring his father or should no longer obey him. But it means that the Torah from this point on becomes his primary guide instead of his loving father. (Lizorkin-Eyzenberg 2021)

After the Bar Mitzvah rite, the ceremony marking the release of the child from his father's responsibility, the boy would be able to participate in public reading of the Torah and lead worship in the synagogue. It was in view of the Bar Mitzvah that the apostle Paul wrote admonishing the Gentile believers about their being free from the Torah as custodians. Writing to the Galatians, he said the following:

> Now before faith came, we were held captive under the law, imprisoned until the coming faith would be revealed. So then, the law was our guardian until Christ came, in order that we might be justified by faith. But now that faith has come, we are no longer under a guardian, for in Christ Jesus you are all sons of God, through faith. (Gal 3:23–26)

The apostle Paul, who was well versed in Jewish Scriptures and traditions, understood this basic principle of close guardian transfer. With the coming of the Jewish Christ, such responsibility transfer was taken to another level. Those who believed in Christ and became sons of God were no longer under the guardianship of the Torah but would be led by the Spirit sent by Jesus Christ (John 14:26). They were not "sons of the Torah," as described by the Bar Mitzvah, but "sons of God through faith," for, as he says to the believers in Rome, "all who are led by the Spirit of God are sons of God" (Rom 8:14). So Gentile believers should be guided by the Holy Spirit:

But I say, walk by the Spirit, and you will not gratify the desires of the flesh. But if you are led by the Spirit, you are not under the law. (Gal 5:16, 18)

Since raising children was a joint responsibility, the father would in his instructions also enjoin his son to follow the instructions and teachings of his mother.

2.9.3. The Woman

In relating to her husband, the woman addressed her husband as "*ba'al*," which is the Hebrew word for "master" or "lord." Peter, addressing matters regarding the relationship between husband and wife, cited the example of Sarah, who related to her husband Abraham with respect, as seen in this Scripture:

> Holy women who hoped in God used to adorn themselves, by submitting to their own husbands, as Sarah obeyed Abraham, calling him lord. (1 Peter 2:5–6)

In God's plan at Creation, the woman was to be a helper—that is, a helpmate of the man. This meant that the husband and wife were to work in partnership and in union, signified by the fact that they had become one flesh. Old Testament history and wisdom books teach that the wife and mother is a wise, hard-working, and diligent woman. In the book of Ruth, we see Naomi as a wise, loving, caring, and responsible woman. Ruth herself is a woman of commendable character, as affirmed by Boaz in the following statement:

> All that you have done for your mother-in-law since the death of your husband has been fully told to me, and how you left your father and mother and your native land and came to a people that you did not know before. (Ruth 2:11)

As we see in the narrative of the book, Ruth was a diligent, devoted, and caring woman. She cared for her mother-in-law and was rewarded with a husband. It was through her that the Davidic king and the ultimate Messiah King, Jesus Christ, came.

Proverbs chapter 31 is a hymn to the virtuous, diligent, and wise woman. Her entrepreneurial skills and homemaking strengths outshine those of many men in many ways, contributing to the success and reputation of her husband. She is generous to the poor and needy. Her wise and godly character wins the admiration of influential men at the gate of the city, making her family praise her, as we read in the following verses:

> Her husband is known in the gates when he sits among the elders of the land. Strength and dignity are her clothing, and she laughs at the time to come. She opens her mouth with wisdom, and the teaching of kindness is on her tongue. Her children rise up and call her blessed; her husband also, and he praises her: "Many women have done excellently, but you surpass them all." Charm is deceitful, and beauty is vain, but a woman who fears the LORD is to be praised. (Prov 31:23, 25–26, 28–30)

In Israel, the city gates were centres of life (civic and economic) and the leaders of the city would gather there to judge matters of the city's inhabitants. The excellent work and noble character of the woman contributed significantly to her husband's success and reputation. And so, the very significant statement of fact: "Her husband is known in the gates" (Prov 31:23). It was customary that the child was known through his father and the woman through her husband. But here we find that the tradition was broken in a positive way. Here it shows that the man found his identity in his wife. This was a win and strong commendation for the woman: Truly, "a woman who fears the Lord is to be praised. And let her works praise her in the gates (Prov 31:30, 31).

2.9.4. Parents

The man and woman, as husband and wife, had the joint responsibility of training and bringing up their children in the fear of the Lord.

Disciplining children is a joint responsibility of both parents. Both father and mother will cooperate and agree in the way they will nurture and discipline the children. This is the basic understanding of Scripture as we read in the following instruction to the child:

> My son, keep your father's commandment, and forsake not your mother's teaching. When you walk, they will lead you; when you lie down, they will watch over you; and when you awake, they will talk with you. (Prov 6:20, 22)

Discipline is training a person and guiding him to act in a way that is acceptable and agreeable. It is training in godly character. The ultimate aim of discipline is to lead the child to allow Christ to control the whole of his life, his words and actions. He should be trained to develop self-discipline. This will enable him to keep following the biblical principles he has been receiving from his parents at home. Of course, the Holy Spirit is at work all the time, right from the time the parents starting instructing him in the Lord. As the child is trained more and more, being exposed to the Word of God—and especially when he has come to believe—the Holy Spirit takes over as he yields to Him. It is at this point that the Spirit starts producing the fruit of love, peace, patience, kindness, self-control, and other virtues in the child.

As discipline is basically instruction and the setting of boundaries, it is understood that both parents will not differ much, since their basis of discipline is the Word of God and training in righteousness, as 2 Tim 3:13–16 clearly states.

Parents in ancient Israel were admonished to discipline children to make sure that they walked in the ways of the Lord. This is what we read in the book of wisdom:

> Train up a child in the way he should go; even when
> he is old he will not depart from it. (Prov 22:6)

And the ways mentioned here are ways of the Lord, given that the ways and desires of the world, which are attractive to young people of this generation, are not the ways of the Lord, as Isaiah 55:8–9, shows. But we should train our children to love the ways of the Lord, and walk in them, for this will make them friends of God. The apostle John warns us not to love the world and its ways because what it offers, its desires and pride, is not from God the Father (1 John 2:15–17).

Having family devotions and worship forms children's minds, hearts, and wills, as they learn in the presence of the Lord, beginning in the family altar. The Lord has promised to be with us, especially when we meet to worship Him. As we study the Word of God together, we store it in the heart, meditating on it and learning to live it out as a family. The children, when they grow up, will follow this pattern and train their own children to do the same.

In Biblical times, disciplining the children with a cane or spanking was a normal thing, as we read in the following Scripture:

> Do not withhold discipline from a child; if you strike
> him with a rod, he will not die. If you strike him
> with the rod, you will save his soul from Sheol. (Prov
> 23:13–14)

So we see that the Bible affirms that there is a place for corporal punishment in child rearing. However, the primary purpose of the parent here should be teaching the child rather than expressing his disapproval in anger. Anger and rage can easily lead to abuse and violence. So parents should guard their ways in order to avoid abuse, for this leads to violence. And there is already a lot of violence in the world. We all know how children have been scarred and even destroyed for life when they are abused. Sadly, children who have suffered abuse tend to use violence in raising their own children, and so the children, in turn, suffer abuse.

There is definitely a difference between discipline, which is instruction and training in righteousness and in the ways of the

Lord, and punishment. Punishment comes in when discipline fails. Punishment is meted out when a child has broken a boundary. With regard to disciplining of children, Kenneth Gangel (1979:57) says the following:

> Discipline is more than punishment. Punishment is what must be used when discipline fails. If discipline is erecting the fences, then punishment is what happens when the fences are broken down, or when the child deliberately transgresses beyond the boundaries. Parents incorrectly conclude that a slap in the face is discipline. It is not. It is rather punishment, and probably a poor form at that.

Gangel further makes some important points about nurturing children in the Lord. He says, for example, that nurturing requires that parents set an example before children and that they have the ability to communicate proper values for life and eternity. He goes on to say that discipline must be applied in a rational rather than an emotional state. And more importantly, he says that nurturing requires a climate of love and security. This is important because for a child to develop well and have confidence, he should feel secure in the home knowing that he is unconditionally loved and accepted even when he makes mistakes.

The area of discipline in child rearing is one of the thorny and confusing domains among Christian parents. Parents should be measured and loving, following the example of God, our Father, who disciplines us in love so we can yield fruits of righteousness and peace.

As stated above concerning the role of the father regarding his son, the parents' primary responsibility is to teach the children and bring them up in the fear of the Lord. The first manual of education and nurturing is the Bible, which contains the very Word of God to man. Early on, before the children of Israel ever entered the Promised Land, God instructed parents to teach their children His Word:

> You shall love the LORD your God with all your heart and with all your soul and with all your might. And these words that I command you today shall be on your heart. You shall teach them diligently to your children, and shall talk of them when you sit in your house, and when you walk by the way, and when you lie down, and when you rise. (Deut 6:5–7)

What God shows us in these instructions is the heart of a godly life, the love of God. To love God with all our hearts, souls, and might means loving God with our whole beings. And all that loving God entails must be engrained in our hearts. The heart represents all that man is in essence. This means that God's love and His Word must infuse us so that we are totally soaked to the point of saturation. It is from this point that we should start to teach our children. This teaching process will be so pervasive that it will know no limit in space or time, day or night. This means that the Word of God will be visible, since it is everywhere around the home, on the doorposts, on the gates, and on our bodies (Deut 6:8). This means that our words and acts should be of God; His love should move us so much that what we do or utter is done in love. This is how we will teach our children; teaching His Word means living His Word so that the children will not only hear but will also see it in our lives. We often ignore the power of the Word of God in our life. We see the import of the Word in the gospel of John. John said, "In the beginning was the Word and the Word was God" (John 1:1). This therefore implies that teaching them and saturating them with the Word will lead them to allow God to dwell in their lives, such that they will be filled through and through with the person of God. This will be made clear when Christ comes and teaches us that He and the Father will come and make their home in us.

Paul exhorts the church at Colossae to live in the same way we have just described. He says the following to the Colossians:

> Let the word of Christ dwell in you richly, teaching and admonishing one another in all wisdom,

> singing psalms and hymns and spiritual songs, with thankfulness in your hearts to God. (Col 3:16)

Paul here provides a teaching model that will be very effective if followed faithfully. The first equipment of the teachers, who are here parents, is the Word of God. If the Word of God is internalized and laid on our hearts, we will have wisdom, which will enable us to instruct and advise those we teach with wisdom. The Holy Spirit, who is the Teacher, will help us in our teaching. The other way of teaching which is effective with both children and adults is using songs and hymns. Children learn more effectively if the truths of the Scriptures are sung. This is why the psalms are meant to be sung. We will then be teaching wholeheartedly, which means we are teaching with love. The commandments of God being on the heart foresees the new covenant (in Jer 31:33), when He will write His laws on the hearts of the people. The Word of God in the hearts of the children makes them ready to walk in righteousness and truth, as the psalmist teaches in the follow verse:

> How can a young man keep his way pure? By guarding it according to your word. I have stored up your word in my heart, that I might not sin against you. Blessed are you, O LORD; teach me your statutes! (Ps 119:9, 11–12)

Memorizing God's Word and talking about it and obeying it will yield fruit in our lives and make us ask God to teach us more. I see from personal experience that memorizing the Word of God and teaching our children to lay God's Word in their hearts has yielded a lot of fruit. My parents were effective in their ministry because they valued the Word and read it daily, memorizing and meditating on it daily, and lived this way all their life. My wife and I learned this from them and have followed their example. This has brought us a lot of joy, as we have seen God use His Word to enrich our lives such that we have been equipped to teach others these same principles. We are glad that we taught our children the same things and they are now teaching their own children. And it is our prayer that they will in turn pass what they themselves learned to succeeding generations.

2.9.5. Children

In ancient Israel, the children respected and honoured their parents, following the commandment of God to them, as we read in Exodus:

> Honour your father and your mother, that your days may be long in the land that the LORD your God is giving you. (Exod 20:12)

Children obeyed their parents. And any child who was disobedient and did not honour his or her parents could be put to death by the community, as we read below:

> If a man has a stubborn and rebellious son who will not obey the voice of his father or the voice of his mother, and, though they discipline him, will not listen to them, then his father and his mother shall take hold of him and bring him out to the elders of his city at the gate of the place where he lives, and they shall say to the elders of his city, "This our son is stubborn and rebellious; he will not obey our voice; he is a glutton and a drunkard." Then all the men of the city shall stone him to death with stones. So you shall purge the evil from your midst, and all Israel shall hear, and fear. (Deut 21:18–21)

In this section, we have seen that God created the man and woman to reproduce and to work and live in harmony. Each member of the family should faithfully carry out his or her God-given duty and relate well to the others: husband and wife, mother and father, and even the children. This tells us that life and God's mission for man is fully realized in marriage and in the family unit. And this is the foundation of a godly and healthy society. Individual families are the building blocks of the community, the nation, and the world.

2.10. Divorce

As we have seen so far concerning marriage and the family, the importance of the family and the closeness of people in their group will obviously explain why divorce was not frequent in ancient Israel. Divorce was a serious matter in those times and was not taken lightly. Though divorce was hard to imagine back then, God, in His foreknowledge, knowing the weakness of man and the depravity of the heart of man, made provision for this state of affairs and so laid down conditions in which divorce could be permitted. This is what we read about the conditions for a divorce:

> When a man takes a wife and marries her, if then she finds no favour in his eyes because he has found some indecency in her, and he writes her a certificate of divorce and puts it in her hand and sends her out of his house, and she departs out of his house, and if she goes and becomes another man's wife, then her former husband, who sent her away, may not take her again to be his wife, after she has been defiled, for that is an abomination before the LORD. (Deut 24:1–2, 4)

Here the law starts by giving the conditions for a divorce. It is a conditional situation, which is hypothetical. And so this is an example of "case law" because it has an *if* clause (when ... then). At Creation, God made the union between the man and his wife so strong that separation would be difficult, and this would be done at the risk of damage to the body that the union had made into one indivisible whole and sealed. The clause "they shall become one flesh" affirms this point. And this is why it would have been rare to consider divorce in ancient Israel. However, it happened not only among the people themselves, but worst of all, it happened between Israel, the betrothed of the Lord, and Israel divorced herself from Him, their husband, and so He decries this situation, as reported by Isaiah in the following Scripture:

> Thus says the LORD: "Where is your mother's certificate of divorce, with which I sent her away? Or which of my creditors is it to whom I have sold you? Behold, for your iniquities you were sold, and for your transgressions your mother was sent away." (Isa 50:1)

So it was because the children of Israel had sinned that they were sent on exile. The most serious sin that the people could commit against God, which came to be called "the great sin," was the sin of idolatry, which the son of Nebat had caused Israel to commit, as we read in the following verse:

> And Jeroboam drove Israel from following the LORD and made them commit great sin. (2 Kings 17:21)

In the Old Testament, people who committed this sin were cut off from God. Idolatry defiles people and makes them impure, and so the children of Israel, the betrothed of the Lord, had covered themselves with indecency and thus had met the condition of a divorce, as we read in Deut. 24:1, cited above. Therefore, it is the sin of idolatry, the great sin that caused Israel to be sent into exile (2 Kings 14:15–16; 17:21–23). As God says in Isaiah 50:1, they sinned themselves into exile and so divorced themselves. God did not divorce them, or He would have given them a certificate of divorce. Several times in the Bible it is said that a person, a king, or the people of Israel sold themselves to sin when they sin in such a way that they are irresistibly given over to sin (1 Kings 21:20, 25; 2 Kings 17:17; Is 52:3). This was the case, for example, for Ahab, as we read in the following verses of Scripture:

> There was none who sold himself to do what was evil in the sight of the LORD like Ahab, whom Jezebel his wife incited. He acted very abominably in going after idols, as the Amorites had done, whom the LORD cast out before the people of Israel. (1 Kings 21:25–26)

As previously stated, when God instituted marriage, His will was that people be married for life, and divorce was granted in the case of immorality, which resulted in unfaithfulness and impurity or indecency.

Jesus, who is a fulfilment of the law, will come to reinforce the fact that marriage is to be a lifelong institution. Paul also teaches the same thing in his writings, as we can read from the following verses:

> To the married I give this charge (not I, but the Lord): the wife should not separate from her husband (but if she does, she should remain unmarried or else be reconciled to her husband), and the husband should not divorce his wife. (1 Cor 7:10–11)

Jesus, confronting the religious leaders who questioned Him about the Law of Moses regarding divorce, pointed them to the intention of God at Creation, when He instituted marriage. Thus, when the Pharisees came up to Him to test Him and asked whether it was lawful for a man to divorce his wife for any reason, He answered them as follows:

> Have you not read that he who created them from the beginning made them male and female, and said, "Therefore a man shall leave his father and his mother and hold fast to his wife, and the two shall become one flesh?" So, they are no longer two but one flesh. What therefore God has joined together, let not man separate." (Matt 19:4–6)

When asked why the law of divorce was given at all if God had not given room for divorce, Jesus replied that it was because of the stubbornness of the people.

The disciples saw the difficulties that could occur in marriage and were trying to evade the risk of a lifelong difficult marriage. This is what a lot of people fear today. People are unwilling to bear hardship, especially when this concerns a close relationship, such as it is meant to be in marriage. But we forget that life is all about commitment and endurance. What makes a marriage last is not just the emotions or sentiments of love; it is the commitment that the spouses make one to each other—their loyalty to each other.

The word "love" in ancient Hebrew does not just relate to having an intense feeling towards a person. It supposes loyalty, and this is the sense that it conveys in the Shema (Deut 6:4–6). Love is connected to Judaism's central prayer, the Shema. Talking about this kind of love towards the Lord God, Schaser (2021) writes,

> Deuteronomy 6:5 states, "You shall love (אהבת; ahavta) the Lord your God with all your heart and with all your life and with all your strength." But what does it mean to "love" God according to ancient Israelite thought? For the biblical authors, love isn't just an intense form of "liking" or some kind of "warm feeling" for another; rather, the most common Hebrew word for "love" (אהבה; ahavah) expresses loyalty.

We previously saw that in ancient Israel people went into a marriage relationship not so much because of emotions, but rather for economic and social reasons. Of course, if we regard marriage as God ordained and accept that it is done in Him and with Him, He will be the one we will look to when the going is rough. It is often the case that God has greatly blessed the work and ministry of those who, though in a difficult marriage, have persevered and stayed married in order to honour God and their vows. We saw in 1.9.2 that the marriage of John Wesley to Mary Vazeille made life very difficult for him. Even though his wife made life very difficult for him, he persevered, endured all the trials, and honoured his vows and stayed married till her death. Wesley's ministry was greatly blessed despite the problems he endured. The Lord used these difficulties to train and refine him for greater use and fruitfulness in his ministry.

Marriage represents the whole of the Christian life. Life was never meant to be easy; Christianity is fraught with difficulties, and it is through hardship that we triumph and are rewarded. Marriage is a school where the discipline of patient endurance is learned, enabling the spouses to develop character, which makes them grow increasingly sanctified till they appear before the Lord perfect and blameless (Rom 5:3–4; Eph 5:27; Jude 24–25).

Jesus, however, conceded one condition that would warrant a divorce: sexual immorality. He states it here:

> And I say to you: whoever divorces his wife, except for sexual immorality, and marries another, commits adultery. (Matt 19:9)

So, according to Jesus, divorce can be allowed when one partner commits adultery. This is so not only for the spouse's sake and jealousy, but especially because of the seriousness of apostasy, which is spiritual adultery. In the Old Testament, marriage was a reflection, at the human level, of the bond that ought to exist between God's people, Israel, and Himself. Idolatry was punishable by death. Therefore, if the law of divorce were relaxed, this would weaken the marriage bond and make people treat unfaithfulness to God lightly. The reason why Jesus allowed divorce in the case of adultery is because it could lead to spiritual adultery, which is unfaithfulness to God. Recall that Israel was the betrothed of God and God was their husband (Isaiah 54:5). In the New Testament, Christ is the Bridegroom and the church is the bride. Addressing the topic of sexual immorality in the church, Paul says the following:

> Do you not know that your bodies are members of Christ? Shall I then take the members of Christ and make them members of a prostitute? Never! He who is joined to the Lord becomes one spirit with him. (1 Cor 6:15, 17)

Paul is telling the Corinthian believers that to commit immorality is to defile one's body and also to defile the members of Christ and so unfaithfulness, as exhibited in immorality, is an outrage and a violation of the sanctity of the body of Christ. When we become Christians, we are in Christ and Christ is in us, and so we are united with Him, and thus we should be faithful to Him.

The social question that arises is, What should be done in an abusive relationship? Studies have shown that a lot of women are killed every year as a result of domestic violence. Statistics on domestic violence, commonly referred to as intimate partner violence (IPV), are alarming. For example, according a study done by the Emory University School of Medicine, nearly 5.3 million incidents of IPV occur among U.S. women aged 18 and older every year. IPV results in nearly 1300 deaths and 2 million injuries every year in the United States and more than 3 women are killed by husbands or boyfriends every day.[24]

It is obvious that when we take the sanctity of life into consideration, we would say that divorce should be permitted in cases where the life of a woman or man is in danger.

However, there are situations where a woman in an abusive marriage may choose to stay for the sake of the children. On the other hand, there are people who strongly believe that divorce should be contemplated only as a last resort. My father, who followed the Bible to the letter concerning divorce, did not allow any of his daughters to file for a divorce. When our eldest sister was in an abusive marriage, he did not encourage her to get out of the marriage. He said that my sister should persevere because God would protect her. And God did protect her, even when there was a threat of murder.

---

[24] https://med.emory.edu/departments/psychiatry/nia/resources/domestic_violence.html
Accessed on 8/01/24

3

BAFUT TRADITIONAL MARRIAGE

Bafut traditional marriage was quite different to what Bafut marriage is today. Marriage demands and practices may differ slightly from one family to another, but basically the customs are in the main the same. Most of the practices found in Bafut traditional marriage are found in the tribes of the Grassfields, including the Bamilekes in the Western Region of Cameroon.

Traditional Bafut marriage was based mostly on economic and social considerations and not so much on emotions. With regard to this Abumbi II (2016:117) writes,

> In the past the notion of courtship was non-existent. Before the girl was five, she was already betrothed to a man who would take her as wife upon her coming of age. The criteria for her father's choice depended on how many heroic activities the man had carried out, his heroism in time of war and trouble, his performance during hunting expeditions and whether or not there had been a suicide in his family. Love, was never a factor worthy of consideration.

Other factors also came into play: It was important to marry within the tribe, and as HRM Abumbi says in the quote above, the standing of the family was important. It was a given in traditional

Bafut that the man would have had built a house of his own, since this was one of the indications that one was of age and therefore prepared to marry and establish a family and a home of his own. It was unthinkable that a man would marry without having built a house of his own, which would mean having to bring his wife to his mother or father's house. Maturity or manhood meant independence, being able to stand on one's own, no longer being dependent on one's parents or on others. Marriage came with a lot of responsibility, and thus marriage itself was a mark of maturity and responsibility. And this is why, in the community, marriage automatically conferred a higher status on the man.

What was expected of the girl was that she be from a good family (meaning one that was respected and in which the children were well brought up). The girl would be able to cook and feed her husband. According to the blog Cameroonian Spy, "A Bafut lady is known for her long hair, knowing how to prepare their traditional meal which is the *"achu"* and also her farming skills" (Cameroonian Spy 2013).

Yes, indeed, a Bafut girl must be able to cook the traditional meal, *àtsugè,* and she should be hard-working and be able to "hold the hoe"—that is, she should be able to work hard on the farm, from where she will feed her husband and children.

3.1. Definition of Terms (yɔ'ɔ́/nɨyɔ'ɔ́, sà'â/nɨsà'â)

It will be helpful to understand the meanings behind the Bafut terms used in the domain of marriage. The general term for "marry" is "yɔ'ɔ́," and the noun derived from it is "nɨyɔ'ɔ́" ("marriage"). This word has several senses, including (1) rub with oil (or ointment), and (2) anoint with oil. Marriage in Bafut takes the second sense of the word *"yɔ'ɔ́."* This sense is also used for anointing a king or successor. The Bafut term for Messiah, *"Àyɔ'ɔ́ Nwì,"* is a derivative of the word *"yɔ'ɔ́,"* and the compound noun means "the anointed of God."

Another term that is used in the domain of marriage is "sà'â," which means "pick" or "choose." It is used when plants are chosen from among the seedlings in a nursery for planting, or when a plantain tree sucker is selected for planting. Thus the phrasal verb "sà'a ŋgwê" means "take a wife." Another sense of this word, which is a negative one, relates to the taking of another man's wife. The noun derived from this verb, "sà'a and m̀fɔ̂" (literally "king/chief,") refers to the betrothed of the "Fon" or king. "Sà'amfɔ̂" is the proper noun derived from this phrasal verb "sà'a mfɔ̂," which literally means, "Pick the fon/chief." This is the reverse of Sà'amfɔ̂, which means that the person who bears the name was seen by the Fon to be fit for him, and so he chose him for himself. My father was given the name Sà'amfɔ̂ because the Fon was pleased with his services when he became a courtier in the palace. He consequently became the confidant and steward of the king and was put in charge of the Fon's affairs and of the palace property.

Another meaning of "sà'â," although close to the first meaning, has a negative connotation. This applies to a man who sees a lady whom he likes and takes her to live with him without going through the customary process of marriage, paying all the dues, or meeting the obligations of marriage. This also describes a man who elopes with a girl.

Yet another term in the domain of marriage is "sà'â." This is a homophone of "sà'â" ("pick"), which is discussed above. The word "sà'â" means "scatter, tear down, or demolish (a building or structure)". And so it is used here to mean "divorce." It collocates with the word "marriage," and so the phrasal verb "sà'à nìyɔ'ɔ̂" means "divorce" or "tear the marriage apart." This is better translated as "separate or put asunder."

3.2. The Betrothal (ŋ̀kòsə̂ màŋgyɛ̀)

The betrothal (ŋ̀kòsə̂ màŋgyɛ̀) is the initial rite of the marriage process. This process is called "knock-door" in Pidgin English. A member of the bridegroom's family and a close friend of the bridegroom come to the bride's parents to introduce the young man and his intention to marry the young girl. On coming, they bring a small calabash of palm wine (mɨ̀lù'ù mɨ fìtəə̀). It is at this stage that the ìghòrə (i.e., the marriage negotiations that fix the terms, dues, and contributions) are initiated. The friend of the bridegroom is the ǹtoò ìghòrə (negotiator or messenger of the family of the young man) in all matters that concern the marriage.

The representative of the family of the young man introduces the reason of their visit by saying, for example, "I have seen a nice goat here in your compound which I like very much, and I have come to beg for it (ǹlɔ̀ntâ)."[25] The father of the girl will ask, "What is the name of the goat?" And the girl will be named. (The girl will be waiting in another room, for she is not supposed to be present, though she would have been told about the event.) The girl is then called and asked whether she accepts to marry the young man. If she accepts, she will be asked to open the wine (ǹtsɔ̀'ɔ́ àjènsə̀ mìlù'ù). After she does this, the wine is then served to all. At this point, the intention is accepted (m̀bîî ìghòrə̀). The father of the girl pays for the wine, giving a token amount. This amount will be part of the brideprice. And that is why it is called a token; the amount will be multiplied several times in return. If, for example, the token were 2,000 frs CFA, the young man would bring 20,000 frs as part of the brideprice.

3.3. Soft Wine (mìlù'ù mî bɔrə̀)

When the family of the young man comes a second time, they will bring more wine than before. This is called the mìlù'ù mî bɔrə̀, which means "soft or fresh wine." This signifies the early stage of the marriage negotiations and arrangement. Before coming, the young man would have given money to the mother of the girl to buy meat and cook food, which will be eaten by those who will be present. The young man comes with more family members and his friends. At this point, the father of the girl will have invited a number of his family and friends. The young man is introduced to the wider family and friends of the father of the girl. There is feasting and rejoicing.

---

[25] Any domestic animal that is attractive (e.g., a chicken, sheep, or cat) could be used as a metaphor.

At this point, the father of the girl and the young man will have talked about the brideprice. In traditional Bafut society, the brideprice is not a fixed amount. They would not tell the family of the young man an exact amount to bring. The father would tell the young man, "Zì nî ŋkabə̀ atû ŋgwɛ ghò tso ŋgàŋkabə̀," meaning he should bring the brideprice like a wealthy man, which indicates he should bring a reasonable amount of money. The custom regulating the brideprice is the principle that the father of the girl should ask only for what he paid for his wife. He could receive up to that amount, but if something has to be added, it should not be much. Also, the in-laws will be asked to make several contributions to family functions and events (e.g., funerals, births, other marriages in the family, social functions) for as long as the marriage lasts. Even when an amount is given, the young man is not required to pay it in full. He gives just a part of it. And thus, in Bafut it is said that *"Kaa bi si ŋkabə̀ atû màŋgyɛ̀ tu maŋsɔ,"* which means that one never finishes paying the brideprice. Part of it is given before the marriage is conducted, and the rest of it may come in kind as the young man and his family support their in-laws in many ways, as needed in the family.

3.4. Big Wine (*mɨ̀lù'ù mî wè*)

This rite is performed when the family of the young man comes a third time with a good amount of wine (mɨ̀lù'ù mî wè), more wine than what was brought on the second occasion. Also at this time, a good part of the brideprice will be brought. And as previously stated, what is paid should not be more or less than what the father of the girl had paid for his wife. Several twenty-litre jugs of wine are given to the father for his friends he will have invited. Some of the brideprice money is also given to the father of the girl, which he will share with his brothers. There will be a lot of feasting and rejoicing during this occasion.

3.5. Duties of the Young Man to His Father-in-Law

At this point, the young man and his friend, the *ǹtoò ighòrә* (messenger), will be asked to perform many duties for the father of the girl.

3.5.1. Clearing the Farm (*m̀bù'û ǹsòo ighòrә*)

The young man is asked to clear a farm for the father of the girl. The young man and his friend, the ǹtoò ighòrә, will arrange for this to be done. They can clear the farm themselves or they might invite other friends to go on a fixed day to do the work.

3.5.2. Splitting Wood (*ǹsàâ ŋkwee ighòrә*)

The young man is also asked to bring firewood for the father of the young girl. They can bring firewood or they can buy a blanket for him.

3.5.3. Roofing Grass (*bwii ighòrә*)

The traditional houses in Bafut were roofed with grass, since Bafut is in the Grassfields. Each year, the man had to go to the hills to cut roofing grass, usually in the dry season. He would then come and renew the roofs of his houses. Now houses are roofed with aluminium-zinc sheets. In the past, the young man would invite his friends to go and cut the roofing grass, which they brought to the compound of the parents of the girl. However, nowadays a young man will roof the house of his father-in-law with aluminium-zinc sheets.

3.6. Sauces and Food for the Women (ǹnù'û ǹjyà)

There are several things that need to be done for women of the family. The young man has to ask his mother-in-law to give him the list of things that he needs to do.

3.6.1. First Marriage Sauce
(ǹnù'û ǹjyǎ atu yì m̀bɔrə̀)

The young man has to provide cooked food and sauce for the mother of the girl. This is called ǹjyǎ mamu mɔ́'ɔ́ (sauce only for mother of child). She will take this and share it with the women and young girls of her family, as well as her friends. This is the making of the first sauce, ǹnù'û ǹjyà yî m̀bɔrə̀. The young man will buy a good amount of meat and plantains. The plantains are cooked separately (nìŋgɔ̀ɔ̀ nì atsɛ'ɛ̀ [single plantains]). The meat is also cooked separately, and the juice is used to prepare the sauce. The sauce is prepared with a lot of palm oil. All those that the mother of the girl has invited to the ceremony (i.e., her sisters, the young girls of her family and her friends) will be in the compound. They will eat the food that has been prepared and then share the plantains and the meat among themselves and take these home. Some of the food will be given to the father of the girl. The young man will have been informed that he is to give an amount (about 5000 frs) to the father, ŋ̀kùsə̂ ǹtsŭ njyà (covering the sauce). He will also give some money to a paternal uncle, an act termed "ǹlə̀ə̂ ǹtɨɨ ndɔ̀ɔ̀nsə̂ ǹdâ," meaning, "satisfying the heart of the uncle."

3.6.2. Oil of Mothers-in-Law
(mìghurə mi nswoŋ bìnɔ̂ ŋsə̀)

The young man will then be asked to bring oil for the married women of the family of the girl's mother. He will bring one twenty-litre tin of oil and two big bunches of plantains. He will also provide meat which will be used in making sauce. The women who are coming for the occasion will each bring cooked food, and this is the food that they will eat. The plantains and the oil will be shared only among the married women of the family. Since this occasion is attended only by the women of the family of the mother of the girl, the young man will be asked to go and see a sister of the girl's father, ŋ̀ghɛ nyə ǹtsŭnda nɔ́ ŋsə̀ (her paternal auntie).

3.7. The Marriage Sauce
(ǹnù'û ǹjyà yî ŋwè[ǹjya nɨyɔ'ɔ̀])

The bridegroom gives money to the mother-in-law to prepare food that will be cooked in the bride's compound for the occasion. They cook enough food to entertain the guests.

The required (lawful) things for this celebration are a big goat (mâ mâ m̀bî) and two big bunches of plantains. People now demand a pig in place of the goat. The neck of the goat (or pig) is cooked separately for the father of the girl. One of the bunches of plantains and a chicken are cooked for the mother of the bride (mother-in-law). All these things are cooked at the bridegroom's home and brought to the bride's compound.

The women from the girl's family also cook food. They bring the food in mìŋkàà (baskets). The mìŋkàà of the family of the mother of the bride will be paid (ǹtukə̂ mìŋkàà). This means that each of the women who bring food will be given money. The mitô (intestines) of the goat are also cooked with plantains (niŋgɔ́ɔ̀ nî tàrə̀) and brought. The rest of the plantains are cooked separately (ǹlàâ niŋgɔ́ɔ̀ ni tsɛ'ɛ̂). The soup is cooked separately too. The family of the mother of the girl divide the plantains and the meat to take home. The father of the girl gives her maternal grandfather an amount of money at his discretion.

When the plantains are divided and the food is eaten, the marriage rite will be performed.

3.8. The Marriage (nìyɔ'ɔ́)

3.8.1. Solemnization of the Marriage

The solemnization of the marriage is fixed on Mumɨ̀tàà (Country Sunday). The marriage rite is conducted after all the food has been eaten and the plantains and meat shared among the women. At this point, all those present at the occasion gather in the family house. The father of the girl asks that the girl be brought. The sisters of the girl, (bɔɔ bɨ maà yì bî bàŋgyɛ̀), bring the girl. These girls are given a token amount of money for bringing the bride. One of them will hold the girl as she is being anointed with red oil by her father.[26] The father advises and blesses the bride while anointing her. For example, he will say:

> Take care of your husband well, for your husband will only have regard for us to the extent that you have regard for him. Therefore, value him and take care of him.

He may also say, "Mɨ̀kòrə̀ mɨ kɔ'ɔ ɨkuu mi nɨkwà, mɨ sɨgə mi nto'o kə mi nɨfwaà." (When four legs go up into the bed, let them come down six or eight.)

The girl is then helped to get up from the kneeling position she took to be anointed. At this point, the audience cheer and utter words of joy and praise. The father of the bride hands her to the family of the groom. Again there is a rapturous shout in jubilation.

The father of the bride gives a carved traditional stool to the bride as a sign of the recognition of her marriage status. The family of the bride gives her a young girl (àdasə̀ [gift]) who will keep her company and do the chores of a child. She will be the first babysitter when the bride gives birth. And she will be brought up

---

[26] If the bride is the first daughter, the marriage solemnization will be done by the paternal grandfather. He will be the one to anoint the bride.

as the couple's firstborn child. In some families, this young girl is also anointed after the bride has been anointed.[27]

3.8.2. Bridal Procession

After the bride is anointed, she will be given to her sisters and her maternal aunts. The aunts will then take their baskets (mìŋkàà) and follow the bride. One paternal aunt and one brother of the girl will join themas envoys of the father of the girl.

The bridal party, including the members of the bride's family and the family and friends of the bridegroom, begin the bridal procession to the bridegroom's compound. Since the ceremony takes place at night, bamboo torches (mìŋkà'à) will have been prepared. At this point they are lit and carried to light their way. On the way, they will be singing and chanting praises of the bride, pointing out some of her virtues (m̀bwìtə mûŋgèn). First, they will chant as follows:

Lead singer: mûŋgen à kɨ kwɛ̂ɛ̂ (Here comes the bride!)
All: À kwɛ̂ɛ̂! (She has indeed come!)
Lead singer: À sɨ ŋwa'à lɛ? (Is her beauty not dazzling?)
All: À ŋwà'â aà! (Her beauty is indeed dazzling!)
Lead singer: À laa, kɨ à sɨ laa lɛ? (Isn't she pure?)
All: À làâ[28] (She is pure!)

All along, as the bridal procession advances, people come out to watch or to greet the bride. Some bystanders join the procession. People hear and recognize a bridal procession because of the chanting, singing, and exhilarating shouts and cries of joy.

---

[27] When our eldest sister was married, I was given to her as her first child. I must have been about three years old, since she had to carry me on her back. I will never forget how slippery her back was because of the oil she had been anointed with.

[28] The Bafut word "laâ" ("clean") in this context means "pure." They are singing the virtues of the bride, saying that she is pure and has not been defiled—that is, she is a virgin. The girl is expected to be a virgin.

As the procession gets closer to the home of the bridegroom, the sisters of the girl and her aunties (*bìjààntɔ̀*) will be looking for ways to be pampered (*ǹnɛ̀'ɛ̂*) (*bì kâ ǹnɛ'ɛ*), then they will be given small amounts of money.

When they get to the gate of the groom's compound, the bridegroom will be required to provide the torches used to light their way (*ǹtsɔ̀ɔ ŋkà'à*). The torches are prepared by splitting raffia bamboo and tying the pieces together (*ǹsɛ̀ntɔ̂ ŋ̀kà'à*).

When they arrive at the bridegroom's compound, there will be much feasting. The food is not specified except for the dish of the bride, (*ŋ̂kwoŋ mûngèn*). It requires a good-size cooked chicken and soup made with a lot of palm oil.[29] This is placed in front of the bride. But she might not eat much of it, because her sisters and the aunts who came to escort her will eat most of it. They will say that the husband will feed her with lots of goodies. So this will be their only chance to eat this special dish.

Ladies of the compound and other married women of the family will go and wash the bride, for she will not sleep with the anointing oil on her body. The sisters will anoint the bride again the following day so that she will continue in the anointing of marriage, which is performed in the paternal home on the night of the marriage.

The money to pay for the torch (*ǹtsɔ̀ɔ ŋkà'à*) will be given to the brother of the bride, who will bring it to the father of the bride.

Marriage in Bafut is a family feast and a union between two families. Although it is two people being united in the bond of matrimony, it is more of a family and community contract than just a union of two people. It promotes cultural and ethical values. The fact that it promotes marriage within the group helps to hold families together.

---

[29] Palm oil in Bafut culture is what olive oil was to ancient Israel. It represents wealth and riches. It is used in anointing, for cosmetics, and for other rites, such as the enthronement of the king.

3.9. Form of Marriage

In traditional Bafut, every person aspired to get married. The ruling idea was therefore to be married. Marriage always began with one wife. So monogamy was the starting point. After a young man got married and engaged in farming, the number of agricultural activities he was involved in and the gain he made from them would then determine whether he needed another wife or other wives. As for a young man, he looked up to his father and would likely follow his father's example with regard to marriage. If his father had several wives, he would aspire to be a polygamist. Thus, polygamy was the traditional form of marriage. However, not many were able to marry more than one wife. The number of wives a man had determined his social status. The Fon, of course, had many wives, followed by princes and noble men.

3.10. Roles and Relationships in the Family

In the family unit, the various members—father, mother, and children—had defined roles.

3.10.1. Father

Authority was vested in the father. He was the family head, and the home was run under his control. He made sure that the family was well provided for and protected. He took care of his wife by providing the farm which she would work to feed the family. He provided the meat, salt, and oil that she needed in order to feed the family. He provided her clothing and other things she needed for her body and well-being.

The father was responsible for training his son to grow up and become like him and to be a responsible man and husband. The boy started working with the father as early as the age of five. The father would take him along to do boys' and men's chores.

3.10.2. Wife and Mother

The woman was to provide food for her husband and the children. She was to respect her husband and obey him. She called her husband Taà (father) because women could not call their husbands by name. When she gave birth, the husband would then be called "father of Neba" or "father of Asoh." The mother trained her daughters and raised them to know how to farm and to cook food. She raised them to be well behaved. The girls would be modelled by the mother such that when people looked at the mother, they would know what kind of wives the daughters would make.

3.10.3. Children

Children were the responsibility of both parents. The parents were responsible for feeding them and bringing them up. The father was responsible for taking care of their clothing, their general welfare, and their health. Discipline began with the mother while the children were infants, and the father came in when they started walking and could understand the consequences of their actions. Some of the means of discipline were spanking and beating, or even depriving the children of food and other amenities and treats. When a child misbehaved or disobeyed in such a way that deserved punishment, the mother would draw the attention of the father to this, and he would administer the appropriate punishment. The children's primary responsibility was to obey and honour their parents and to do the chores that were given to them. They had to help their parents in the house and on the farm. The mother went to the farm with the girls, and the father went with the boys to do men's work.

3.11. The Need to Have Children

The primary aim of marrying was to have children, and so a couple, especially the woman, would be very miserable if she did not have children. It was customary to blame the woman if a child did not come. In some cases, a woman would be sent away because she did not give the man children. However, sometimes the man resorted to taking a second wife. In such cases, it could be said that polygamy was good for the family because it reduced the chances of divorce in the community.

3.11.1. Boys and Girls

Both boys and girls were valued, and so a couple would love to have both. Women often preferred to have a girl first, while men preferred to have a boy.

3.11.2. The Need to Have a Boy

It was very important for the man to have a boy. Girls grew up to be married into other families, while boys would remain in the family. And so a man badly needed to have a boy to inherit his property and to perpetuate his name. In some cases, the man would see the need of taking a second wife if the first wife did not give him a son.

3.12. Levirate Marriage

In Bafut society, the woman was married into the family and the brothers of the man, the brothers-in-law of the woman, called the woman their "wife." The woman called her brothers-in-law her "husbands."

It is therefore customary that the woman belonged to the family. This is in no way a kind of polyandry, for everyone understood who the literal husband of the woman was. This was a custom built within marriage to further cement the family bonds.

Given the bonds in the family that marriage created, the woman was already integrated into the family; and so, at the death of her husband, she would not expect to be left alone. First, it was the responsibility of her parents-in-law to take care of her, since, through marriage, the woman had become their daughter. The brothers of her husband were also to take the responsibility to see that she was taken care of after the death of her husband. In this case, depending upon the situation of her brothers-in-law and the relationships that had been established with the wife, especially a caring attitude, the family would decide who should take the widow to be his wife. So it was normal and expected that the widow of a man who died while the wife was young, and especially if she were still likely to bear children, would be married to one of the brothers of her husband.

3.13. Divorce (ǹsà'á nìyɔ'ɔ́)

Marriage in traditional Bafut, as we have seen, was a family and communal institution. Marriage brought together families and communities. Marriage was not based on emotions or erotic love but on practical economic and social factors that met people's needs and promoted welfare and peaceful coexistence. This is why cases of divorce were fairly rare in traditional Bafut society.

If there were a conflict in a marriage, and if it happened that the wife was wronged and could not be appeased, she would leave the marriage home (ǹsàá) and go back to her parents. In this case, the parents of the woman and the parents of the man would by all means seek a solution to restore peace between the couple. For the woman to come back to the marriage home, the man had to bring a calabash of wine to the father of the woman to beg him to give back his wife. If it was a case of domestic violence or a case of irresponsibility, the man would be admonished, and he would have to promise to treat his wife with consideration. This shows that everything was done to save marriages because of the children and because of the commitment of the two families. Divorce was therefore not a desirable option in marriage. If anything, divorce was only condoned because the family was deemed very important. And generally family bonds, first between the two families and also within the wider community, were solid. Bonding within the group was very strong. Divorce was a violation of the family union and peace. And therefore, this was a violation of Bafut customary law. This is what Abumbi II (2016:120) says about the perspective of Bafut traditional law and customs:

> According to Bafut customs and traditions, marriage is a life union, and divorce is an abomination. However, when the marriage is irreversibly broken down on traditionally acceptable grounds, divorce may be granted.

This means that divorce was exceptionally allowed under Bafut traditional law and customs. There had to be strong grounds, supported by facts that did not violate social cohesion and the sanctity of life.

4

ANCIENT ISRAEL AND TRADITIONAL BAFUT MARRIAGE: CULTURAL AND RELIGIOUS IMPORT

4.1. Similarities and Differences

As shown in this study so far, even though there are cultural and religious differences between ancient Israel and traditional Bafut, there are a lot of similarities between the marriage customs of ancient Israel and those of traditional Bafut.

Looking at marriage in both ancient Israel and traditional Bafut, we find a lot of commonality. The rites of betrothal, marriage, and the bridal procession are very similar. While the bride was anointed in Bafut, she was not anointed in ancient Israel.

Marriage is a family celebration and a commitment in the customs of both communities. The marriage rites in both societies translate the joy that is in marriage and among peoples when they are united as one family. The motif of bride and bridegroom—the adornment, the beauty, and the joy of the occasion—were acknowledged by God and used both in the Old and New Testaments such that, at the consummation of salvation, John described this in his revelation as follows:

> And I saw the holy city, New Jerusalem, coming down out of heaven from God, prepared as a bride adorned for her husband. (Rev 21:2)

4.2. Redemptive Analogies

Just as there were values, institutions, and symbols in ancient Israel that God redeemed and used to bring deliverance to the people and nation of Israel, so there are values and symbols in Bafut culture and traditional religion (BTR) that God has placed there to serve as redemptive analogies. These are concepts in the traditions and customs of the people that serve as beachheads for the gospel, the good news of salvation.

4.2.1. The Family

The Bible uses the family to point people to what life in God can be when the family is connected to God, our Father, who is in heaven. As previously stated, God created the man and woman in His image. So it is expected that man should reflect who God is.

4.2.1.1. *God the Father*

The fatherhood of God is seen in various Old Testament Scriptures beginning in Exodus. He is seen as father to the people of Israel as a whole:

> Then you shall say to Pharaoh, "Thus says the LORD, Israel is my firstborn son, and I say to you, 'Let my son go that he may serve me.' If you refuse to let him go, behold, I will kill your firstborn son." (Exod 4:22–23)

When David wanted to build the house of the Lord, God told him that his son, Solomon, would build the temple and told David concerning this, as we read in the following verses:

> I will raise up your offspring after you, who shall come from your body, and I will establish his kingdom. I will be to him a father, and he shall be to me a son. (2 Sam 17:12, 14)

So in the Old Testament it was already established that God was father and the people of Israel, the covenant faithful, were His children. And as children, they were able to enjoy the protection, guidance, love, and grace of a father, as David brings out in the following verse:

> As a father shows compassion to his children, so the LORD shows compassion to those who fear him. (Ps 103:13)

It was the father's care for his children that Jesus wanted to teach His disciple. He affirmed the fatherhood of God in His teaching ministry. And so when the disciples asked Him to teach them how to pray, He told them, "Pray then like this: 'Our Father in heaven …'" (Matt 6:9). Jesus had such a close relationship with His Father that He would also want His disciples to enter into such a relationship. Before this time, although God had revealed Himself as Father, the Jews revered Him so much as Creator, and as so holy, that they did not even dare to pronounce His personal name. For Jesus to teach His disciples to call God Father and relate to Him as such was quite revolutionary and countercultural. Thomson and Pitt (2021:2) also see this teaching as a paradigm shift in the Jewish view and understanding of God:

> At the time these words were spoken, this was a seismic shift in the people's understanding of God. This was the first time in Scripture anyone had been taught to pray to God as their own Father.

In the Lord's prayer, Jesus taught the disciples to look at God not just as holy but also as one to whom they could go personally for every need of theirs, and not only for the needs of the kingdom.

And when He appeared to Mary after His resurrection, He gave her a message for the disciples:

> Go to my brothers and say to them, "I am ascending to my Father and your Father, to my God and your God." (John 20:17)

In this declaration, Jesus makes an important revelation which is very astonishing. He makes the disciples understand that they had become His siblings, included in the Father's family. In their relationship, the disciples had moved from servants to friends, and now to brothers.

And Paul also taught us the same truth—that God is our father and that every family is named after Him:

> For this reason I bow my knees before the Father, from whom every family in heaven and on earth is named. (Eph 3:15–16)

In Bafut, the child is named after his father, and this speaks of his biological origin and his identity. In the same way, Hebrew children were named after their father. So, too, we who have come to believe in God find our identities in God, our Father.

If in the family of God, God is the father, then who is the mother? Theologically, God is the Father of all created beings. He is our Father, especially the father of all those who trust Him. Our federal father is Adam, while Abraham—the patriarch—is our covenantal father (Gen 12:3; 17:5; Gal 3:29; Micah 7:20). David, being the father of the Davidic Messiah, is also our father. Jesus Christ is also our father, since He is Creator (John 1:2)—the father of humanity. If there is a father of children, there is naturally a mother. From Scripture we can establish who the mother of humanity is. The Bible speaks of motherhood following different contexts and definitions. Eve is the federal mother of humanity, while Sarah is the covenantal mother of the people of God (Gen 17:6; Gal 4:29). Israel, symbolized by Sarah, is the mother of all God's people, as can be read from the following verses of Scripture:

> But the Jerusalem above is free, and she is our mother. For it is written, "Rejoice, O barren one who does not bear; break forth and cry aloud, you who are not in labour! For the children of the desolate one will be more than those of the one who has a husband." So, brothers, we are not children of the slave but of the free woman. (Gal 4:26–27, 31)

The children of the free woman here in the quote are the children of Sarah. All those who believe in Christ belong to the heavenly Jerusalem; even those who were not yet born at the time these words were spoken, including the Gentiles, would become God's people, the new Jerusalem and the new Israel. The woman in Revelation who gave birth to the son, Christ, who defeated the dragon symbolized Israel.[30]

4.2.1.2. Children

When God created the man and woman, He gave the order to reproduce—to "bear fruit." Adam and Eve having children made them the first human family. This reflects the fact that God, being Father, bears children, though not in the same way that a man does. God being a father presupposes children. John, the gospel writer, who teaches us most about God and who He is, will tell us how we become God's children, as we read in the following quotation:

> He came to his own, and his own people did not receive him. But to all who did receive him, who believed in his name, he gave the right to become children of God, who were born, not of blood nor of

---

[30] The woman in Revelation 12:1–2, by virtue of her clothing, symbolizes Israel. She is clothed with the sun, a crown of twelve stars on her head and the moon under her feet. This depicts Israel as the royal nation, shining with the glory of the Lord and the Star of David; the twelve stars represent the twelve tribes of Israel and the twelve apostles.

the will of the flesh, nor of the will of man, but of God. (John 1:11–13)

Both in the culture of Israel and Bafut, children were brought up after their parents. The father trained his sons to grow and become like him. So also we find in the Bible that we, as children of God, should reflect our heavenly Father. This is what Paul teaches in the following text:

> Therefore be imitators of God, as beloved children. And walk in love, as Christ loved us and gave himself up for us, a fragrant offering and sacrifice to God. (Eph 5:1–3)

The Father is good to all, forgiving and gracious, kind even to the ungrateful, and so we should be like Him, doing good even to our enemies, forgiving them, meeting their needs, expecting nothing from them. So Jesus exhorts us:

> Love your enemies, and do good, and lend, expecting nothing in return, and your reward will be great, and you will be sons of the Most High, for he is kind to the ungrateful and the evil. Be merciful, even as your Father is merciful. (Luke 6:35–36)

Jesus came to show us who the Father is and to make us His children. He showed and demonstrated by His life how He related to the Father. He revealed God's character and lived it out for His disciples to see. He said repeatedly that He loved them as the Father loved Him. He lived a perfect live. The purpose of the Sermon on the Mount was to show His followers that it was possible to live as God expected His children to live. He set high standards which pointed to the Father, and amazingly, He wants us to be perfect. And so He urged, "You therefore must be perfect, as your heavenly Father is perfect" (Matt 5:48).

And Paul describes the process where we daily grow into the image of God our Father:

> Now the Lord is the Spirit, and where the Spirit of the Lord is, there is freedom. And we all, with unveiled face, beholding the glory of the Lord, are being transformed into the same image from one degree of glory to another. For this comes from the Lord who is the Spirit. (2 Cor 3:17–18)

John goes a step further and foresees what we, as children of the Father, will be when Christ returns and we are glorified:

> See what kind of love the Father has given to us, that we should be called children of God; and so we are. Beloved, we are God's children now, and what we will be has not yet appeared; but we know that when he appears we shall be like him, because we shall see him as he is. And everyone who thus hopes in him purifies himself as he is pure. (1 John 3:1–3)

So there is a purpose for which God created us in His image: that we will become like Him, bearing His image, and that we will be pure and holy, just as He is (Lev 11:44; 1 Peter 1:16). It is from this background that we have the proverb "Like father, like son."

4.2.1.3. Son, Heir

As previously stated, both in Israel and Bafut, it was important that people have children, and especially that a man have a son to inherit his property. So it will be easy for people in this cultural setting to understand what the Bible teaches about God the Father and His Son, Jesus. Jesus' sonship was predicted by the prophet Isaiah (Isa 9:6). Paul, who was steeped in Jewish culture and religion, brings out the meaning of a son and the implications of Jesus being the Son of the Father.

> For you did not receive the spirit of slavery to fall back into fear, but you have received the Spirit of adoption as sons, by whom we cry, "Abba! Father!"

> The Spirit himself bears witness with our spirit that we are children of God, and if children, then heirs—heirs of God and fellow heirs with Christ. (Rom 8:15–17)

Paul, using the concepts of sonship, adoption, and inheritance, brings to mind all of salvation history. While we were slaves to the world and sin, Christ saved us, and through faith in Him, we became children of God by adoption. Just as adopted children had the right of inheritance, so we, too, who become God's children, will have the right of inheritance, just like Jesus, the Son of God. And we become coheirs with Christ. Paul continues to emphasize the purpose of God in recreating us to become His children in view of our eternal inheritance by saying,

> He saved us, not because of works done by us in righteousness, but according to his own mercy, by the washing of regeneration and renewal of the Holy Spirit, whom he poured out on us richly through Jesus Christ our Saviour, so that being justified by his grace we might become heirs according to the hope of eternal life. (Titus 3:5–7)

By becoming God's children, we are made members of His family. We also become brothers of Jesus Christ, who makes this clear in the following text:

> And he answered them, "Who are my mother and my brothers?" And looking about at those who sat around him, he said, "Here are my mother and my brothers! For whoever does the will of God, he is my brother and sister and mother." (Mark 3:33–35)

Jesus, by this public statement, teaches us that those who do the will of God form the true members of the family of God. In actual fact, becoming members of the family of God, as John writes, has nothing to do with biological affinity or natural birth (John 1:10–13). It has everything to do with God's decision and following His will. It is especially a spiritual act, carried out by the Holy Spirit. The work of the Holy Spirit was clearly seen in the conception of Jesus when He overshadowed Mary.

At another point in his ministry, Jesus teaches us that it is those who desperately need Him, those who trust Him wholeheartedly, who are members of His family. A woman who had a desperate need and completely trusted in Jesus said in her mind,"If I touch even his garments, I will be made well" (Mark 5:28). Seeing her desperation and trust, Jesus said to her, "Daughter, your faith has made you well; go in peace, and be healed of your disease" (Mark 5:34).

When Jesus saw how much this woman needed Him, He called her "my daughter," thus giving her a different identity—that of a daughter. She is no longer, an outcast, shunned by society because of her condition, but someone significant in the eye of the Master, a member of God's family. Jesus did not only heal her; He rehabilitated her.[31]

The concept of family, as we see in ancient Israel and Bafut traditional society, points us to a spiritual and eternal reality realized here and now on earth, and in the end, to a fully-fledged heavenly reality in glory, when, as John says, people from every tribe, tongue, and nation will gather before the throne, worshipping the Father and saying, "Salvation belongs to our God, who sits on the throne, and to the Lamb."

4.3. Husband, Betrothed, Wife, Bridegroom, and Bride

The roles of the husband, wife, betrothed, bride, and bridegroom in the customs of Israel and Bafut have been examined. These roles are reflected in the Old Testament and New Testament Scriptures.

---

[31] The Greek word "*sozo*" means "heal" or "save." So the faith of the woman brought her not only physical healing but also spiritual healing; she was saved by Christ, the Saviour, who forgives sins and saves. Her salvation made her a daughter of God.

4.3.1. Yahweh, the Bridegroom and Husband

In the Old Testament, God presents Himself as the Bridegroom, and the people of Israel are His betrothed, as we read in the following Scripture. The Lord told unfaithful Israel that they would turn away from Baaland call Him "My Husband," as He declares:

> "And in that day, declares the LORD, you will call me 'My Husband,' and no longer will you call me 'My Baal.'And I will betroth you to me forever. I will betroth you to me in righteousness and in justice, in steadfast love and in mercy. I will betroth you to me in faithfulness. And you shall know the LORD." (Hosea 2:16, 19–20)

God had made a covenant with the people of Israel at Mt Sinai, and they promised to be faithful to God but subsequently repeatedly broke the covenant though God, who was their husband, had been faithful to it, as He states:

> ... my covenant that they broke, though I was their husband.(Jer 31:32)

God now promises to make a new covenant with them which will not be broken. God will write His laws on their hearts and cause them to obey Him and be faithful to Him as their husband.

So we see that the terms "husband," "betrothed," and "bride," as used in ancient Israel and traditional Bafut, are reflected in the Old Testament. We saw that in ancient Israel, the bride had to keep herself pure for her husband and the bridegroom was the hope and joy of the young lady. And marriage was a celebration and a joyful situation. So casting Christianity and the kingdom of God in the mould of marriage gives it a joyful, celebratory perspective. That is reflected in Bafut, in which the term "sà'amfɔ" means "the betrothed of the Fon." So because God, in His foreknowledge, put this term in the culture of the Bafut people, this ties them to the fact that the people of Israel were the betrothed of God, their King. So to the Bafut people, Israel is called "sà'amfɔ." Given the implication of this term, the people of Bafut will naturally envy the position of Israel. It is no small matter to be the betrothed of the king. As we saw in 3.1, the position that my father held, by virtue of his name, *Sà'amfɔ* (meaning "the betrothed of the king") was enviable because of the special relationship he had with the Fon. Paul will come to exploit this concept when he tells the Corinthian believers that they are the betrothed of Christ, as we read in the following verse:

> For I feel a divine jealousy for you, since I betrothed
> you to one husband, to present you as a pure virgin
> to Christ. (2 Cor 11:2)

Paul, in his writings, tries to teach and reinforce the position of the individual Christian and the church as the bride of Christ. This position comes with responsibilities and privileges. Paul's responsibility (as well as that of any leader of the church) was to teach and build up the believers so they would grow up and be presented pure and blameless to Christ, their Bridegroom. If we catch just a glimpse of the bride of Christ at the Marriage Supper of the Lamb (Rev 19:6–9), every believer will marvel at the prospect of just being part of the feast, let alone being in the position of the bride of the Lamb. The fact that Christians are the bride of Christ goes with the responsibility of being faithful to Him and keeping themselves pure and holy.

4.3.2. Jesus Christ, the Bridegroom

In the New Testament, Christ presents Himself as the bridegroom and the church as His bride, as we read in the following verse:

> And Jesus said to them, "Can the wedding guests
> mourn as long as the bridegroom is with them? The
> days will come when the bridegroom is taken away
> from them, and then they will fast. (Matt 9:15)

When the disciples of the Pharisees wondered why they were fasting and His disciples were not, He told them that, inasmuch as a wedding was a time of joy, so the presence of the Messiah, which was in a sense the kingdom of God brought down on earth, was a moment of rejoicing. So long as Christ was with His own, this was the time during which they would know His joy and their joy would be full (John 15:11). He said that a time was coming when He, the bridegroom, would be taken away (when he would be crucified), and even when He was going to be taken up to heaven, they would mourn and be sorrowful (John 16:20; Acts 1:10–11). Regarding this joy, John the Baptist said that the joy that he experienced when he was in the presence of Christ could be compared only to that felt by the friends of the bridegroom (John 3:28–29).

The presence of the Lord and, finally, His kingdom is always cast in the image of a wedding—and not just that of any wedding, but that of a royal (king or prince), for God is the King reigning and ruling in His kingdom. And so we read in the following Scripture, "The kingdom of heaven may be compared to a king who gave a wedding feast for his son" (Matt 22:2).

In the end, when the earth and the heavens (that is, the old cosmic order) are renewed at the coming of Christ, the new earth will be made so beautiful that it can be compared only to a bride adorned for the bridegroom, as we read in the following Scriptures:

> Then I saw a new heaven and a new earth, for the first heaven and the first earth had passed away, and the sea was no more. And I saw the holy city, New Jerusalem, coming down out of heaven from God, prepared as a bride adorned for her husband. (Rev 21:1–2)

What should be highlighted in the picture of the new world is the fact that the New Jerusalem, the renewed Zion, the Mountain and the sanctuary of the Lord, is seen in the light of marriage, the bride and her husband. Here the motif of marriage is brought to the forefront in order to draw our attention to the Bridegroom. This prepares the ground for the Marriage Feast of the Lamb, the Last Supper of the Lamb and His bride, the church. This implies that we are to prepare ourselves and the whole body of Christ in such a way that we, and the church, will be presented to Christ, the Bridegroom, in splendour, holy and without blemish, just as He himself intended (Eph 5:25–28). So we should be in the mood of a wedding. Just as we prepare ourselves when we are going to attend a wedding, we should be looking forward to the return of the Lord and our meeting with Him, which is described as His wedding. Normally we would go to a wedding in our best attire, and so we should be ready and well dressed both outwardly and inwardly (in terms of our character, which is our inner beauty). Our inner beauty and adornment is more important because just as the person who did not have the proper wedding robe was thrown out of the banquet hall (Matt 22:11–14), the wayward will be kept out of the kingdom because they lack character—the robe of righteousness and inner beauty:

> But as for the cowardly, the faithless, the detestable, as for murderers, the sexually immoral, sorcerers, idolaters, and all liars, their portion will be in the lake that burns with fire and sulfur, which is the second death. (Rev 21:8)

Peter also warns the church, exhorting it to hasten the coming of the Lord (and the Day of God, which will be for the judgment of the ungodly). The believers were to live holy and godly lives in view of their blissful reunion with Christ so that He would find them without spot or blemish, and at peace (2 Peter 3:11–14).

4.3.2.1. *The Marriage Supper of the Lamb*

The marriage of the Lamb, the ultimate marriage, which is also the end of all marriages, takes place in heaven, the heavenly sanctuary. And Jesus Christ, the King, is the bridegroom. His bride, the chosen bride, is the perfect and righteous bride. John describes the majesty, splendour, and joy of this marriage as follows:

> Then I heard what seemed to be the voice of a great multitude, like the roar of many waters and like the sound of mighty peals of thunder, crying out,

> "Hallelujah!
> For the Lord our God
>   the Almighty reigns.
>   Let us rejoice and exult
>   and give him the glory,
> for the marriage of the Lamb has come,
>   and his Bride has made herself ready;
>   it was granted her to clothe herself
>   with fine linen, bright and pure"—
>
> for the fine linen is the righteous deeds of the saints. (Rev 19:6–8)

What we see here is the marriage of the King, Jesus Christ. His bride, the chosen one, is the church—the bride of Christ.

4.3.2.1.1. Robes and Clothing

Robes and clothing are motifs that we find in the Scriptures from Genesis to Revelation, from the first Adam to the second Adam, Jesus Christ. Moses was asked to make "holy garments for glory and beauty" for Aaron and his sons (i.e., the priestly robes) (Exod 28:2). Joshua, the high priest, who was standing before the Lord clothed with filthy garments, was given pure garments:

> And to him he said, "Behold, I have taken your iniquity away from you, and I will clothe you with pure vestments." And I said, "Let them put a clean turban on his head." So they put a clean turban on his head and clothed him with garments. (Zech 3:4–5)

Jonathan, the son of Saul, heir to the throne, gave his robe to David:

> And Jonathan stripped himself of the robe that was on him and gave it to David. (1 Sam 18:4)

In this case, Saul would be following the custom of primogeniture, whereby the first or oldest son inherits the family property, as we see by the way he treated Jonathan. And this meant that Jonathan would be the next king after him. So by this symbolic act, Jonathan was showing that the throne would rightfully go to David. This was thus a sign of Jonathan's abdication, foreshadowing his transfer of the kingship to David. It should be said here that the robe is a symbol of royal authority.

Jesus came to the world as the king of the Jews (Matt 2:2), but after the resurrection He came to reveal Himself as the King of the whole world, King of Kings, as recorded in Revelation. John saw Him clothed with a robe:

> And in the midst of the lampstands one like a son of man, clothed with a long robe and with a golden sash around his chest. (Rv 1:13)

The Bridegroom in Revelation 19:6–9 is Jesus Christ, the King, and the brideis no ordinary virgin. She is arrayed in purity. It was granted her to be clothed in special bridal raiment and adornment. The bride is thus a royal, since the bridegroom is the King. This is indeed a royal wedding. As with all royals, it is the King who clothes his bride. In royal marriages, the bride would be a princess and would be in splendid attire, just as described in the following song:

> All glorious is the princess in her chamber, with robes interwoven with gold. In many-coloured robes she is led to the king, with her virgin companions following behind her. (Ps 45:13–14)

The motif of clothing is underlined by Jesus in the parable of the wedding feast in Matthew 22:11–14. The king holding the feast queries one of the guests:

> Friend, how did you get in here without a wedding garment? (v.12)

The king orders the man to be cast away into outer darkness, where the wicked suffer and gnash their teeth. This scene has kept people wondering about the action of the king. Bible scholars have explained this by saying there is evidence that in the ancient world kings supplied garments to their guests. Joseph did so to his brothers (Gen 45:22), and the one the king would honour was to be given royal robes (Esther 6:8–9). So it is likely that the guest did not put on the wedding garment provided by the king for guests attending the party.

The motif of the robe (clothing) here and in other Scriptures calls to memory the clothing (covering) of the man and woman, Adam and Eve, in the Garden of Eden (Gen 3:21).[32] The Garden of Eden then was the sanctuary of God on earth. It foretold the erection of the tabernacle in the desert, which brought the presence of God to His people. The presence of God overshadowed His people for protection, covering, and refreshing from the scorching heat of the desert. Eventually, the temple in Jerusalem, Zion, was built.

In the Old Testament, the motif of clothing carried with it the impartation of a new nature, including attitudes, character, and a new way of life, as we can see in the following text:

> I will greatly rejoice in the LORD; my soul shall exult in my God, for he has clothed me with the garments of salvation; he has covered me with the robe of righteousness, as a bridegroom decks himself

---

[32] It is important to note that it is the Lord who clothes us, because the clothing or garments that man makes for himself are not effective. We see that the effort Adam and Eve made when they "sewed fig leaves together and made themselves loincloths" did not effectively cover their nakedness (their sin). And this is why God had to make garments of the skins of animals to effectively cover them. Here we should note that the lives of the animals, their blood, were taken. This foreshadows the atonement, which involves the deaths of the animals (Lev 16:11; 17:14; Heb 9:22) and eventually the atonement effected by the sacrificial death of Christ. Christ's blood (which was indeed His life) was shed to atone for our sins, for as the Scriptures say, without the shedding of blood there cannot be the forgiveness of sins (Heb 9:22). And so the clothing is the imputation of Christ's righteousness to His bride.

like a priest with a beautiful headdress, and as a
bride adorns herself with her jewels. For as the earth
brings forth its sprouts, and as a garden causes what
is sown in it to sprout up, so the Lord GOD will cause
righteousness and praise to sprout up before all the
nations. (Isa 61:10–11)

Again we see the working of the grace of God right in the Old Testament: It is the Lord who takes the initiative to impart righteousness to His rebellious and stiff-necked people, Israel, clothing and adorning her in the beauty of a bride. Salvation and righteousness are imputed to God's people by grace. It is not the doing of the people; it is the Lord's doing. And as stated previously, just as our clothing is not an effective covering (for our sins), our deeds of righteousness are not good enough, for they are like dirty rags (Isa 64:6). Just as the garden causes what is sown in it to sprout, so the Lord causes righteousness to dawn on His people. The righteousness and salvation that God gives us cause us to rejoice and be glad.

It is also the image of clothing that Paul uses to talk about renouncing our sinful ways of life and adopting the new life of Christ with all the virtues of our imputed righteousness:

> Put on then, as God's chosen ones, holy and beloved,
> compassionate hearts, kindness, humility, meekness,
> and patience, bearing with one another and, if one
> has a complaint against another, forgiving each
> other; as the Lord has forgiven you, so you also
> must forgive. And above all these put on love, which
> binds everything together in perfect harmony. (Col
> 3:12–14)

What we should note here is the difference between ancient Israel, under the old covenant, and the believer of today, who walks in the new covenant. As stated previously, whereas in the old covenant it was impossible to keep the law of God, in the new covenant God Himself wrote His laws on the people's hearts and caused them, by His Spirit, to keep His commandments. It is thus that Paul was able to bring this home to the believers in Christ. God imparts righteousness in us and makes us do the good works that He prepared beforehand (Eph 2:8, 10). Paul goes ahead to tell us that it is God who makes us willing and able to do what he requires us to do, in order to be pleasing and acceptable to Him (Phil 2:13; Rom 12:2). We, the bride of Christ, are able to do what we do for Him because He is in us and is working through us, thus making us willing and enabling us to do the works of righteousness, the things that please Him.

It is in the light of this background of imputed righteousness that the bride of Christ is prepared. She has prepared herself for the Bridegroom. This reminds us that we, the church, should be ready at all times for the Bridegroom, unlike the foolish virgins in the parable of the ten virgins (Matt 25:1–13). The clothing of the bride, the fine, bright, and pure linen, as John explains, represents the righteous deeds of the saints, and these deeds are those that God prepared beforehand for them to do (Eph 2:10).

4.4. Virtues

In my study of ancient Israeli customs and culture, I have noticed a number of values held in common with traditional Bafut. Since God created man (and woman) in His image, so, in all cultures there are values that reflect godly virtues.

4.4.1. Purity

In both communities, purity was very important, and so a girl was to jealously guard her virginity. The bride was expected to be a virgin in both communities. James presents purity as the primary virtue (James 3:17).

Immorality was abhorred and severely punished in ancient Israel. As previously stated, adultery was punishable by stoning. In the Bafut community, a girl who got pregnant outside wedlock brought shame on herself and on the family. Such a girl was dubbed *swùŋədàŋ,* "a lewd and wayward girl."[33] This kind of girl was not anointed with palm oil, because she had lost her virginity and so was morally impure.

4.4.2. Love, Obedience, and Trust

Love meant a different thing in ancient Israel than what we understand it as in everyday parlance. It was not so much a matter of emotions and romance, but it had much more to do with loyalty and doing things that promoted the good and welfare of the object of love. This kind of love looks back to the declaration of the name and character of the Lord to Moses in Exodus 34:6. This is God's steadfast love. The steadfast love of the Lord is the character trait which shows Him as merciful, gracious, and faithful to those who trust Him. It had to do with trust or faith. A good demonstration of love, which at the same time serves as a commentary on true love, such as that depicted in 1 Corinthians 13, is given in a scene from the film *Fiddler on the Roof*.[34] The main character, Tevye, asks his wife, Golde, whether she loves him. Golde, who is surprised by the question, blurts out, "Do I what?"[35] She then goes on to tell her husband that, after twenty-five years of working together to raise their children and struggling together to make their home, if that is not love, then she doesn't know what it is. Monica la Rose, commenting on Golde's reaction says the following:

> The scene both reflects the joy of being loved and a commitment to living out the kind of love that is

---

[33] The word is a complex form composed of two morphemes, "*swùŋə̂* "("pull or drag") + "*daŋ*" ("nothing or other"). Literally, it means "One who is dragged for nothing or by another or others." The word suggests that the girl is dragged away from parental protectionand moral order by ways or people other than the established order of life.

[34] The film is based on the book *Fiddleron the Roof*, by Jerry Bock.

[35] *Fiddler on the Roof*, DVD, a 1971 musical *film* produced and directed by Norman Jewison.

forged through discipline and commitment. That's a perspective on love that's much bigger than romance; it's the kind of active, self-giving love that, in the New Testament, believers are invited, over and over, to live out. (la Rose 2022)

Marriage in both Israel and Bafut required a lot of trust or faith on the part of the young girl to be given in marriage. The girl had to trust her parents because, in most cases, it was the parents who made the negotiations. The girl had also to have faith in the young man she was going to marry, believing that he would be a good husband for her—a man who would do her good and be kind to her. In the case of Rebekah, she had not met or known Isaac, but she accepted being his wife.

The word "love" is used primarily as a verb in Bafut and is rendered in various forms—for example, "kɔŋɜ̂" ('love!'— the imperative form) and "ŋ̀kɔŋɜ̂" ("loving" [gerund] and "to love"[infinitive])—and has shades of meaning that are morecurrent, such as "favour," "kindness," "like," or "want." The will of God is translated with the word "love" or "want," as in *"ànnù yìi Nwi akɔŋə aà"*("what God likes" or "what pleases God"), or as *"ànnù yìi Nwi lɔ̀ɔ̀ aà"* ("what God wants.")

The derivative of the word "kɔŋɜ̂"("love!"), "àkɔŋnə̀" (noun) means "steadfast love," "mercy," or "grace," the terms which God used in Exodus 34:6 to proclaim His name and character. And so the concept of love in Bafut reflects the biblical view, and it also reflects who God is to His people: one who is being faithful to, doing good to, and showing kindness to the object of love. Thus, love is viewed similarly in both ancient Israel and in traditional Bafut society. And for this reason, it will be easier for both the Jew and the Bafut person to understand the biblical concept of love. This will bring him, particularly, to the love of God and allow him to relate to Him.

The command to love the Lord God "with all your heart and with all your soul and with all your might" (Deut 6:4) entails giving oneself wholeheartedly to God, which translates into devotion, trust, and loyalty.

Jesus came as a visual manifestation of the love of God. And it is shown in the key verse of the redemption story, found in John 3:16, where love, at its fullest, manifests itself in giving: "God so loved the world that He gave His One and Only Son" to save us.

Later in His ministry, Jesus taught His disciples that love translates into obedience:

> If you love me, you will keep my commandments. Whoever has my commandments and keeps them, he it is who loves me. Whoever does not love me does not keep my words. (John 14:15, 21, 24)

Jesus further told the disciples that if they loved Him and obeyed Him, He would send the Holy Spirit to guide and lead them so they would grow in love, knowledge, and understanding.

> And I will ask the Father, and he will give you another Helper, to be with you forever, even the Spirit of truth. (John 14:16–17)

Ruth Reilly-Smith throws more light on how this works out in our lives, as we read in the following quote:

> It is by the work of the Spirit, who is with us and in us, that we can learn to obey Jesus and "keep His commands," responding to the promptings experienced throughout. (Smith 2021)

As stated above regarding the dispensation of the new covenant, God is committed to seeing us obey His commands, loving Him and His children willingly. God is love itself, and we are able to love because He loves us and abides in us (1 John 4:12, 16, 19). And so, when God's love abides in His people, it gives them the desire to love and to please Him. This will make them eager to obey Him, and so his commandments are not burdensome but a delight (1 John5:2–3; Ps 119:92, 97, 103, 111). For example, Jacob's love for Rachel made him eager to serve, and serve delightfully, as we read in the following Scripture:

> So Jacob served seven years for Rachel, and they seemed to him but a few days because of the love he had for her. (Gen 29:20)

Obeying God's commandments means loving His children, which means loving one another (John 13:34; 15:12; 1 John 3:11,14). So if God's commandments are rightly understood and followed, they will bring believers great joy and the freedom to love and to do good to one another, for as the Bible says, love is a fulfilment of the law (Rom 13:9). So love and obedience to the law are complementary.

In Bafut and in ancient Israel, children honoured their parents and showed that they loved and honoured them by obeying them. And in ancient Israel, as stated earlier, disobedience by children could lead to the death penalty. This stresses the fact that love, loyalty, and obedience are important relational values that must be taught, understood, and fostered in life.

4.4.3. Love Means Caring for One Another

Jesus will teach his disciples to show their love to one another and that this kind of love will be the mark of discipleship.

> A new commandment I give to you, that you love one another: just as I have loved you, you also are to love one another. By this all people will know that you are my disciples, if you have love for one another. (John 13:34–35)

And as we have seen above in our word study, this kind of love in Bafut is represented by the word "àkɔ̀ŋɔ̀." And so love in this sense means caring for one another; thus "to love one another" is rendered in Bafut as "Nɨ̀ ka ŋkɔŋnə ghuu bu nɨ bù." The apostle John knew what it meant to love, for Christ showed it to him, since he referred to himself as the one whom Jesus loved. He teaches us what loving one another means. In his epistles, he teaches us that love is shown by the way we care for the needy as we read:

> But if anyone has the world's goods and sees his brother in need, yet closes his heart against him, how does God's love abide in him? Little children, let us not love in word or talk but in deed and in truth. (1John 3:17–18)

So we see that true love, just like true faith, expresses itself in deeds. James echoes the same truth in his epistles (James 2:14–16).

4.4.4. Erotic Love

God created the man and woman with their emotions. God feels for us, His people. Jesus experienced the feelings of love, tiredness, and pain. The feelings of love that God and Jesus express are not sensual, for God and Jesus cannot be associated with erotic love. As we have seen in our study of love, divine love is steadfast and compassionate love. God's feeling of love is the love for His people. This kind of love that exists between God and His people is called "agape love." The love of God for His rebellious and sinful people makes Him grieve and moves Him to discipline them so that they will repent and continue in His covenantal love. We can see this expressed in the testimony of David in the following verses of his penitential psalm:

> For when I kept silent, my bones wasted away through my groaning all day long. For day and night your hand was heavy upon me; my strength was dried up as by the heat of summer. I acknowledged my sin to you, and I did not cover my iniquity; I said, "I will confess my transgressions to the LORD," and you forgave the iniquity of my sin. Therefore let everyone who is godly offer prayer to you at a time when you may be found. (Ps 32:3–6)

In these verses, David testifies that the purpose of God's heavy hand on him was to bring him to confess his sin, which he did. He then advises the godly to be wise and immediately confess their sins to God, who is their hiding place, the one who preserves them from the storms of life (vv. 5–7). He realizes that it is the love of the Lord that works and moves Him to guide and discipline the godly, those in a covenant relation with Him, to come back to Him—their refuge, home, and resting place. And so the Psalmist states the following:

> Many are the sorrows of the wicked, but steadfast love surrounds the one who trusts in the LORD. (Ps 32:10)

So this confirms and underlines the nature and purpose of God's love: to do good to His children, making them to enjoy His kindness, grace, and favour. And so the writer of the Hebrews, quoting Proverbs 3:12, writes, "For the Lord disciplines the one he loves, and chastises every son whom he receives" (Heb 12:6).

And, as the writer to the Hebrews affirms, God's love and discipline train God's people to live upright and righteous lives. God's discipline demonstrates the Father's love, proves that we are truly God's children (Heb 12:7–8) and, finally, "yields the peaceful fruit of righteousness to those who have been trained by it" (Heb 12:11).

And so we see that God's love is different from erotic love. It is a yearning and warmth of feelings that enfold and lead to doing good and the protection of His people, as expressed in Isaiah 54:10 and 40:11. We can see His love and yearning for His beloved in the following verses:

> The LORD appeared to him from far away. I have loved you with an everlasting love; therefore I have continued my faithfulness to you. Is Ephraim my dear son? Is he my darling child? For as often as I speak against him, I do remember him still. Therefore my heart yearns for him; I will surely have mercy on him, declares the LORD. (Jer 31:3, 20)

As we will see below, the expression of erotic love is sensual. The feelings of love and sexual excitement are intended to enrich a love relationship and strengthen the marital bonds. The Song of Songs expresses the feelings of erotic love (i.e., sexual desires and pleasure). This is evident as we read through the book.

4.4.4.1. *Sensual Love*

Sensual feelings are emotions that God gave our bodies, and these can be rightly directed and used appropriately. Solomon expresses these feelings in his relationship with the one he loved, as we can read here in the following verses:

> Your two breasts are like two fawns,
> twins of a gazelle,
> that graze among the lilies.
> His left hand is under my head,
> and his right hand embraces me! (Song 4:5; 2:6)

4.4.4.2. *The Beauty of Love*

Love, and all that it entails, is a beautiful feeling. The love of God refreshes us, comforts us, and renews us. It gives us a feeling of joy, as the prophet Zephaniah describes in Zephaniah 3:17. The adage "Beauty is in the eye of the beholder" can be verified in life. And so the love one has for someone makes him or her beautiful in the eyes of the one who loves. This is the feeling we have when we read the Song of Solomon, as we see in the following verses:

> Behold, you are beautiful, my love,
> behold, you are beautiful!
> My beloved speaks and says to me:
> "Arise, my love, my beautiful one,
> and come away." (Song 4:1; 2:10)

4.4.4.3. *The Power and Value of Love*

If anything, the world has come to experience the power of love. This is why it is important for us to realize how to harness the beautiful feelings that God has given us, so as to use them to our advantage. Paul knew the power of love. He knew how to use the love he had for Christ to fuel his work and ministry. He told the

Corinthians, "For the love of Christ controls us" (2 Cor 5:14). In his song of love, he says the following:

> Love is patient and kind; "Love bears all things, believes all things, hopes all things, endures all things." (1 Cor 13:4, 7)

We can see the power of love when it exists in the heart in the following description:

> Sustain me with raisins;
> refresh me with apples,
> for I am sick with love.
> Many waters cannot quench love,
> neither can floods drown it.
> If a man offered for love
> all the wealth of his house,
> he would be utterly despised. (Song 2:5; 8:7)

4.4.4.4. *Erotic Love Should Be Controlled*

The emotions of love can be so intense that we may be blinded or controlled by them. God, who gave us the feelings of love, has also given us the spirit of self-control. The girl in the Song of Songs who experienced the power of love can now advise other young girls as follows:

> I adjure you, O daughters of Jerusalem,
> by the gazelles or the does of the field,
> that you not stir up or awaken love
> until it pleases. (Song 5:8)

As stated previously, love is a beautiful feeling, and it can arouse in us all kinds of emotions. These are God-given and so should not be suppressed but rather be controlled.

4.5. Authority, Submission, and Head

Both in ancient Israel and in Bafut traditional society, authority was vested in the father and husband, and he was the head of the family. The order and authority that we find in the family, both in ancient Israel and Bafut, reflect the order and authority in the Godhead, as well as in the church. With reference to this, Paul says, "But I want you to understand that the head of every man is Christ, the head of a wife is her husband, and the head of Christ is God" (1 Cor 11:3).

As we see in Scripture, there is order in the Godhead, and the three persons exist in a relation of authority (i.e., in the order in which they are named: God the Father, the Son, and the Holy Spirit). In the same way, in the family there exists an ordered authority relationship of father, mother, and child (children). The father is the head of the family. The children are to honour, respect, and obey their parents. They are to be under the authority of their parents. The wife is to submit to the authority of her husband and honour him. In ancient Israel, a girl was under the authority of her father until she got married, and she would then be under the authority of her husband.

4.6. Unity

Unity was best demonstrated at Creation in the institution of marriage, when God said the two would become one flesh. We have seen that in both ancient Israel and in Bafut traditional society, unity was very important. Marriage was a means of uniting two families. It was important to marry within the group, for this further fostered unity in the group.

In traditional Bafut, it was the belief that disunity could allow a witch to come into the family and so deprive the family of the fruit of the womb. We read this in the following Bafut proverb:

> Kaa ndâ ǹtsǔ ntsù ɨ̀ sɨ mu kwe'e.
> (A divided house cannot carry a child on the lap.)

Here is what Jesus said about a divided house:

> If a kingdom is divided against itself, that kingdom cannot stand. And if a house is divided against itself, that house will not be able to stand. (Mark 3:24–25)

Unity in the body of Christ was so important that Christ made it a topic of His priestly prayer, as we read in the Gospel of John:

> I do not ask for these only, but also for those who will believe in me through their word, that they may all be one, just as you, Father, are in me, and I in you, that they also may be in us, so that the world may believe that you have sent me. (John 17:21)

4.7. Light

Light, the first thing that God created, included the heavenly light bodies: the sun, moon, and stars:

> And God made the two great lights—the greater light to rule the day and the lesser light to rule the night—and the stars. (Gen 1:16)

These light bodies, including rain, dew, snow, and such, were regarded in ancient Israel as the gifts and blessings of God to mankind. In the traditional Bafut religion and worldview, light and rain were regarded as gifts of the gods, and of God Almighty, the God of the world, the one who created all things. While ancient Israel viewed thunder, storm and particularly the rainbow as phenomena displaying God's glory, majesty, and goodness, Bafut traditional society viewed these as foreboding, ominous and evil.

Israel saw lightning and thunder as the manifestations of God showing His power and wrath, sent to warn people and instil His fear in them. And traditional Bafut people see these as forces of evil harnessed by an enemy using mystical power to destroy his opponent.

The patriarchs came to interpret the heavenly bodies—the sun, moon, and stars, as symbols of the family: The sun, the "greater light," stood for the husband and father; and the moon, the "lesser light," stood for the wife and mother, while the stars stood for the children. This we read from the interpretation of Joseph's dream, where he saw the sun, moon, and eleven stars bowing down before him (Gen 37:9). Jacob's reading of the dream is as follows:

> His father rebuked him and said to him, "What is this dream that you have dreamed? Shall I and your mother and your brothers indeed come to bow ourselves to the ground before you?" (Gen 37:10)

The motif of light runs all through the Scriptures. Light represents life and virtue, while darkness represents evil and death. The reign of God is the kingdom of light, and the reign of Satan and his forces of evil is called the dominion (or domain) of darkness (Col 1:13).

The lampstand was the second of the three furnishings in the Holy Place, the sanctuary. God said to Moses,

> You shall make a lampstand of pure gold. You shall make seven lamps for it. And the lamps shall be set up so as to give light on the space in front of it. (Exod 25:31, 37)

Light represented the presence of God, or theophany, and the glory of God. And the people of God can reflect the light of the glory of the Lord. This was foreseen in the Old Testament and realized in the New Testament, as we can read in the following verses:

> Arise, shine, for your light has come, and the glory of the LORD has risen upon you. For behold, darkness shall cover the earth, and thick darkness the peoples; but the LORD will arise upon you, and his glory will be seen upon you. (Isa 60:1–2)

> And we all, with unveiled face, beholding the glory of the Lord, are being transformed into the same

> image from one degree of glory to another. For this comes from the Lord who is the Spirit. (2 Cor 3:18)

In the revelation of Jesus Christ, the seven golden lampstands represent the seven churches (Rev 1:20), and so the light motif and symbolism are carried into the New Testament. Light represents the presences of Christ, as we see in the dramatic conversion of Saul:

> Now as he went on his way, he approached Damascus, and suddenly a light from heaven shone around him. (Acts 9:3)

In ancient Israel lamps were used in the home to light the house and also outdoors, in the night, to light the way.[36] As we saw earlier in the bridal procession, lamps were used. In the parable of the ten virgins, Jesus highlights the need of having lamps in readiness to meet the bridegroom. We also saw that in a Bafut bridal procession, people used torches to light their way.

4.7.1. God Is Light

In ancient Israel, it was believed that light came from God. The New Testament writers acknowledge the truth of Genesis 1:3—that God is the creator of light—as we can read from James:

> Every good gift and every perfect gift is from above, coming down from the Father of lights with whom there is no variation or shadow due to change. (Jas 1:17)

The Bible does not only say that God is light itself; it says that He clothes Himself with light, as we read in the following verses:

---

[36] In ancient Israel, the lamp was an oval-shaped clay vessel that had two openings: one for fuel, and the other for a wick. Normally it was in wall alcoves or set on a lampstand. A lamp was small enough to sit on the palm of the hand so that it could be used outdoors to light one's way.

> This is the message we have heard from him and proclaim to you, that God is light, and in him is no darkness at all. (1 John 1:5)

> Bless the LORD, O my soul! O LORD my God, you are very great! You are clothed with splendor and majesty, covering yourself with light as with a garment, stretching out the heavens like a tent. (Ps 104:1–2)

For David, light is fundamentally a reflection of who God is—the Creator and King, in His splendour, majesty, power, might, and holiness. All these attributes, converging in the brilliance of light, metaphorically clothe or envelop the Lord God, as seen in Ps 104:1–2, quoted above.

> Bless the LORD, O my soul! O LORD my God, you are very great! You are clothed with splendour and majesty, covering yourself with light as with a garment, stretching out the heavens like a tent. (Ps 104:1–2)

When David said God was his light, he would have also looked back to recall the light in the sanctuary and how the God of light would appear on the mercy seat unto deliverance and for salvation. And he would have also recalled how God had delivered him on several occasions, dawning on him as light. The light seen in the historical sanctuary and the light of occasional deliverance that David experienced was a foretaste of the light of the eternal salvation and riches in Christ that were still to come.

4.7.1.1. *Salvation and Righteousness as Light*

Having seen and experienced God as light, it follows that the salvation that He brings to the world is light, for it transforms life and opens the eyes of the faithful to behold the riches of His glorious inheritance in them as a result of their sanctification and adoption (Eph 1:18; Rom 8:17). This image of salvation is well depicted by the psalmist as follows:

> The LORD is my light and my salvation; whom shall I fear? The LORD is the stronghold of my life; of whom shall I be afraid? (Ps 27:1)

As God, Christ, and the Holy Spirit speak and infuse life, the Salvation that we experience makes us stand out as light for the world to see. Isaiah paints a glamorous and powerful picture of the salvation of God's people in the following striking verses:

> For Zion's sake I will not keep silent, and for Jerusalem's sake I will not be quiet, until her righteousness goes forth as brightness, and her salvation as a burning torch. (Isa 62:1)

God will glorify Himself in His saints, who have been washed, sanctified, and renewed in increasing glory. The evidence of our salvation is seen in our godly and righteous lives as the Spirit produces fruit, such as goodness and good works that shine as light for people to see.

4.7.2. Jesus Is Light

Jesus' coming as light, the light of salvation, was a fulfilment of the prophecy of Isaiah 9:1–2. And so when Jesus's ministry started in Capernaum, in the region of Galilee, as the narrator of the gospel says, it was a fulfilment of what Isaiah had predicted and written about Him:

> The land of Zebulun and the land of Naphtali,
> the way of the sea, beyond the Jordan, Galilee of the Gentiles—
> the people dwelling in darkness
> have seen a great light,
> and for those dwelling in the region and shadow of death,
> on them a light has dawned. (Matt 4:15–16)

As Bible scholars and commentaries explain, the region of Zebulun and Naphtali (Matt 4:13) had experienced a lot of turmoil and suffering under oppressive Assyrian rule, and the Jewish inhabitants had longed for liberation from their Gentile rulers.[37] And as it happened, they were then the first to see the great light of God's deliverance in Jesus Christ when he started His ministry in their region, preaching the gospel of the kingdom of God. Just as these people saw in Jesus the light of deliverance and salvation, we today, who are also living in tumultuous times, can see in Jesus (or the Godhead) the light of hope. What Schuldt (2021) says in the following quote is very appropriate:

> Many of us live with similar worries, which produce anxiety and stress. When the darkness presses in on us, we can find peace because we know God is with us too. The divine flame of the Holy Spirit lives in us to light our path until we meet Jesus face to face.

John, writing about Jesus, also said He was the light, as we read in his Gospel:

> In him was life, and the life was the light of men. The true light, which gives light to everyone, was coming into the world (John 1:4, 9)

The good news about Jesus the Messiah coming into the world as light, as predicted by the prophets Isaiah and Malachi, was that He was bringing healing and peace to a world of sickness, war, total darkness, and death, as we read in the following verses:

> But for you who fear my name, the sun of righteousness shall rise with healing in its wings … Because of the tender mercy of our God, whereby the sunrise shall visit us from on high to give light to those who sit in darkness and in the shadow of death, to guide our feet into the way of peace. (Mal 4:2; Luke 1:78–79)

---

[37] ESV Study Bible.

Jesus Christ Himself said that He was the light of the world and that He came to enlighten the world. And as such, He gave people understanding so they would know God through Him and His teachings. He brought this out when He addressed the Jews:

> Again, Jesus spoke to them, saying, "I am the light of the world. Whoever follows me will not walk in darkness, but will have the light of life." (John 8:12)

By saying this, Jesus must have had in mind the prophecy of Isaiah, where God speaks of sending His Servant, "a light for the nations, to open the eyes that are blind" (Isa 42:6–7). Jesus would open the eyes of the people, thus making them know God. The purpose of God's grace when He delivered His people from captivity was to eventually use the liberation from Babylonian exile as an image of spiritual liberation.

Again Jesus spoke to the Jews who were questioning His identity and wondering whether He was the expected Messiah:

> The light is among you for a little while longer. Walk while you have the light, lest darkness overtake you. The one who walks in the darkness does not know where he is going. While you have the light, believe in the light, that you may become sons of light. (John 12:35–36)

When Jesus is out of our world, the light of God is withdrawn from us, as seen at the crucifixion:

> It was now about the sixth hour, and there was darkness over the whole land until the ninth hour, while the sun's light failed. And the curtain of the temple was torn in two. (Luke 23:44–45)

Our duty as God's people is to work from the vantage point of the cross and death of Christ to point people back to the light, drawing them out of the darkness of death. The death of Christ paradoxically brought about eternal life by opening a direct way to

God, who is Light eternal. And it is only through Christ that people can now go directly to God the Father and have life (John 14:6). The curtain barring the way to the Holy Place was torn, opening the way for people to go to God, thanks to Christ and His suffering on the cross to bear our sins and secure forgiveness not only for the Jewish and Roman authorities who crucified Him but also for us (Luke 23:34). This is the privilege and blessing of access, for thanks to Christ and His reconciling work on the cross, we can go directly to the Father, as Paul says, "For through him we both have access in one Spirit to the Father" (Eph 2:18).

When we look at the way things are in the world, it is as though the church of Christ is sleeping and not awake to the fact that living in the dark is still crucifying the Christ, who came to give us light. Believers need to realize that they are no longer in darkness. They have nothing to do with the works of darkness and the desires of the flesh but are led by the Spirit (Gal 5:18, 22–23). So Paul is sounding the clarion call in the following words:

> At one time you were darkness, but now you are light in the Lord. Walk as children of light (for the fruit of light is found in all that is good and right and true), and try to discern what is pleasing to the Lord. Anything that becomes visible is light. Therefore it says, "Awake, O sleeper, and arise from the dead, and Christ will shine on you." (Eph 5:8–10, 14)

It is my prayer and desire that this book, like the others in the Awake series, would be a wake-up call to the church, that the church would wake up to its responsibility as "the light of the world."

4.7.3. The Word of God Is Light

It was with great light—flashes of lightning, thunder, and fire—that God appeared on Mount Sinai to give the law to the people of Israel through Moses (Exod 20:18; Heb 12:18–21). And David asserts this in the psalms when he says, "Your word is a lamp to my feet and a light to my path" (Ps 119:105), while Peter expresses this even more vividly in the following quote:

> And we have the prophetic word more fully confirmed, to which you will do well to pay attention as to a lamp shining in a dark place, until the day dawns and the morning star rises in your hearts. (2 Pet 1:19)

The Word of God gives us the truth, enabling us to gain knowledge in the things of the Spirit and matters of God. In this way, our minds are enlightened. This is what David meant when he wrote the following:

> The unfolding of your words gives light; it imparts understanding to the simple. (Ps 119:130)

4.7.4. Believers Are Light

It is mind-boggling just to imagine that we can be the light of the world! On the other hand, it should not surprise us, since at Creation we were imparted with the nature of God, because man was created in the image of God. Secondly, the light and glory of the Lord shine on those He has chosen in order that they will shine. In view of this, Isaiah writes,

> Arise, shine, for your light has come,
> and the glory of the LORD has risen upon you.
> For behold, darkness shall cover the earth,
> and thick darkness the peoples;
> but the LORD will arise upon you,
> and his glory will be seen upon you. (Isaiah 6:1–2)

Jesus tells his disciples the following in the Sermon on the Mount:

> You are the light of the world. A city set on a hill cannot be hidden. Nor do people light a lamp and put it under a basket, but on a stand, and it gives light to all in the house. In the same way, let your light shine before others, so that they may see your good works and give glory to your Father who is in heaven. (Matt 5:14–16)

This is a great responsibility, since we live in a world where everything makes it difficult to live what is taught in the Sermon on the Mount. However, this is what Christians have to be. Our mission is to let the light of Christ shine on the world as we preach and live the gospel truths. Peter, in his epistle, reinforces this teaching of Christ, explaining why we must make an impact on the world:

> But you are a chosen race, a royal priesthood, a holy nation, a people for his own possession, that you may proclaim the excellencies of him who called you out of darkness into his marvellous light. (1 Peter 2:9)

James Banks, in the following quote, helps us see how we can be a light to the world through what Christ has done in our lives:

> When we look to Jesus for salvation and follow His teaching we're restored in relationship with God, and He gives us new power and purpose. His transforming life and love—"the light of all mankind"—shines in us and through us and out to a dark and sometimes dangerous world. (Banks 2022)

4.8. Oil and Anointing

In both ancient Israel and Bafut traditional society, oil was important, for it was a symbol of riches, wealth, and the joy of life. In Bafut, having oil all the time for cooking, for ceremonies, and for social transactions is important for a man's reputation, because oil is a mark of wealth and well-being. The household is poor and the husband poor if the wife cooks without oil.

In Israel, too, olive oil was a symbol of wealth. And we find this reflected in several passages of the Bible. For example, talking about the blessings of Asher, indicating how blessed in riches he would be among his brothers, Moses says,

> And of Asher he said, "Most blessed of sons be Asher;
> let him be the favourite of his brothers, and let him
> dip his foot in oil. (Deut 33:24)

Oil was used in religious practices, with offerings, and for anointing. For example, when Jacob met God at Luz, he called that place "the house of God," raised up a pillar there, and poured oil on the top of it. Apostate and rebellious Israel, in defiance of the covenant agreement, poured out libations and drink as an offering to foreign gods, the gods of the land, as we read in the following Scripture:

> Among the smooth stones of the valley is your portion; they, they, are your lot; to them you have poured out a drink offering, you have brought a grain offering. Shall I relent for these things? (Isa 57:6)

In Bafut traditional religion, oil is also used for libations and sacrifices to the gods and ancestors of the tribe. For example, at a traditional marriage ceremony, oil is held as sacred and so is used for sacrifice. In addition to the functions described in chapter 3, it was used for libations. For example, any oil that spills on the floor when oil is being distributed is said to be an offering to the gods. Religious shrines are also identified with pillars, and during religious sacrifices these are anointed with oil. However, for sacrifices, rather than using red oil, *bìrə̀ntɔ'ɔ̀,* which is deep red, fine powder from camwood, is used. Camwood powder is sacred and is produced in the palace following strict rules, and it is the equivalent of the holy anointing oil which was unique and made strictly following a recipe and rules (concerning the ingredients) given by God (Exod

30:22–33). It was used for anointing the holy vessels and priests. Oil is used in Bafut for anointing kings and for blessing people. When a noble is being honoured with the naming rite (*Mii Mfɔ*), he or she is anointed with camwood. The successors of nobles or important chieftains are anointed with camwood. When princesses are married off by the Fon, they are anointed with camwood.

While oil is an important foodstuff, it is more significant because it is a symbol of riches and wealth. The olive tree, with its fruit and oil, was equivalent to the palm in Bafut traditional society.

4.8.1. Functions of Oil

Oil was used for the body, for cosmetics, and for anointing, both in Bafut traditional society and in ancient Israel. It was also used for lighting. As we have seen the preceding chapters, it was used in lamps. Oil brought joy and gladness to life, as we read in various places in the Bible:

> Oil and perfume make the heart glad, and the sweetness of a friend comes from his earnest counsel. (Prov 27:9)

> The Spirit of the Lord GOD is upon me, because the LORD has anointed me ... to grant to those who mourn in Zion— to give them a beautiful headdress instead of ashes, the oil of gladness instead of mourning, the garment of praise instead of a faint spirit; that they may be called oaks of righteousness, the planting of the LORD, that he may be glorified. (Isa 61:1, 3)

Oil is used regularly in the Old Testament to anoint the head (Matt 6:17; Mark 14:3), for cosmetic purposes, and to anoint the feet (John 12:3), as a show of hospitality and honour to guests. In the New Testament, we read about women anointing Jesus as an act of devotion to Him. When Mary anointed Jesus, she meant to honour Jesus and show her deep devotion to Him. Jesus also interpreted this as the preparation of His body to be offered as a sacrifice for our sins (John 12:1–9). Oil was also used to anoint and prepare the body for burial. Jesus commended the woman who came and poured the expensive ointment over His head, and He said,

> Leave her alone. Why do you trouble her? She has done a beautiful thing to me. She has done what she could; she has anointed my body beforehand for burial. And truly, I say to you, wherever the gospel is proclaimed in the whole world, what she has done will be told in memory of her. (Mark 14:6, 8–9)

Oil mixed with perfumes was used as cosmetics. Anointing oils were applied on special occasions. These were made from crushed aromatic blossoms or resins mixed with oil and boiled to produce ointment. Such oils were used for romantic purposes, as we read in the following Scripture:

> Let him kiss me with the kisses of his mouth! For your love is better than wine; your anointing oils are fragrant; your name is oil poured out; therefore virgins love you. (Song 1:2–3)

Oil was also used for medicinal purposes, to treat wounds (Luke 10:34) and for healing (anointing the sick), as we read in James 5:13–14.

As stated above, oil was used in the Bible for religious purposes (for anointing vessels, altars, priests, and such), and it was part of the sacrifices and offerings. Oil was used in anointing kings in Israel (1 Sam 10:1; 16:3, 12–13). And in Bafut, camwood powder was used for religious purposes, for sacrifices, and for anointing kings. And as stated previously, oil was used to anoint brides.

4.8.2. Anointing of the First Kings of Israel

From the beginning, God was the king of Israel, and so Israel was a theocracy. God was the Lord of hosts (God of the armies) because

God was the one who ruled and fought the wars of the people of Israel (Josh 5:13–14). However, with time the people of Israel longed to have a king to rule over them and fight their wars. The Lord, being omniscient, had foreseen this and made provision for this, and consequently he gave Moses the laws of kings in Israel (Deut 17:14–20). And so the Lord said,

> When you come to the land that the LORD your God is giving you, and you possess it and dwell in it and then say, "I will set a king over me, like all the nations that are around me," you may indeed set a king over you whom the LORD your God will choose. (Deut 17:14–15)

It is important to note that there is a proviso: Yes, the children of Israel could set a king over them, but with the proviso that this king would be one chosen by God. It was expected that the king would be obedient to God and be faithful to the covenant.

And as we shall see, the anointing of the king in Israel was a significant prophetic act that pointed to God's redemptive plan for the world.

4.8.2.1. *The Anointing of Saul as King*

As the Lord had foreseen, it came to pass that the children of Israel asked Samuel to set a king over them to judge them like the other nations (1 Sam 8:5). Although this thing—that the people would prefer to have a king rather than the Lord—displeased Samuel, God asked him to listen to the people. And so with time the Lord revealed to Samuel that Saul was the one He had chosen to be prince over Israel, and He then asked him to anoint him king over Israel (1 Sam 8:7; 9:15–17; 10:1).

So when Samuel "took the flask of oil and poured it on the head of Saul" he said, "Has not the Lord anointed you to be prince over his people Israel?" (1 Samuel 10:1) He then told Saul, "The Spirit of the Lord will rush upon you, and you will prophesy and be turned into another man" (v. 6). In this case, as we will see in the case of David, the anointing signalled God's choosing and appointing of Saul into the office of king. And the Spirit came upon him to equip and empower him for the service of God as "prince over his people Israel." The statement that Saul would be turned into another man is not to be taken literally, for Saul did not suddenly become another man. This signified that he would from that point on be a different man because he was being equipped with special power for a different or new role. The importance of the office of king would completely change the status of Saul, who saw himself as very little and as from the least of the tribes of Israel.

With regard to the choice of Saul, a note in the ESV Study Bible gives the following important point:

> The onrush of the Spirit of the Lord upon Saul is predicted, but not manipulated as in the Canaanite practices; it is necessary in order to dispel any doubts Saul might have about his choice and as a public demonstration that he was now the "prince." It is related to his election as king.

The office of king was sacred in Israel (2 Sam 1:14). It is because David recognized the sacredness of the king, the anointed of the Lord, that he refused to kill Saul, as we read in the following verse:

> He [David] said to his men, "The LORD forbid that I should do this thing to my lord, the LORD's anointed, to put out my hand against him, seeing he is the LORD's anointed." (1 Sam 24:6)

The office of the king had been announced in the days of Abraham and Sarah when God made His covenant with Abraham and announced the role he would play in the history of Israel and the nations. God changed his name from Abram to Abraham, saying that He would make him into nations and that kings would come from him (Gen 17:1–6). Saul was going to be the first king of Israel, a position which carried a lot of weight. He is the one whom all Israel desired the most (1 Sam 9:20). Since Israel had cried for a king to lead them (1 Sam 8:6–7, 18–22), the one who was going to fill this post would be the envy of everyone. At the place of worship where people were gathered to eat after having sacrificed to the Lord, Samuel gave Saul the sacred portion of the meat, the leg, that he had set aside (1 Samuel 9:23–24). The leg was the priest's portion (Exod 29:27), and the bread that Samuel told Saul to accept (1 Sam 10:4) would have been intended as an offering and would have been eaten by the priest as part of the "consecrated things" given to them by the Lord as their portion (Num 18:8). The fact that these sacred things were given to Saul to eat was an indication of the sacredness of the kingship, at the same time prefiguring the king–priest office of the Messiah.

The king, God's anointed, was first and foremost to do the will of the Lord. But Saul, who started well, failed woefully and disobeyed the Lord out of greed and pride. First he offered a burnt offering to the Lord, which was the duty of Samuel the priest. This was the first act of disobedience, and the beginning of his downfall, and so Samuel said to him,

> You have done foolishly. You have not kept the command of the LORD your God, with which he commanded you. For then the LORD would have established your kingdom over Israel forever. But now your kingdom shall not continue. The LORD has sought out a man after his own heart, and the LORD has commanded him to be prince over his people, because you have not kept what the LORD commanded you. (1 Sam 13:13–14)

Despite this failure, God still gave Saul another chance and sent him on mission to go and fight against the Amalekites, devoting them to destruction. But again Saul failed to obey the command of the Lord. And the Lord expressed His disappointment to Samuel:

> I regret that I have made Saul king, for he has turned back from following me and has not performed my commandments. (1 Sam 15:11)

At this point, Saul had become very greedy. And because God had caused him to win many battles, he became proud. When he defeated the Amalekites, he kept the best of the things for himself on the pretext of offering them to God as sacrifice. When he returned from the battle, he set up a monument for himself at Carmel, showing that his heart had turned from following the Lord. This made God regret that He had made him king, and consequently He utterly rejected him. Samuel was very sad about what Saul had done and queried him, saying,

> Why then did you not obey the voice of the LORD? Why did you pounce on the spoil and do what was evil in the sight of the LORD? Has the LORD as great delight in burnt offerings and sacrifices, as in obeying the voice of the LORD? Behold, to obey is better than sacrifice, and to listen than the fat of rams. You have rejected the word of the LORD, and the LORD has rejected you from being king over Israel. (1 Sam 15:19, 22, 26)

It is a very sad thing when someone who has tasted the grace and goodness of the Lord deliberately turns from following Him. It is a greater evil and even a curse when the Lord has rejected someone. This person becomes sold to sin, delighting in doing evil rather than doing the will of the Lord. From this point, when Saul turned away from God by rejecting His word, he was bent on doing evil, seeking particularly to destroy David, the one God had anointed in his place. The culmination of his sin occurred when he killed the priests at Nob, as we read in these verses:

> Then the king said to Doeg, "You turn and strike the priests." And Doeg the Edomite turned and struck down the priests, and he killed on that day eighty-five persons who wore the linen ephod. And Nob, the city of the priests, he put to the sword; both man and woman, child and infant, ox, donkey and sheep, he put to the sword. (1 Sam 22:18–19)

The irony is that while Saul failed to carry out the ban against the Amalekites, he treated Nob, the city of the priests, like an enemy city that has been "devoted to destruction" (15:13). He thus destroyed part of his kingdom (because he failed to destroy David). This sin further made him abominable before God. And as if this were not bad enough, he proceeded to another abomination: When the Philistines gathered to fight against Israel, he was terribly afraid. And since God had rejected him and would not answer him, he went and consulted the medium of Endor, asking her to bring up Samuel, the one who had asked the Lord for him before. In doing this, Saul was deliberately going against the command of God not to consult mediums or necromancers (Deut 18:10–12). The wrongness of his act was evident from the response of Samuel. He asked Saul, "Why have you disturbed me by bringing me up?" (1 Sam 28:15) Samuel only repeated the message of his rejection and told him how he and his sons would die, saying to him,

> The LORD has done to you as he spoke by me, for the LORD has torn the kingdom out of your hand and given it to your neighbor, David. Because you did not obey the voice of the LORD and did not carry out his fierce wrath against Amalek, therefore the LORD has done this thing to you this day. Tomorrow you and your sons shall be with me. The LORD will give the army of Israel also into the hand of the Philistines. (1 Sam 28:17–19)

So, because of his numerous acts of disobedience and the horrible and abominable acts of cruelty, he died a violent and shameful death. He killed himself, committing suicide so that the Philistines, from whom he was running away, would not capture him alive. The Philistines came and stripped him, cut off his head, and hanged his body on the wall of Beth-shean (1 Sam 31:4–10). The chronicler, citing his last act of disobedience, explains why Saul died:

> So Saul died for his breach of faith. He broke faith with the LORD in that he did not keep the command of the LORD, and also consulted a medium, seeking

guidance. He did not seek guidance from the LORD. Therefore the LORD put him to death and turned the kingdom over to David the son of Jesse. (1 Chr 10:13–14)

4.8.2.2. *The Anointing of David as King*

When Saul disobeyed God and was rejected, the Lord asked Samuel to anoint David, the son of Jesse, to be king over Israel.

> Now he was ruddy and had beautiful eyes and was handsome. And the LORD said, "Arise, anoint him, for this is he." Then Samuel took the horn of oil and anointed him in the midst of his brothers. And the Spirit of the LORD rushed upon David from that day forward. (1 Samuel 16:12–13)

After Samuel had anointed David king of Israel, "the Spirit of the Lord rushed upon David." The anointing with oil and the ensuing anointing with the Spirit links the oil to the Spirit and equally links the action to the effect. The anointing with oil affirms the choosing and election of David by the Lord for the function of king, while the anointing with the Spirit empowers him for the role and duties he is being called to perform as king. This episode parallels what happened to Saul when He was chosen and anointed king. (1 Sam 10:1, 6)

It should be noted here that because of conflicts and divisions in Israel, David had to be again anointed by the people in order to legitimize his rule and make him acceptable to both the people of Judah and Israel. In the divided kingdom, rather than choosing a relative of Saul, who was from the tribe of Benjamin, the people of Judah wanted to rally behind one of their own, David, since he was from the tribe of Judah. David gathered his men, and they came to live in Hebron:

> And the men of Judah came, and there they anointed David king over the house of Judah. (2 Sam 2:4)

An attempt by the followers of Saul to make his son king failed. They reasoned, however, that though there were differences between Israel and Judah, David was one of them. So all Israel at last acknowledged David as one chosen by God. And so the leaders of all of Israel came to David and said,

> "Behold, we are your bone and flesh. In times past, when Saul was king over us, it was you who led out and brought in Israel. And the LORD said to you, 'You shall be shepherd of my people Israel, and you shall be prince over Israel.'" So all the elders of Israel came to the king at Hebron, and King David made a covenant with them at Hebron before the LORD, and they anointed David king over Israel. (2 Sam 5:1–3)

The choice of David by the Lord and his being anointed as king was of utmost significance. The fact that David was taken from the field as a shepherd boy, taking care of the sheep, prefigured the motif of shepherd that God would take on with regard to His people and the subsequent choice of David as the under-shepherd, as we read in the following verses:

> I myself will be the shepherd of my sheep, and I myself will make them lie down, declares the Lord GOD. And I will set up over them one shepherd, my servant David, and he shall feed them: he shall feed them and be their shepherd. (Eze 34:15, 23)

It would be from his personal experiences as a shepherd boy and the protection and care of the Lord God for him that David would pen what has become the best-loved hymn in the whole Bible, the twenty-third psalm. In it we read these reassuring verses:

> The LORD is my shepherd; I shall not want.
> He makes me lie down in green pastures.
> He leads me beside still waters.
> Even though I walk through the valley of the shadow of death,

I will fear no evil, for you are with me;
your rod and your staff, they comfort me. (Ps 23:1–2, 4)

God promised, as predicted in the Old Testament prophecies that the Messiah will come from the line of David, as we read in the following Scripture:

> Behold, the days are coming, declares the LORD, when I will raise up for David a righteous Branch, and he shall reign as king and deal wisely, and shall execute justice and righteousness in the land. (Jer 23:5)

God is faithful and will honour His covenant with David, as we read in 2 Samuel 7:4–29. These verses, where the Davidic covenant was made, constitute a key text in the history of salvation, for it is here that the Lord promises to raise the Messiah from the line of David. The Lord promises to make one family—that is, the family of David—the representative of his people forever. Verses 8–17 are often described as the "Davidic covenant" based on the promise recorded in Ps 89:3, where the Lord declares, "I have made a covenant with my chosen one."

When David asks to build a house for the Lord, the Lord promises instead to build him a house, and makes a solemn promise to him, declaring:

> I will raise up your offspring after you, one of your own sons, and I will establish his kingdom. I will be to him a father, and he shall be to me a son. I will not take my steadfast love from him, as I took it from him who was before you, but I will confirm him in my house and in my kingdom forever, and his throne shall be established forever. (1 Chron 17:11, 13–14)

It is this promise that would come to be known as the Davidic covenant. God promises to raise up Solomon, his son, the one who will build His house as an act of obedience, and so He would establish his kingdom. God promises him His steadfast love (Hb.

"*hesed*"), which will not be withdrawn from him as it was from Saul. It is worth noting that God calls the Davidic house and kingdom "my house ... and my kingdom." This means that God's eternal heavenly kingdom (Ps 103:19; 145:13) will be present and realized through the Davidic kingdom. Hebrews 1:5 applies the words "I will be to him a father, and he shall be to me a son" to Christ, since as Messiah, He, the offspring of David, inherits the Davidic throne and takes on the role of the representative of God's people. David himself captures his choosing and anointing as king in Psalm 89, as follows:

> You have said, "I have made a covenant with my chosen one; I have sworn to David my servant: 'I will establish your offspring forever, and build your throne for all generations.'" —I have found David, my servant; with my holy oil I have anointed him, my faithfulness and my steadfast love shall be with him, and I will make him the firstborn, the highest of the kings of the earth. My steadfast love I will keep for him forever, and my covenant will stand firm for him. I will establish his offspring forever and his throne as the days of the heavens. (Ps 89:3–4, 20, 24; 27–29)

Again, here the words in the above quote—"I will establish his offspring forever and his throne as the days of the heavens"—point away from David and his earthly kingdom to the Messiah and His eternal kingdom. And so the choice of David as king fits in the eternal purpose of salvation history: David, the king priest foreshadowing the Incarnation, which brings the Messiah, the King Priest, to us here on earth. It was known in the Old Testament that the Messiah, the deliverer, would come from the Davidic line. And so in the New Testament, people recognized Jesus as the son of David, which is a Messianic title (Matt. 2:2; 9:27; 21:9). And so when Jesus came, He was recognized as the promised Messiah and King of Israel (Matt 2:2). Christ was called the branch from the stump of Jesse (Isa 11:1). And Christ calls Himself "the root and the descendant of David, the bright morning star" (Rev 22:16).

Again, as we have already seen, it is important to know that the purpose of God for the king, which would also be the goal of the king, was to fulfil the will of God. This is illustrated by the choice and anointing of Cyrus, as we read:

> Thus says the LORD to his anointed, to Cyrus, whose right hand I have grasped, to subdue nations before him and to loose the belts of kings, to open doors before him that gates may not be closed: "He is my shepherd, and he shall fulfil all my purpose;" saying of Jerusalem, "She shall be built," and of the temple, "Your foundation shall be laid." (Isa 45:1; 44:28)

Saul was rejected because he failed in his primary duty; that is, he failed to do the will of God and fulfil His purposes. God wanted a man who would accomplish all his purposes; and He found this man in David, as testified in the following Scriptures:

> Then they asked for a king, and God gave them Saul the son of Kish, a man of the tribe of Benjamin, for forty years. And when he had removed him, he raised up David to be their king, of whom he testified and said, *"I have found in David the son of Jesse a man after my heart, who will do all my will."*[38] Of this man's offspring God has brought to Israel a Saviour, Jesus, as he promised. (Acts 13:21–23)

It is important to note that David is said to have a heart like that of God, and that he will accomplish all of God's will. David, as we know from his life, was not perfect, since he was a man and, like all men, was tempted and sinned. But Jesus Christ, the ultimate son of David, will be perfect and will have the heart of God: a compassionate and loving heart. And His desire will be to do the will of God (Heb 10:7; John 6:38).

---

[38] Emphasis is mine.

4.8.2.3. *The Anointing of Solomon as King*

As stated previously, God made a covenant with David which stipulated that his son would be established on his throne. And so, towards the end of his life, David decided who his successor would be and started to groom him for the high office.

Since David was aware of the conditions of the covenant, he wanted to make sure that the son he had chosen to succeed him would walk closely with God in obedience to His statutes, rules, and commands. And these are his instructions, of a father to a son, the one who will succeed him:

> And you, Solomon my son, know the God of your father and serve him with a whole heart and with a willing mind, for the LORD searches all hearts and understands every plan and thought. If you seek him, he will be found by you, but if you forsake him, he will cast you off forever. Be careful now, for the LORD has chosen you to build a house for the sanctuary; be strong and do it. (1 Chr 28:9–10)

As a father, and one who walked closely with the Lord and followed Him wholeheartedly, he was concerned that his son should follow in his footsteps. And he wanted Solomon to know and wholeheartedly serve God, whom he assuredly calls, "the God of your father." And his last instructions and charge to Solomon reiterated this last charge, as we read in the following words:

> I am about to go the way of all the earth. Be strong, and show yourself a man, and keep the charge of the LORD your God, walking in his ways and keeping his statutes, his commandments, his rules, and his testimonies, as it is written in the Law of Moses, that you may prosper in all that you do and wherever you turn, that the LORD may establish his word that he spoke concerning me, saying, "If your sons pay close attention to their way, to walk before me in faithfulness with all their heart and with all

their soul, you shall not lack a man on the throne of Israel." (1 Kings 2:2-4)

The first task that God would give to David's chosen heir to the throne was to build His house.

David had in mind to build the house of the Lord, and so he made all the preparations necessary. But God told him that he would not build Him a house, because he had been a man of war and shed a lot of blood. However, God promised to build and establish David's house (i.e., his family), assuring him that his throne would be occupied by his own son until it would ultimately come to the rightful offspring and heir of David, the ultimate Son of David, Jesus Christ, the Messiah. This was even a greater reward because the physical house, the temple that Solomon was to build in Jerusalem, would be destroyed in favour of the true house—that is, the temple that is Christ's body, which would be indestructible (John 2:18–22).

Even though God had said to David that it would be his son who would build His house, David wanted to help his son succeed in this monumental task, the first God-given task to Solomon. The act of building the house of God was of utmost importance to David and the people. And the history of the Christian church will reveal that this was divine providence, given that the motif of building the temple, or house of God, would be carried over to the New Testament to mean building the church, the body of Christ, and building up the individual Christian members of the church.

David threw his whole weight behind the project. He provided a lot of the material needed for the temple and encouraged the people of Israel to do the same (1 Chron 29:1–9). He said,

> Solomon my son, whom alone God has chosen, is young and inexperienced, and the work is great, for the palace will not be for man but for the LORD God. So I have provided for the house of my God, so far as I was able, the gold for the things of gold, the silver for the things of silver, and the bronze for the things of bronze, the iron for the things of iron, and wood for the things of wood, besides great quantities of onyx

and stones for setting, antimony, coloured stones, all sorts of precious stones and marble. Moreover, in addition to all that I have provided for the holy house, I have a treasure of my own of gold and silver, and because of my devotion to the house of my God I give it to the house of my God. (1 Chron 29:1–3)

David was so overwhelmed and humbled by the generosity and willingness of the people to help Solomon build the house of God that he said to God, "But who am I, and what is my people, that we should be able thus to offer willingly?" (1 Chron 29:14). This brings out a clearly important trait of the character of David—humility, true humility, which is from God. Despite the military victories of David and his being hailed by the people as a mighty man of war and a good leader, he attributes all this to God. And so he speaks from his heart of hearts:

> Yet the LORD God of Israel chose me from all my father's house to be king over Israel forever. For he chose Judah as leader, and in the house of Judah my father's house, and among my father's sons he took pleasure in me to make me king over all Israel. And of all my sons (for the LORD has given me many sons) he has chosen Solomon my son to sit on the throne of the kingdom of the LORD over Israel. He said to me, 'It is Solomon your son who shall build my house and my courts, for I have chosen him to be my son, and I will be his father. I will establish his kingdom forever. (1 Chron 28:4–7)

David saw the favour of the Lord playing out in His life from the moment he was chosen as king. Even prior to that, God had, in His providence and grace, chosen the tribe of Judah to be leader and said that the king of Israel would come from him (Gen 49:10), and this notwithstanding the kind of person Judah would be. Also, God had made a covenant with David, assuring him that Solomon would be king after him. Reviewing this, it suddenly hit him hard and so he marvels:

> Who am I, O Lord GOD, and what is my house, that you have brought me thus far? (2 Sam 7:18)

And as we have stressed and will continue to see, God decides to carry out His perfect will and purposes through the family. He connects the family of David to Himself, making Solomon, His son, in the covenant he made with David (1 Chron 28:7).

David was caught off guard when he received bad news from his wife and Nathan, the prophet, that Adonijah, one of his sons, had proclaimed himself king. On hearing this, David was alarmed and angry with Adonijah, the usurper, who would have gone against the Lord's will for the heir to the throne. Bathsheba urged David and said to him, "And now, my lord the king, the eyes of all Israel are on you, to tell them who shall sit on the throne of my lord the king after him" (1 Kings 1:20). At this David swore, saying:

> As the LORD lives, who has redeemed my soul out of every adversity, as I swore to you by the LORD, the God of Israel, saying, "Solomon your son shall reign after me, and he shall sit on my throne in my place,' even so will I do this day." (1 Kings 1:30)

Immediately King David called Zadok the priest, Nathan the prophet, and Benaiah and said to them,

> Take with you the servants of your lord and have Solomon my son ride on my own mule, and bring him down to Gihon. And let Zadok the priest and Nathan the prophet there anoint him king over Israel. Then blow the trumpet and say, "Long live King Solomon!" You shall then come up after him, and he shall come and sit on my throne, for he shall be king in my place. And I have appointed him to be ruler over Israel and over Judah. (1 Kings 1:33–35)

So they went and did as David had instructed:

> Zadok the priest took the horn of oil from the tent and anointed Solomon. (v. 39)

Then they blew the trumpet, and all the people said, "Long live King Solomon!" The people then returned to King David in the city, playing pipes, and there was great rejoicing. And King David then praised the Lord and said, "Blessed be the LORD, the God of Israel, who has granted someone to sit on my throne this day, my own eyes seeing it" (v. 48).

4.8.3. Anointing of the Monarch of the United Kingdom

4.8.3.1. *Anointing the first Kings of England*

In England, Christianity is a state religion, given that the Church of England was patronized and protected by the monarch. The monarch is Supreme Governor of the Church of England.

The earliest English coronation that is recorded in detail is that of the Anglo-Saxonking Edgar, crowned in Bath in 953. Subsequent kings and queens were eager to maintain aspects of the pomp and ceremony of the coronation pageantry in order to maintain the historical link and to ensure their legitimacy.

Other early monarchs that came after Edgar were Edward the Confessor (1042–1066), Henry III (1216–1272), and Charles II (1660–1685).

Political historian Mark Cartwright[39] says the coronation ceremony of British monarchs as we see it today involves many elements that have been a part of the pageantry ever since the eleventh century. Features of the ceremony that have been carried out in Westminster Abbey since 1066, when William the Conqueror

---

[39] Cartwright, Mark. 2020. "The Coronation Ceremony of the British Monarchy." World History Encyclopedia. 30 March 2020. The Coronation Ceremony of the British Monarchy." World History *Encyclopaedia* https://www.worldhistory.org/article/1533/the-coronation-ceremony-of-the-british-monarchy/
Accessed 19 November 2022

was crowned, have been maintained by successive monarchs right down to Queen Elizabeth II and her own coronation on 2 June 1953. These features have been maintained because all the rulers were keen to show they were part of a long-standing tradition. The purpose of the crowning ceremony was to see the monarch swear an oath to uphold the Church and rule with honour, wisdom, justice, and mercy.

The anointing of British monarchs goes back even further in biblical history, to the time of King Solomon, who was anointed by Zadok, the high priest, in the tenth century BC, as we read in the following quote:

> The tradition goes back to the Old Testament where the anointing of Solomon by Zadok the Priest and Nathan the Prophet is described. Anointing was one of the medieval holy sacraments and it emphasised the spiritual status of the sovereign. Until the seventeenth century the sovereign was considered to be appointed directly by God and this was confirmed by the ceremony of anointing. Although the monarch is no longer considered divine in the same way, the ceremony of Coronation also confirms the monarch as the Head of the Church of England.[40]

The fact that the work of Handel titled *Zadok the Priest* has been performed as a coronation anthem down through the years confirms the fact that the crowning of British monarchs is intended to link the ceremony to its spiritual and biblical roots. Handel's oratorio tells the story in music and paints a picture in words that echo the biblical narrative in 1 Kings chapter 1, as we can see in the following lines of the work:

---

[40] Royal Collection Trust, "The Coronation Spoon," accessed 20 November 2022, https://www.rct.uk/collection/31733/the-coronation-spoon. Accessed, 20 Nov 2022

> Zadok the priest
> And Nathan the prophet
> Anointed Solomon king
> And all the people
> Rejoiced, rejoiced, rejoiced
>
> Long live the king
> God save the king
> May the king live
> For ever, for ever, for ever,
> Amen, amen, alleluia, alleluia, amen, amen[41]

4.8.3.2. *The Anointing Oil*

Anointing the monarch is the most sacred part of the coronation ceremony. This, as we have seen above, has been carried over from the ordination of priests, including the anointing of Aaron and his sons by Moses (Exod 29 and Lev 8). The crowning of the monarch is also taken from the rite of ordination in Scripture, where the turban is set upon the head of the priest and the "holy crown upon the turban" (Exod 29:4). The robe of the monarch is symbolic of the garments of the priests.

We thus see that the crowning of the monarch is full of spiritual and biblical symbols. In Scripture, the sacred anointing oil was unique, carefully made according to the recipe given by God, and no other oil was to be made like it (Exod 30:32). It was used to consecrate and to set apart the priests for the service of God, as we read in the following verse:

> You shall anoint Aaron and his sons, and consecrate them, that they may serve me as priests. (Exod 30:30)

---

[41] https://mojim.com/usy213206x1x3.htm
Zadok the Priest (1996 Remaster) lyrics © Universal Classics & Jazz A.d.o.Univers
Music by **Royal Choral Society, London Philharmonic Orchestra & Sir Andrew Davis**
Accessed, 14/01/24

And so all British monarchs, on the basis of biblical sources, would seek to make the oil used for anointing sacred and unique. The composition of the anointing oil and its production was assigned to special perfumeries and kept a secret. And so the oil used to anoint the monarch is deemed special, even mystified, in order to strengthen the belief in its divine origin. For example, it was believed that the oil used at the coronation of Henry IV of England in 1399 was miraculously given to the Archbishop of Canterbury, Thomas Becket.

The scented oil used for the coronation of Queen Elizabeth II was made from a secret mixture of sesame and olive oil, containing ambergris, civet, orange flowers, roses, jasmine, cinnamon, musk, and benzoin.[42]

Monarchs were eager for affirmation, and so they sought to be approved and legitimized not only as civil rulers but also as servants of God.

4.8.3.3. *Anointing of the Monarch*

The anointing is done in private, and this is a time for the monarch to take time to reflect on the import of the whole exercise and the heavy responsibility that comes with the crown. Since the anointing is seen as a sacred rite, this part of the ceremony will be a time spent before God to implore His help and the grace needed for the exercise of the royal and priestly duties that the sovereign is to perform as head of the Church of England. In view of the sacredness of the office, the anointing and crowning are done at a religious service before God. The anointing is done by the Archbishop of Canterbury, who pours a small quantity of the holy oil from an ampulla into the

---

[42] https://www.google.com/search?client=firefox-b-d&q=The+scented+secrets+of+the+Queen%E2%80%99s+coronation+anointing+oil
The scented secrets of the Queen's coronation anointing oil... - The Perfume Society.pdf
Accessed, 9/10/22
See also: https://www.telegraph.co.uk/news/2018/01/14/secrets-oil-used-anoint-queen-coronation/
Accessed 15/01/24

coronation spoon and anoints the sovereign on the head, breast, and palms. And it is at this point that the sovereign is crowned.

When a king is crowned, the whole congregation acclaims the new monarch, shouting and saying, "God Save the King [or Queen]." At this time, the bells of Westminster Abbey ring out, and there is simultaneously a sixty-two-gun salute from the Tower of London.

The crowning of the seating monarch is the climax of the entire ceremony. The monarch then swears an oath to uphold the Church and rule with honour, wisdom, justice, and mercy.

4.8.3.4. *The Crown, Sceptre, Sword of Justice, and the Orb*

The St. Edward's Crown, which has been used in coronations since the seventeenth century, is gold and weighs 2.3 kilos (5 pounds). Since this crown is so heavy, after the crowning it is normally replaced by a lighter crown, such as the Imperial State Crown.

The Imperial State Crown, which was created for the coronation of Queen Victoria in about 1838, is a lighter alternative to the St. Edward's Crown. This crown is a very spectacular, as it contains over 2,800 diamonds, 17 sapphires, 11 emeralds, 4 rubies, and 269 pearls.[43] The British crown jewels make the crown the most valuable crown in the world. The value and beauty of the British royal crown can serve to deepen our appreciation of the value that God places on His people, when we read the following Scripture:

> You shall be a crown of beauty in the hand of the LORD, and a royal diadem in the hand of your God. (Isa 62:3)

To further establish the link between the anointing and crowning of the British monarch and the kings of ancient Israel, we can cite the following Scripture:

---

[43] Mark Cartwright, "The Coronation Ceremony of the British Monarchy," World History Encyclopedia, 30 March 2020, https://www.worldhistory.org/article/1533/the-coronation-ceremony-of-the-british-monarchy/ Accessed 19 November 2022

> And they ate and drank before the LORD on that day with great gladness. And they made Solomon the son of David king the second time, and they anointed him as prince for the LORD, and Zadok as priest. (1 Chr 29:22)

In ancient Israel, the priest and the king worked together to govern the people, the priest exercising his priestly function while the king, exercised his regal functions. In the above text, we see that both the king and the priest were anointed. And so it is that the Archbishop of Canterbury and the king work closely together. Just as in Israel where it was the priest who anointed and crowned the king, it is the Archbishop of Canterbury who anoints and crowns the king.

It is also good to note the significance of the crown and its symbolism in Scripture. The crown signified life, honour, victory, rule, royalty, righteousness, and the like. What is more relevant for us here is the mark of royalty. Already in early times it was said of Israel, "You shall be to me a kingdom of priests and a holy nation" (Exod 19:6). This meant that the priests had the character, powers, and privileges that belong to royals. Peter makes this clear when he talks of the priesthood of all believers and says to them, "You area royal priesthood" (1 Peter 2:9).

After the monarch is anointed and crowned, he is given the sceptre and staff, which are traditional symbols of royal authority and justice. Two swords are also given to the monarch by the Archbishop of Canterbury: the Sword of State and the Jewelled Sword of Offering. The Archbishop of Canterbury then makes the following proclamation:

> With the sword do justice, stop the growth of iniquity, protect the holy Church of God, help and defend widows and orphans, restore the things that are gone to decay, maintain the things that are restored, punish and reform what is amiss, and confirm what is in good order.[44]

---

[44] Ibid.

The Archbishop of Canterbury next places in the monarch's left hand the Sovereign's Orb, which is topped by a cross and is symbolic of the Christian monarch's domination of the secular world.

It is significant that British monarchs have sought to maintain the link of this exercise to the Bible. We have sought to make the point that God assigned to mankind regal and priestly functions. As to the function of the king, the monarch rules as God's representative. And as we have seen above regarding the anointing of the biblical monarchs Saul, David, and Solomon, these were appointed by God. So if the British monarchs saw themselves as God's appointees, there would be the expectation and hope that they would rule in a godly way, just as David did. But in most cases, this was not so.[45] However, there were some who ruled with God in mind, just as David did, being lamps so that the Davidic flame would burn before the Lord (1 Kings 11:36), until the messianic King, the Christ, would come to be the light of the world. And as we will see in the next section, Queen Elizabeth II was mindful of the sacredness of the monarch's office and consequently reigned in the fear of God.

4.8.4. The Anointing of Queen Elizabeth II

Princess Elizabeth and her husband, the Duke of Edinburgh, were in Kenya, visiting the Aberdare National Park and staying at the Treetop Hotel when her father, King George VI, died on 6 February 1952. At the news of the death of her father, she cut short her visit and returned to England to accede to the throne. The coronation of Queen Elizabeth II took place on 2 June 1953 in a deeply symbolic church service with Holy Communion.

At the most sacred moment, the Queen was shielded under a canopy from press cameras and public gaze, and she was clothed in

---

[45] This is not surprising, since it was the same with the kings of Israel. When we read the history books of the Bible, especially, 1 and 2 Kings and 1 and2 Chronicles, we find that although there were some godly kings, a majority of them were not godly, and so the phrase "the way of the kings of Israel" came to denote the evil and rebellious ways of these kings. See 2 Kings 8:18.

a simple white dress with no jewels or the crown. The Archbishop of Canterbury anointed her with oil and prayed for her, praying over her, asking God to set her apart for His service. While anointing her, he prayed thus:

> And as Solomon was anointed king
> by Zadok the priest and Nathan the prophet,
> so be thou anointed, blessed, and consecrated Queen
> over the Peoples, whom the Lord thy God
> hath given thee to rule and govern,
> In the name of the Father, and of the Son, and of the
> Holy Ghost. Amen.[46]

Just before her coronation, the Queen walked past the throne, went straight, and knelt at the high altar and prayed silently.

After the coronation, the Queen kneeling down at the faldstool, the Archbishop said the following Blessing over her:

> Our Lord Jesus Christ,
> the Son of God,
> who by his Father was anointed with the Oil of gladness
> above his fellows,
> by his holy Anointing pour down upon your Head and Heart
> the blessing of the Holy Ghost,
> and prosper the works of your Hands:
> that by the assistance of his heavenly grace
> you may govern and preserve
> the people committed to your charge
> in wealth, peace, and godliness;
> and after a long and glorious course
> of ruling a temporal kingdom
> wisely, justly, and religiously,
> you may at last be made partaker of an eternal kingdom,
> through the same Jesus Christ our Lord. Amen.[47]

---

[46] https://www.oremus.org/coronation/1953/ Accessed 15 January 2024

[47] Ibid.

As with other coronation services in the past, the orb, sceptre, ring, and crown used in the coronation ceremony of the queen each include a cross, which is meant to symbolize the rule of Jesus Christ over the world. Also, the Bible was presented to her and described as "the most valuable thing that this world affords," and this would come to mean much in the exercise of her royal duties.

It should be noted that giving the Word of God, the book of the law, to the monarch is in line with Scripture, as we can read in the following verses concerning the laws of the kings of Israel:

> And when he sits on the throne of his kingdom, he shall write for himself in a book a copy of this law, approved by the Levitical priests. And it shall be with him, and he shall read in it all the days of his life, that he may learn to fear the LORD his God by keeping all the words of this law and these statutes, and doing them. (Deut 17:18–19)

It is evident that the Queen had a definite theology of coronation and a spirituality of the monarchy that flowed from her inner being. And this spirit will mark her whole reign. The Queen expressed her personal faith in Jesus Christ in public and in several of her Christmas broadcasts. And in these she would always bring out an impactful truth of the Christian faith. In her first Christmas broadcast as Queen in 1952, she made the following prayer request:

> Pray for me ... that God may give me wisdom and strength to carry out the solemn promises I shall be making, and that I may faithfully serve Him and you, all the days of my life.[48]

I always looked forward to her Christmas messages. In her Christmas broadcast in December 2000, she testified as follows:

---

[48] Christianity. "Queen Elizabeth's Faith." Christian Enquiry Agency. https://christianity.org.uk/article/queen-elizabeths-faith. Accessed 2 November 2022

> For me the teachings of Christ and my own personal accountability before God provide a framework in which I try to lead my life.[49]

The above testimony bore witness to her personal faith in Christ. Her faith has been testified by members of her family and the Christian community. During the memorial services organized for her and at her funeral service, many people, including religious leaders and world leaders, paid tribute to her, speaking well of her faith. During the thanksgiving service organized before her funeral, the Archbishop of York, in his tribute, referred to her faith in Jesus Christ as "a fountain and a well upon which she drew deeply and by which she was replenished through to the challenges and joys of life." And Dame Cindy Kiro, Governor-General of New Zealand, said this about the Queen:

> She had been a constant and provided continuity and stability, a real symbol of dedication to service.

A reporter of ITV News said, "The Queen was the UK, and the UK was the Queen."

The Queen considered herself a servant, serving the Lord Jesus Christ, her nation, Great Britain, and the Commonwealth of Nations. This servant theme ran through her coronation service and her reign. This was testified to by various officials during her memorial services, as can be verified by the following quotes:

> The theme of service runs throughout the coronation and, during the Queen's long reign, she has been inspired by the sacrificial life of Jesus Christ, who said of himself: he "did not come to be served, but to serve."[50]

The Queen was tireless in her service to the sick, poor, and needy. Whether she was sick or well, she went out of her way,

---

[49] Ibid.

[50] Ibid.

travelling by train and land, by sea, and by air, visiting, as has been corroborated by one of her aides:

> What people didn't see is the work she put in, day in, day out, in the freezing winters of the United Kingdom where she would get on an ordinary train, travel somewhere quite remote to visit ordinary people in hospitals, in schools. Her whole life was about service. She never took sick days. She very rarely cancelled anything.[51]

Even during her last days when she was frail, she was determined to serve till her last moments. This was clearly demonstrated and verified. Just two days before her death, she was pictured performing one of her official duties as Crown Head of her government, swearing in the appointed prime minister of Britain. Again the follow quote confirms her servant spirit:

> Her life was set apart for the service of others. Her majesty's sense of vocation, of duty and calling, was not something she could pick up and put down again. It was deeply embedded in her understanding. In a message she wrote on Ascension Day she wrote: "In this special year as I dedicate anew to your service and hope we will be reminded of the power of togetherness and the convening strength of family, friendship and good neighbourliness"[52]

Samantha Cohen, who served the Queen for seventeen years, first as her press secretary, then as her assistant private secretary,

---

[51] Samantha Cohen, the Queen's former press secretary. "Humble, funny, feisty: Queen's former aide speaks out on her legacy" https://www.youtube.com/watch?app=desktop&v=oeHoVdmM_Zo

[52] Royal Family Channel, "LIVE: St Paul's Service of Thanksgiving to Honour the Queen," YouTube, 9 September 2022. https://youtu.be/1CFPcpVeRWU.

had unique insight of who the Queen was. Her personal testimony is very telling:

> With the passing of the Queen people have lost someone who represented a value system that is more difficult to find these days and a framework for life. She taught me that you have to be true to your values and you have to be true to yourself. The Queen was an anchor; she was such an emotional anchor because her value system was so clear that you felt very sure of the world when she was in it. I think that she was just there for so long that we don't know a world without her in it really.[53]

As can be seen in the testimonies given by those who knew Queen Elizabeth II, she was a remarkable person, able to face life with faith, courage, composure, and dignity. Even one year after her death, her legacy still speaks to and impresses those who knew the Queen personally, as we read in the testimony of Sarah Ferguson, quoted by Mary Jury Jane (2023):

> I am heartbroken by the passing of Her Majesty the Queen. She leaves behind an extraordinary legacy: the most fantastic example of duty and service and steadfastness, and a constant steadying presence as our head of state for more than 70 years.

Her faith was strong and sure. However, as with all human beings, she surely had her struggles and weaknesses. She faced a lot of problems in her family. The heir to the throne had a troubled marriage that ended in a divorce, and his remarriage to Camilla was troubling. Her grandchildren had several regrettable scandals and even went through litigation.

---

[53] "Humble, funny, feisty:" Queen's former aide speaks out on her legacy | 7.30 | ABC News
https://www.youtube.com/watch?app=desktop&v=oeHoVdmM_Zo Accessed 20/12/2023

Given the importance of the family in advancing the purposes of God's kingdom, what can we say is the spiritual legacy that Queen Elizabeth II leaves behind in her family? It might not be immediately obvious how her life impacted her immediate family. It is not clear how many of her family are committed Christians, walking with the Lord and upholding the faith that the Sovereign solemnly vows to defend during the coronation service. It could be said that one of the reasons she held fast to the throne till the very end was the fact that she was not sure of the faith and steadfastness of the crown prince. It could well be said that her life and faith in the end impacted the heir to the throne, King Charles III. Those who know of his life would likely agree that the death of the Queen, his mother, must have shocked and changed him. In his first address as Sovereign to the nation, King Charles III promised to carry on the legacy of his mother and serve in her example:

> As the Queen herself did with such unswerving devotion, I too now solemnly pledge myself, throughout the remaining time God grants me, to uphold the Constitutional principles at the heart of our nation. I shall endeavor to serve you with loyalty, respect and love, as I have throughout my life.[54]

He acknowledged the impact of his mother on the family, as we can see from the following quote:

> Throughout her life, Her Majesty the Queen—my beloved Mother—was an inspiration and example to me and to all my family, and we owe her the most heartfelt debt any family can owe to their mother; for her love, affection, guidance, understanding and example.[55]

---

[54] King Charles III address the nation Full Transcript - The New York Times https://www.nytimes.com/2022/09/09/world/europe/king-charles-speech-transcript.html
Accessed 20/12/2022

[55] Ibid.

The deep love and respect King Charles had for his mother can be read in these moving farewell words he said to the Queen:

> And to my darling Mama, as you begin your last great journey to join my dear late Papa, I want simply to say this: Thank you. Thank you for your love and devotion to our family and to the family of nations you have served so diligently all these years. May "flights of Angels sing thee to thy rest."[56]

The death of his mother also evoked in him the faith that had kept her going. And so, looking back into his life with a sense of duty and satisfaction, he acknowledged the Monarch's particular relationship and responsibility towards the Church of England, the church in which, as he said, "my own faith is so deeply rooted. In that faith, and the values it inspires, I have been brought up to cherish a sense of duty to others."

The turnaround of King Charles speaks much about the impact that the faith and loving care of a mother can have on her child even at her death. The legacy of a godly parent on her children and those she leads is more than words alone can tell.

4.8.5. The Anointing of King Charles III

At the moment Queen Elizabeth II died in Balmoral Castle on 8 September 2022, King Charles became the monarch of the United Kingdom of Britain and Northern Ireland, as well as the head of state of the Commonwealth countries. On the following day, 9 September, the King made his first address as monarch, pledging to carry on the legacy of his mother and to serve with loyalty, respect, and love.

The coronation of King Charles III and Queen Camilla took place on 6 May 2023 at the Westminster Abbey in London at a solemn church service presided over by the Archbishop of Canterbury, Justin Portal Welby. This service followed the format of a typical

---

[56] Ibid.

coronation service of the British monarchs, similar to what we have already described above. As has been the case in previous coronation services, the orientation and spirit of the whole service was to portray the king as a servant of God who would rule in the fear of God, after the order of the kings of ancient Israel, the anointed of the Lord. In order not to repeat things already described, I will limit myself to what was particular to King Charles' coronation or different from the other coronations.

The first thing we notice that was different from previous coronations is the greeting of the king in the first part of the order of service:

A chorister said to be "representing the youth, hope, the future, and the nation," came forth and stood before the King and addressed him in the Coronation Theatre.

"Your Majesty, as children of the kingdom of God we welcome you in the name of the King of kings."

The King replied, "In His name, and after His example, I come not to be served but to serve."

This opening scene was well calculated to set the stage, highlight the theme of the solemn service, and suggest the rule of the new monarch. In this opening scene, the king is portrayed as one who identifies himself with the kingdom of God.

This scene reveals several things:

1. The children present themselves as "children of the kingdom of God." This is in line with Jesus' teaching: "Let the children come to me; do not hinder them, for to such belongs the kingdom of God" (Mark 10:14). These young members of the kingdom are already serving the king. They are messengers of Christ, sent by Christ as his ambassadors. They come in the name of Christ, the King of kings, to welcome the new monarch. This says that King Charles is coming into a kingdom that indeed belongs to God, and waiting for the end-times fulfilment, as we read in the Bible: "The kingdom of the world has become the kingdom of our Lord and of his Christ, and he shall reign forever and ever" (Rev 11:15). This goes to reinforce the truth as we read in the Bible: that

the king was meant to rule as the representative of God, the King of Kings. And in the end, when Christ would have completed His mission on earth, the enemy defeated and the work of redemption completed, "Then comes the end, when he delivers the kingdom to God the Father after destroying every rule and every authority and power" (1 Cor 15:24).

2. The king sees himself as an apostle—one sent out by Christ, who was Himself the apostle of God: "Consider Jesus, the apostle" (Heb 3:1). And the new monarch comes in the name of Christ. He thus takes his cue from the "sending" Scriptures in the gospels, as we read:

> These twelve Jesus sent out. (Matt 10:5)

> And he appointed twelve (whom he also named apostles so that they might be with him and he might send them out to preach. (Mark 3:13)

> And he called the twelve together and gave them power and authority. (Luke 9:1)

> Go into all the world and proclaim the gospel to the whole creation. (Mark 16:15)

We see here that, like the earlier British monarchs, King Charles III wants to legitimize his authority, right at the onset of the coronation service. And so the anointing and coronation will be the public and official acknowledgement and proclamation of him as the legitimate king of Great Britain and the Commonwealth nations.

3. The King sees himself as a servant, and as such, he is coming in the example of the Servant King. He, too, would be a servant king. And so he is appropriating the words of Jesus, who said, "For even the Son of Man came not to be served but to serve" (Mark 10:45). King Charles is by this confirming the pledge he made in his first address as monarch to follow

the legacy of his mother. And by making servanthood the hallmark of his rule, he reflects what Isaiah said in one of his servant songs: "Behold my servant, whom I uphold, my chosen, in whom my soul delights; I have put my Spirit upon him; he will bring forth justice to the nations" (Isaiah 42:1). And as the servant king, he is also committing himself to serve in the spirit of David and his heir, the Messiah-King, whose aim was to do the will of God:

> I delight to do your will, O my God; your law is within my heart. (Ps 40:8)

> For I have come down from heaven, not to do my own will but the will of him who sent me. (John 6:38)

The next significant step in the coronation service was the presentation of the Bible to the King. Prior to this, the King was presented to the congregation in the following words, as quoted by Torrance (2023:58): "I here present unto you King Charles, your undoubted King: Wherefore all you who are come this day to do your homage and service, are you willing to do the same?"

Those present at the service responded by declaring, "God Save King Charles!" And the King acknowledged with a bow. Given that the King has declared that he comes as servant in the name of the King of Kings, he will govern according to God's rule, with justice and righteousness, doing the will of God. And because of the laws of kings found in the Scriptures (Deut 17:14–20) it becomes a matter of necessity that he be given the book of the law of God. And so the next significant step of the service occurred when the monarch was presented the coronation Bible. The Moderator of the general assembly of the Church of Scotland, the Rt Rev Dr Iain Greenshields, presented the Bible to the king with the following words, quoted by Torrance (2023:58):

> Sir, to keep you ever mindful of the law and the Gospel of God as the Rule for the whole life and government of Christian Princes, receive this Book,

the most valuable thing that this world affords. Here is Wisdom; this is the royal Law; these are the lively Oracles of God.

To God and in ancient Israel, the law, as contained in Scripture, was the source of wisdom and identity for both the king and the people and nation of Israel. And this was clearly stated by Moses, as we read in the following verses:

> Keep them and do them, for that will be your wisdom and your understanding in the sight of the peoples, who, when they hear all these statutes, will say, 'Surely this great nation is a wise and understanding people.' For what great nation is there that has a god so near to it as the LORD our God is to us, whenever we call upon him? And what great nation is there, that has statutes and rules so righteous as all this law that I set before you today? (Deut 4:6–8)

Since the monarchs of Britain want to rule by the Book, this is to be commendable, especially now that the Bible and Christianity are being challenged in many Western nations.

The order of the whole coronation service was planned to make both the king and people see the will and purposes of God for the king. The Word of God was the centrepiece of the service, and so the texts read during the service reinforced the aim, making sure that the goal would be reached. The King was to work in his realms to usher in the kingdom of God, upholding the faith and protecting the church. The Gospel of Luke 4:16–21 describes the work of Christ, the anointed of God, who came to proclaim the gospel of the kingdom—freedom from oppression and sin, in the power of the Spirit. The epistle of Colossians 1:9–17 was a prayer for the king to know the will of God, to do it, and to enter into the work of Christ in a covenant relationship, as that between God and David. Through the work of Christ, we have been brought into the kingdom of Christ and now have an inheritance in the eternal kingdom of God. The motif of kingdom is the strand that is woven through the whole service and celebration.

After taking the Coronation Oath and receiving the wording of the Accession Declaration Oath on a card, the King needed the one thing that would make him effective in the position he was being inducted into—*prayer*. Considering all that accession to power meant for him, bearing in mind his regal and spiritual responsibilities, and the pledges made under oath, the King had indeed to go into prayer in order to be empowered to carry out his duties effectively and in a way pleasing to God, who was calling him into this very high office. The King's prayer was meant to be truly personal in that it allowed the monarch to express his spiritual convictions and respond to the promises he had just made in the two statutory oaths. The prayer, as cited by Torrance (2023:60) was the following:

> God of compassion and mercy whose Son was sent not to be served but to serve, give grace that I may find in thy service perfect freedom and in that freedom knowledge of thy truth. Grant that I may be a blessing to all thy children, of every faith and belief,[57] that together we may discover the ways of gentleness and be led into the paths of peace; through Jesus Christ our Lord. Amen.

The two important sources of grace in the coronation service were prayer and the Word of God. Lambert Palace and Buckingham Palace planned this service together, King Charles and Archbishop Welby worked in consultation so that the whole programme would reflect the tenor they wanted to give to the coronation service. It was to bring out something about the spirituality of the new monarch and also be in line with the other historical coronation services.

---

[57] As crown prince, Prince Charles said that as king he would be the defender of faiths, not the defender of *the* faith—the faith of Christianity that the Anglican Church stood for. Reformulation of his prayer not only reflects this but also introduces a liberal and erroneous belief couched in the phrase "thy children, of every faith and belief." This suggests his belief in a kind of universalism that teaches that all people are children of God and so are saved. Biblically, the children of God are those who have put their faith in Christ and the trusted redemptive work of the cross, His death and resurrection.

4.8.5.1. *The Mark of a Good King*

> Let him who boasts boast in this, that he understands and knows me, that I am the LORD who practises steadfast love, justice, and righteousness in the earth. For in these things I delight, declares the LORD. (Jer 9:24)

Since the king is the representative of God and rules for Him, he is expected to rule in a way that will please his Lord, the King of Kings, who has appointed him into this high and holy office. He should therefore be marked by the qualities listed in the above verse:

1. The king should know and understand God.
2. He should be wise, ruling with God given wisdom.
3. He should be marked by steadfast love, the covenantal loving kindness.
4. He should love the people unconditionally.
5. He should do justice and righteousness.
6. He should judge the cause of the poor and needy.

The kings of Israel who ruled well and pleased God took their cue from King David, and so the Davidic kings, who prefigured Jesus Christ the King–Messiah, were expected to rule by God's standards, which He spells out in the following verses:

> Do you think you are a king because you compete in cedar? Did not your father eat and drink and do justice and righteousness? Then it was well with him. He judged the cause of the poor and needy; then it was well. Is not this to know me? declares the LORD. (Jer 22:15–16)

This tells us that the most important character trait that enables the king or any servant-leader to rule well is the knowledge of God. If one knows God, one will fear Him and rule in a godly way. Also, it is important that one should ask God for wisdom, just as Solomon, the wisest king, did. He said to the Lord:

> Give your servant therefore an understanding mind to govern your people, that I may discern between good and evil, for who is able to govern this your great people?" (1 Kings 3:9)

God granted Solomon understanding and wisdom beyond measure, as we read in the following verses:

> And God gave Solomon wisdom and understanding beyond measure, and breadth of mind like the sand on the seashore, so that Solomon's wisdom surpassed the wisdom of all the people of the east and all the wisdom of Egypt. For he was wiser than all other men. (1 Kings 4:29–31)

God is the source of all wisdom and understanding (Prov 2:6). He Himself is wisdom and Christ is our wisdom (1 Cor 1:30). James advises those who lack wisdom to ask for it from God (James 1:5). Those who know God and seek to rule with Him will surely govern well because it will be with His wisdom that they will rule. And this is assured by Scripture, as we can read in the following verses, where God speaks in wisdom:

> "I, wisdom, dwell with prudence, and I find knowledge and discretion. I have counsel and sound wisdom; I have insight; I have strength. By me kings reign, and rulers decree what is just; by me princes rule, and nobles, all who govern justly. I love those who love me, and those who seek me diligently find me. (Prov 8:12, 14–17)

And so if King Charles III aims to rule well and make the kingdom a blessing, he will seek first to know the Lord and ask Him for wisdom, and consequently he will rule with righteousness and justice, defending the rights of the poor and needy.

It was stated previously that the scene at the beginning of the service was set to present King Charles as one coming into a kingdom that indeed belongs to God, and waiting for the end-times fulfilment, as we read in the Bible, when the kingdom of the world will become the kingdom of the Lord God and of his Christ (Rev 11:15). Elizabeth Hooton was the first woman preacher of the Quaker movement, which was started by George Fox in the 1600s. She was a fearless firebrand preacher, who was frequently thrown into English prisons because of her faith. Even when she went to Boston, in order to preach the gospel, she found herself behind bars again and again. When she returned to England in 1671 she wrote to King Charles II saying:

> Oh that thou would give up thy kingdom to ye Lord, God of heaven and earth, whose it is, and thy strength and power to Jesus Christ, who is King of kings, and then thou wilt be more honourable than ever thou wast. (Cited by Robert Morgan:1977)

This message was not well received by King Charles II. It now begs the question, "How would King Charles III receive the message of Elizabeth Hooton today?" We must admit that there is truth in Elizabeth Hooton's message: King David became the greatest king because he recognized that the throne belonged to God and the Messiah, Jesus Christ.

4.8.5.2. *In Retrospect*

Stepping back to have a look at the life of King Charles III, we will see a stark contrast between his life and that of his mother, Queen Elizabeth II. King Charles III was a champion of many humanitarian and environmental works for years and performed several royal duties in the stead of his mother before acceding to the throne. However, his personal and family lives have left a lot to be desired. His mother's life was ruled by her fear of God and her devotion to her family, which included her seeking to influence her children for Christ; but King Charles' life has all along been ruled by a passion for the world and its environment—all for social and humanitarian reasons. He has loved the attractive and glamorous things of life. When he and Lady Diana visited Cameroon and inaugurated a British-built electric power plant on 22 March 1990, many people were thrilled and honoured to greet him. My brother, Samuel Mfonyam, ostentatiously displayed a picture of Prince Charles and himself in his living room. This shows how the fame of King Charles has spread far and wide, even among members of my family.

However, in view of the issues with his marriage and family, King Charles' marriages and family life have been plagued by a series of problems, at times bordering on scandal and ending in disaster. His marriage life has been marked by flirtation, unfaithfulness, and divorce. His life has markedly affected his family such that his sons have been plagued by conflicts and controversies. We have seen bitter quarrels, fights, and rebellion in the family, leaving some estranged from the rest of the family and cut off from the royal family, as in the case of Prince Harry and his wife, Meghan. This, of course, has come to grieve King Charles III a lot, such as it grieved their grandmother, Queen Elizabeth II, and others.

However, as stated previously, the death of Charles III's mother, whom he fondly addressed as his dear mama, greatly affected his life and seems to have caused a U-turn in his life. It seems as if he was shocked into a different spiritual reality. God has surely been at work in his heart as a result of the prayers of his mother and God's people. We do trust God's grace, mercy, and forgiveness, which never are exhausted, as we read in the following promises:

> For the Lord will not cast off forever, but, though he cause grief, he will have compassion according to the abundance of his steadfast love. The steadfast love of the LORD never ceases; his mercies never come to an end; they are new every morning; great is your faithfulness. (Lam 3:31–32, 22–23)

In the light of this change, we can see the coronation service as the beginning of a new life and as a transformation for King Charles, his family, and the kingdom he has pledged to rule in faithfulness to

God. And at this point it will be the duty of the church, the believers in the Anglican Church, to pray for their King, the anointed of the Lord, as in the example of the faithful of Israel, praying for their king, David, as we read of in Psalm 84:

> O LORD God of hosts, hear my prayer; give ear, O God of Jacob! Behold our shield, O God; look on the face of your anointed! (Ps 84:8–9)

In the prayer of the pilgrim who faces the dangers on his way to worship in God's house in Jerusalem, he refers to the king, the anointed of the Lord, as his shield. Yes, the king was the protector of the people and was called to represent the people of Israel before God and to model faithfulness to the people and keep them secure in order to serve God. In this light, Paul also calls on the church to pray for kings and others in high positions so that believers may "lead a peaceful and quiet life, godly and dignified in every way" so they can proclaim the gospel, so that people may be saved and come to the knowledge of the truth (1 Tim 2:1–4). The fact that Jesus, through His sacrificial death, made us a kingdom and priests unto God the Father (Rev 1:6) makes us dutifully bound to intercede for the king and people. There is a sense in which people make their king by praying him into a godly, just, and righteous life. So it is hoped that praying for King Charles did not end with the coronation service but that this would be a daily and constant exercise and discipline for the Christians of England and Great Britain, and the Commonwealth of nations.

4.8.5.3. *Relevance of Kingship in the Study of Marriage and Family*

How is kingship relevant in the study of marriage and family? If we do not realize how this relates to our lives here on earth, we will never fully understand our identities and so will not fully accomplish our missions, because we will miss the abundant lives we are called to live. We are royals and must accomplish our royal and regal duties. Though we live lowly lives here on earth, in the manner of our Lord and Master Jesus Chris, our citizenship is in heaven, as Paul rightly points out to the believers in Philippi. In the new covenant, we are not only priests; we are princes and princesses, sons and daughters of the King of kings. As John says, Christ has made us kingdoms and priests unto God (Rev 1:6). And as Peter tells us in his epistle, we are a nation set apart for God. As children of God, we live our lives from a heavenly perspective, and so this should inspire us to live the life that is worthy of the King of kings and not to cringe at the view of the glamour of the world. And as the eyes of the world are on the working royals of Great Britain, so the eyes of the world are on believers—sons and daughters of God and Christ the King. This is who we are! And if this does not impact us and the world, then we are missing out on our calling.

Why is kingship important in the mission of God—the mission that He sent His Son, Jesus Christ, the Messiah, to accomplish? The answer is obvious. God is King—the King of kings. Jesus Christ came as the King of the Jews (Matt 2:2) and died a king, the King of Jews (John 19:19). And His death made Him King of the whole world, especially of those who have believed and turned over their lives to Him. He, too, like the Father, is described as the King of kings. God had purposely planned in eternity that the Messiah would come from the line of kings, the line of King David, the man after God's heart—one who would serve God wholeheartedly and would be the exemplary human king.

Jesus was born into a family, as we will further explain, born to "a son of David" (Matt 1:20). Jesus came to preach the kingdom of God. And so we are people of the kingdom, called to live kingdom life and to bring people into the kingdom of God. In the end, when all is accomplished here on earth, as Christ tells us, those who have followed Him will sit on thrones and rule with Him. If we have been made priests and kings, it is important to know our spiritual and heavenly heritage.

The mission of kings is very important as concerns carrying out the whole plan and purposes of God. It is therefore important that all kings should know their duties before God, so as to live for the will and glory of God.

For the king to be blessed and effective in his mission, he should recognize first of all that God is King. This is what David fully realized as we see in his prayer:

> Give attention to the sound of my cry, my King and my God, for to you do I pray. (Ps 5:2)

First God, as King, rules the whole universe as a sovereign, and He rules with sovereign power. Second, God is king over His people, Israel, and that is why the nation of ancient Israel was a kingdom and also a theocracy. And this is why both the king and the priests were anointed, as we see in the following text:

> And they ate and drank before the LORD on that day with great gladness. And they made Solomon the son of David king the second time, and they anointed him as prince for the LORD, and Zadok as priest. (1 Chr 29:22)

So both the king and the priest were chosen by God and set apart to rule and to enforce the rules and statutes of God, the king of Kings. They both ruled as representatives of God before the people and represented the people before God.

It was important for the king to know that the throne he was sitting on was the throne of God, as we read in the following verses:

> Then Solomon sat on the throne of the LORD as king in place of David his father. And he prospered, and all Israel obeyed him. And the LORD made Solomon very great in the sight of all Israel and bestowed on him such royal majesty as had not been on any king before him in Israel. (1 Chr 29:23, 25)

God gives royal majesty and authority to the king who sits on the throne. When the Davidic kingship functioned well and did not usurp the divine kingship, it brought glory to God, and as a result, the people were blessed. So the king has to rule as God would. But when he is faithless and is not faithful to God, he misleads the people. And it is not only him who is punished, but also the people (1 Sam 12:12–15).

And as the Bible says, all rulers are appointed by God. This is why I have taken time in this study to examine the kings of Israel and ended with the kings of the United Kingdom. King David wrote, "Zeal for your house consumed me" (Ps 69:9), and Paul, quoting this text in Romans 15:3, applied it to Jesus, who is the supreme example of living for the glory of God, as shown by the quotation. This shows that Jesus, being the ideal Davidic king, gives us the blueprint of the calling of every king and ruler.

As previously stated, the institution of the kings of England is rooted in the Bible and modelled on the kingship as established in ancient Israel. Jesus, our King, serves as the example to be followed by kings. They are expected to live and rule in the way of the Lord. Anxious that the king should rule in a godly manner, God gave the laws of the kings of Israel in Deuteronomy 17.

It has been heartening to see the spiritual legacy of Queen Elizabeth II. Because of her profound faith in Christ and her sense of calling and duty, world leaders have a lot to learn from her, another human leader like King David. We have seen evidence of the spiritual legacy of Queen Elizabeth II on her son, King Charles III.

Given the orientation of the coronation service of King Charles III, it is my hope that he will follow the example and legacy of his mother, Queen Elizabeth II, patterning his rule after that of the Servant King—a rule of justice, righteousness, and truth. The office and mission of the king is important, since God intended the king to rule as His representative before the people.

4.8.6. Biblical Symbolism of Anointing, Kingship, and Servanthood

We have seen the importance of the symbolism and prophetic acts, such as, oil, anointing with oil, anointing with the Spirit, the crown and coronation, the king, and kingship. Kingship (the office of the king), as we have seen before, was viewed as a sacred office. These symbols foreshadowed the promised Messiah–King, His person, (nature and character), and His mission as the suffering Servant and sin bearer (equipped for service, serving the people, and ministering to God the Father). The Messiah is literally the anointed, the chosen one of God. And as previously stated, Saul was anointed by the Lord (1 Sam 10:1).

The anointing oil and the act of anointing prefigured the Holy Spirit and His empowering work. The role of the Holy Spirit and how He will work in the New Testament was in some ways already seen in the Old Testament and predicted in prophecy, especially in the servant songs in Isaiah, as we can read in the following passage:

> There shall come forth a shoot from the stump of Jesse, and a branch from his roots shall bear fruit. And the Spirit of the LORD shall rest upon him, the Spirit of wisdom and understanding, the Spirit of counsel and might, the Spirit of knowledge and the fear of the LORD. (Isa 11:1–2)

Some of the metaphors and symbols used in the Old Testament regarding the Holy Spirit and His action are used consistently inthe New Testament; for example Judges 6:34 states, "The Spirit of the LORD **clothed**[58] Gideon," and Jesus uses the same words in Luke 24:49, saying, "Stay in the city until you are **clothed**[59] with power from on high." The Spirit working in Jesus was described in terms of anointing, as we read in the Acts of the Apostles: God *anointed* Jesus of Nazareth with the Holy Spirit and with power. (Acts 10:38).

And as we read in the Isaiah text quoted above, the Spirit gives wisdom and understanding, and it is the same Spirit that Jesus would send to teach the disciples (John14:26). We also see the power and influence of the Holy Spirit on David, the ruler. It will be recalled that when David was anointed king, the Spirit of God came upon him; and we know that the Spirit of God gives His servants wisdom, and that is why David was a wise king. The wise woman of Tekoa sent by Joab gave this testimony about David when she met and talked with him:

---

[58] Emphasis mine

[59] Ibid.

> And your servant thought, "The word of my lord the king will set me at rest," for my lord the king is like the angel of God to discern good and evil. The LORD your God be with you! But my lord has wisdom like the wisdom of the angel of God to know all things that are on the earth. (2 Sam 14:17, 20)

We also see the effect of the Spirit on Daniel, who, though captured and brought to Babylon as a prisoner of war or slave, became a renowned ruler in the kingdom. This is what we read about him:

> There is a man in your kingdom in whom is the spirit of the holy God. In the days of your father, light and understanding and wisdom like the wisdom of the gods were found in him, an excellent spirit, knowledge, and understanding to interpret dreams, explain riddles, and solve problems were found in this Daniel, whom the king named Belteshazzar. - Then this Daniel became distinguished above all the other high officials and satraps, because an excellent spirit was in him. And the king planned to set him over the whole kingdom. (Dan 5:11–12; 6:3)

And as stated previously, oil and anointing in the Old Testament prefigured the Holy Spirit, who overshadows, empowers, and teaches the chosen servants of God. John, in his epistles, makes this very clear in the following Scriptures:

> But you have been anointed by the Holy One, and you all have knowledge. But the anointing that you received from him abides in you, and you have no need that anyone should teach you. But as his anointing teaches you about everything, and is true, and is no lie—just as it has taught you, abide in him. (1 John 2:20, 27)

Given the important role of the Holy Spirit's mission, as we seek to accomplish the will and purposes of the Lord, it is important to seek to be empowered by the Spirit. Pentecostal churches place a lot of emphasis on the Holy Spirit and gifts of the Holy Spirit—so much so that this goes over the top and tends to be unscriptural. They often ignore the mind and the cognitive approach to the study of the Scriptures. This approach to Christianity produces people who are carried away by emotions and fantasy. They grow a breed of Christians who are heavy in profession but short on practice. And so they are stunted and not growing in sanctified lives. On the other hand, the mainstream churches do not give enough importance to the Holy Spirit, the fruit (of the Holy Spirit), and the spiritual gifts but rather put a lot of stress on the mind: knowledge, understanding, and a scholarly study of the Scriptures. They tend to not pay attention to the need of being regenerated, illuminated, empowered, and equipped by the Holy Spirit. These should learn from Paul who, when he came with the gospel to the Corinthians, said:

> And I, when I came to you, brothers, did not come proclaiming to you the testimony of God with lofty speech or wisdom. My speech and my message were not in plausible words of wisdom, but in demonstration of the Spirit and of power, so that your faith might not rest in the wisdom of men but in the power of God. (1 Cor 2:1, 4-5)

They do not seek the gifts of the Holy Spirit which will make them fruitful and more effective in ministry. The fruit of the Spirit, which in essence is the character of the Lord, is not seen in their lives, which explains the fact that, in general, both the leaders and Christians in the mainline churches are, in the main, nominal, without having encountered the Lord and received Him by faith in their lives.

This group or section of the church does not grow with regard to sanctified lives, since it is the Holy Spirit that enables people to grow in character into the image of God and become partakers of His divine nature (2 Peter 1:3–11). They emphasize the need for sound doctrine and the meticulous exposition of the Scriptures and adherence to sound doctrine. This tendency to stick to the letter of the law and not discern the spirit of the law leads to a ministry that is dry, unfruitful, and unspiritual. And so it fails to transform lives. This is characteristic of the way of the Scribes and Pharisees, who were very good at interpreting the law and lacking in practice. This results in nominal Christianity, which goes against the teaching and life of Christ, who told the disciples, "It is the Spirit who gives life; the flesh is no help at all. The words that I have spoken to you are spirit and life" (John 6:63). And Paul, who was formerly a Pharisee of the strictest order, said, "The letter kills, but the Spirit gives life" (2 Cor 3:4). And he adds that the law brings condemnation while the Spirit is the Lord and transforms lives (vv. 17–18). Paul will reinforce this truth by showing that the law of God was in man before it was ever given as a written code through Moses.

God places a high value on the meditation, study, and teaching of the truths of the Scriptures and obedience. Jesus was a recognized rabbi, a teacher of the truths of the Scriptures. In ministry, both the mind and spirit must be trained and exercised, such that sound teaching will result in people experiencing the grace and the transformative work of the Holy Spirit in their lives.

Jesus was the teacher par excellence. He taught using what was known in the culture of His audience so that they would understand the points He was making. God, in His foreknowledge and foresight, putin every culture concepts, objects, symbols, and values that could be used as beachheads to preach the gospel of salvation. This is what we have seen in the cultures and customs of Israel and Bafut. In Bafut, "Messiah" is translated as "Àyɔ'ɔ̀ Nwì"—that is, "the one anointed by God." And so, given that the concepts of oil and anointing, and particularly the fact that the king is anointed, will make it easy for the Bafut people to understand the significance of the Messiah and His role as King—ruler, deliverer and Saviour. It will therefore be easy for the Bafut people to embrace Jesus as their King, the deliver and the mediator, since in the Bafut kingdom, the Fon (king) is the supreme ruler, the high priest, and the mediator between the living and the deceased ancestors, whose spirits are regarded as gods.

The values and virtues that existed in both ancient Israel and Bafut traditional society, as earlier discussed, including purity, love, obedience, faith, unity, and light, originated with God at Creation, and so these were carried over in time and history into the various cultures of peoples, as we have seen in Israel and Bafut. And consequently, these speak of God and can be perceived, appropriated, and realized in the lives of the people in these societies. In this way, Christianity is not received in a vacuum, and neither will it be rooted in a void.

Hiebert (1985:54) affirms this fact in the following quote:

> Although the gospel is distinct from human cultures, it must always be expressed in cultural forms. Humans cannot receive it apart from their languages, symbols, and rituals. The gospel must become incarnate in the cultural forms if the people are to hear and believe.

The foundations of marriage and the family were laid by God Himself at Creation. When we have this perspective, which is divine and Christian, we will understand that Christianity is not a Western concept or religion as such. It is universal and divinely inspired, coming from above, just as Jesus told the rabbi Nicodemus. He came from heaven to teach heavenly things by using earthly things so that people, even the rabbi, would understand the deep spiritual things (John 3:11–13).

4.9. Summary

We have so far looked at marriage and the family (1) at Creation, when marriage was instituted; (2) in ancient Israel; (3) in Bafut traditional society; (4) pointed out the similarities and differences between ancient Israel and traditional Bafut customs (where it was shown that while there are differences in their cultures, customs, and traditions regarding marriage and family life, there is a lot that the people in both communities held in common); and (5) noted the values and practices that they have in common. God placed values, concepts, symbols, and institutions in each of these cultures that reveal a lot about the nature, character, and purposes of the Lord in creation. These things serve as a testimony to the person, works, wonders, glory, majesty, and wisdom of the living God. And this confirms what David tells ancient Israel in the following Scripture:

> The heavens declare the glory of God, and the sky above proclaims his handiwork. Day to day pours out speech, and night to night reveals knowledge. There is no speech, nor are there words, whose voice is not heard. (Ps 19:1–3)

Both Israel and Bafut saw the lights of the heavens and rain as gifts; while Israel saw these as the blessings of God, traditional Bafut saw these as the blessings of the gods.

And in the New Testament times, Paul also told the Gentile believers in Rome about the revelations of God in nature and in life, as we read in the following verse:

> For what can be known about God is plain to them, because God has shown it to them. For his invisible attributes, namely, his eternal power and divine nature, have been clearly perceived, ever since the creation of the world, in the things that have been made. So they are without excuse. (Rom 1:19–20)

Yes, as stated previously, God's nature in man predisposes him to be aware of the things that please or displease him, as the spirit and conscience in him speak to him in his heart. The virtues of love, goodness, and unity say something about the Godhead. Things like light or lamp, rain and water, the food that man produces from the ground, and the fruit of the womb, speak loud and clear about the love, compassion, and care of God. The primary purpose of God for man, both in early Israel and Bafut, was to see His creation and works, recognize Him as the Lord and Creator, and turn to Him and be saved. Bafut and Israel are included in the love of God that moved Him to send His one and only Son, Jesus Christ, to come and live among man and die to save him.

Marriage and the family are the institutions and frames best suited for the mission of God on earth. God created man and woman in His image so that they would effectively carry out His purposes for mankind. And when it comes to the New Testament and the new covenant, Paul says this about the divine image in man:

> For those whom he foreknew he also predestined to be conformed to the image of his Son, in order that he might be the firstborn among many brothers. (Rom 8:29)

The image of the Son and the adoption process that ensued give the believer the privileges, or blessings, and responsibilities of a son. Adoption gives them the right to share in the life and sufferings of the Christ, the obedient and intimate Son, in order to also enjoy with Him the privileges of inheritance that accrue to the Son (Rom15–17).

God gave man regal duties to develop and dominate or govern the world. He also gave him priestly duties to serve and minister in such a way as to bring others to know, serve, and worship Him, their Creator.

With regard to the sacred priestly office occupied by Aaron, his children, and the Levites, God apportioned this to them as a gift. It was noted previously that the office of the king was also regarded as sacred because he was chosen by God to represent Him and rule in righteousness and justice. In this regard, oil and anointing have been previously examined, along with their significance in ancient Israel and Bafut. Kings, kingship, oil, and anointing were symbols foreshadowing the promised Messiah-King and His mission.

4.10. Marriage and the Family in Salvation History

Marriage and the family are the basic and fundamental institutions that God has given to man to reflect what the church, community, nation, and world could be. When people marry and forge a family in the Lord, it will reflect what God had intended for marriage and the family since Creation, and thus, there will be no telling of the impact the family can have on the church and society.

4.10.1. Symbolism and the Import of the Familial Terms

The familial terms "father," "mother," "son," "daughter," "child," ("bridegroom," "bride,") "husband," and "wife" are used throughout the Scriptures. When these are used literally, they signify a family or marriage relationship, or biological descent and the bonding that results from the relationship. The familial terms convey the strong relationship that exists among people. And when these terms are used metaphorically, they become symbols of marriage or the family, which are the primary and fundamental institutions or units of God's creation. The purpose of salvation is to bring people into the family of God by adoption through faith in Jesus and the regenerative work of the Holy Spirit. So every use of the familial term suggests this relationship and reveals the identity of the people of God. The familial relationship is governed and cemented by the covenant that God made with Abraham, and then with the people of Israel in the old covenant, and subsequently by the new covenant made by Jesus with the church, which becomes the new Israel, descendants of Abraham.

Let us look at some of the main usages of the key familial terms in the Scriptures with primary and secondary meanings. As regards the key terms "father," "mother," "son," or "wife," we have no difficulty understanding that Abraham was the husband of Sarah and that he and his wife gave birth to two sons, Ishmael and Isaac. Whereas the two sons had one father, Abraham, they had two different mothers. And when it comes to the biological relation of Jesus to His parents, Matthew unequivocally puts it as follows:

> Jacob [was] the father of Joseph the husband of Mary, of whom Jesus was born, who is called Christ. (Matt 1:16)

The familial terms take on different shades of meaning, which are extensions of their primary meanings. Also, more importantly, these terms will come to have symbolic and spiritual connotations. Just as Paul says that the physical came first (1 Cor 15:46), so the natural or biological relationships in marriage and family are used in Scripture to illustrate spiritual truths. Jesus and Paul used the physical and natural world to explain spiritual truths. For example, Paul found it difficult to make the Roman believers understand freedom in Christ—that is, the truth that Christ's sacrificial death liberated them from the enslavement of sin: the freedom that Christ brings to those who believe in Him. He found it helpful to use the analogy of enslavement of the people by their earthly lords to explain what he meant. And He told them why he was resorting to a human illustration:

> I am speaking in human terms, because of your natural limitations. (Rom 6:19)

In the same light, the fatherhood of God can be better understood by people who have good relationships with their fathers. So when God presents Himself as Father, He does not come into our lives as though it were a kind of anthropomorphism, make-believe, or a fairytale fantasy. It is actually the transcendent God revealing Himself with human emotions and exemplary and perfect character traits. And He goes further in the revelation of Himself in human nature by sending His Son, who takes on the form and nature of a human being. And given the import of the father figure, the term, "father" has been used accordingly in Scripture. Just as God is the Father of mankind, this familial term can be used with any significant thing or key concept, because all have their origin in God, as we can see in the following examples: "the Father of lights" (James 1:17) (i.e., Creator of lights), "the Father of mercies" (2 Cor 1:3) (i.e., the source of, or the one who has, mercy). It is in view of the fact that the father has power and authority to protect, guide, and so forth, that the title of "father" is used to designate spiritual and governing authorities, as in the following Scriptures:

> I said, "I will not put out my hand against my lord, for he is the LORD's anointed." See, my father, see the corner of your robe in my hand. As soon as David had finished speaking these words to Saul, Saul said, "Is this your voice, my son David?" And Saul lifted up his voice and wept. (1 Sam 24:10–11, 16)

Although Saul had been disgraced and stripped of the kingship and the royal authority conferred on him, he still regarded himself as king, and David as his subject or servant, and so Saul called him his son. In the same vein, David still respected and honoured him as the anointed of the Lord. He saw himself as the servant of Saul, and so as subject to him. And this is why he called King Saul his father. In Bafut, the Fon, the king, sees himself as the father of his people, and his subjects call him "father." In the same sense, the president or head of state in African nations is called "father of the nation."

In the following examples, the spiritual authority signalled by the term "father" is in focus:

> Now when Elisha had fallen sick with the illness of which he was to die, Joash king of Israel went down to him and wept before him, crying, "My father, my father! Thechariots of Israel and its horsemen!" (2 Kings 13:14)

> And Micah said to him, "Stay with me, and be to me a father and a priest, and I will give you ten pieces of silver a year and a suit of clothes and your living." And the Levite went in. (Judg 17:10)

In the above examples, Elijah wields spiritual authority over the king, and that is why he calls him father. And as regards the priest, since the priestly function is to stand before the Lord on behalf of the people, he is a father figure to the people.

A father or fatherhood signals a progenitor (forefather), head (of a family line), or authority, and so it stands as the symbol of authority, guidance, wisdom, provision, and protection.

A mother symbolizes, origin and birth, care, and comfort (Isa 49:16; 66:13).

In the following text, Israel under the old covenant represents the woman who does not bear children because of her rebellion:

> "Sing, O barren one, who did not bear; break forth
> into singing and cry aloud, you who have not been
> in labour! For the children of the desolate one will

be more than the children of her who is married," says the LORD. (Isa 54:1)

Under the new covenant, the people of God, believers in Christ, who belong to the heavenly Jerusalem, the new Israel, become the mother of a growing family of God, as Paul tells us in Gal 4:25–28:

> But the Jerusalem above is free, and she is our mother. So, brothers, we are not children of the slave but of the free woman. (Gal 4:26, 31)

By extension, the term "mother" is used to describe the origin and core of something—for example, the "mother of all evil" or, as Socrates wrote in his dialogue *Republic*, "Our need will be the real creator." It came to mean what is expressed in the English proverb "Necessity is the mother of invention." And as a logical conclusion, people came to reason that "if necessity is the mother of invention, then play is its father." Although this innovation of the proverb finds no logical explanation, it is clear that the familial terms are used to establish a natural relationship and collocation in language, culture, and life.

The filial terms "son" and "daughter" are used in their extended meanings in Scripture. The extended meaning of the term "daughter" is more restricted in its usage in Scripture than the term "son." It collocates with Zion and Jerusalem, as we see in the following Scriptures:

> Rejoice greatly, O daughter of Zion! Shout aloud, O daughter of Jerusalem! Behold, your king is coming to you. (Zech 9:9)

"Daughter of Zion" is a metaphor for Jerusalem. It is a term of endearment for Jerusalem. When used positively in this sense, Jerusalem is likened to a daughter under the watch or guardianship of a father figure. Jerusalem (Zion) is likened to the daughter of a king, and so she can count herself secure and safe. Jesus/God, in this case, is her father. And as such, she feels safe even when threatened by a would-be abuser, as we can read in the following verse:

> This is the word that the LORD has spoken concerning him: "'She despises you, she scorns you— the virgin daughter of Zion; she wags her head behind you— the daughter of Jerusalem'" (Isa 37:22)

In the above verse, Jerusalem, "the virgin daughter of Zion," wags her head and mocks her would-be attacker because she knows he would be defeated (by the Lord).

In comparison, the familial term "son" is more extensive in its usage than daughter. A singular use of the term "son" or "sons" is found in the book of Lamentations, with a specific meaning as we see in the following example:

> The precious sons of Zion, worth their weight in fine gold, how they are regarded as earthen pots, the work of a potter's hands!(Lam 4:2)

In the above lament, Jeremiah is bemoaning the affliction of the children of Israel during the invasion of Jerusalem before the exile into Babylon. While the children were so precious to their parents, they had no value to the destroying invaders. However, in ancient Israel, the precious sons of Zion were worshippers of God— those who came to worship God in the temple. Jesus redefined the worshippers of God, making the term to apply to all believers who worship God in Spirit and in truth (John 4:21–23).

Other usages of "son"/"sons" that are found in various contexts in Scripture are as follows:

> The sons of God saw that the daughters of man were attractive. And they took as their wives any they chose. (Gen 6:2)

> Now there was a day when the sons of God came to present themselves before the LORD, and Satan also came among them. (Job 1:6)

The identity of "sons of God" in Genesis 6:2 is uncertain. It has been suggested that both in the Genesis and Job texts, "sons of God" refers to heavenly beings—angels. In the case of Genesis 6:2, "sons of God" refers to fallen angels (just like those in 2 Peter 2:4 and Jude 6). And this is why they would contradict Mark 12:25, where Jesus says that angels in heaven do not marry. These angels would be under the command of Satan, the prince of demons, and so would therefore be doing his bidding.

The Hebrew idiom "sons of ...," as used in Scripture, can designate a group that is led by a father figure that members of the group look up to and call their "father," such as the band of prophets in 1 Sam 10:12, 2 Kings 2:7, 15, and 6:1, for example:

> Fifty men of the sons of the prophets also went and stood at some distance from them, as they both were standing by the Jordan. Now when the *sons of the prophets*[60] who were at Jericho saw him opposite them, they said, "The spirit of Elijah rests on Elisha." And they came to meet him and bowed to the ground before him. (2 Kings 2:7,15)

The idiom "children of ..." is used with the same meaning as "son of ...," just as we find in the following examples:

> And you were dead in the trespasses and sins, following the prince of the power of the air, the spirit that is now at work in the sons of disobedience, carrying out the desires of the body and the mind, and were by nature children of wrath, like the rest of mankind. (Eph 2:1–30)

Paul uses the familial terms "sons of disobedience" and "children of wrath" here because he sees Satan at work in the lives of those who disobey God, just as the Serpent caused Adam and Eve to disobey God. The Hebrew figure of speech "sons of disobedience," just like "sons of this world" (Luke 16:8), refers to those who rebel against God. These people belong to the same family, having Satan as their father (John 8:44). These are by nature

---

[60] Emphasis mine

"sons" and "daughters" of Adam, born in sin (Ps 51:5) and subject to God's condemnation. They are therefore called "children of wrath." Jesus called James and John "boanerges," (i.e., "sons of thunder") (Mark 3:17) because they wanted to call down fire from heaven to consume the Samaritans who did not want Jesus to pass through their town (Luke 9:54). Jesus told them that they would be yielding to the power of a different spirit if they did that.

These terms, "sons of ..." and "children of...," when used in a positive sense, are used in relation to the Godhead, His character and divine nature, or the kingdom and kingdom values. As sons and daughters, children of God the Father, we are expected to have the nature and character of our Father and be like Him and imitate Him (Eph 5:1–2; 1 John 3:2). What the sons and daughters of God do is thus governed by who the Father is. It is in view of this that Jesus said in the Sermon on the Mount that we should reflect the Father in His character and deeds:

> You have heard that it was said, "You shall love your neighbour and hate your enemy." But I say to you, Love your enemies and pray for those who persecute you, so that you may be sons of your Father who is in heaven. For he makes his sun rise on the evil and on the good, and sends rain on the just and on the unjust. You therefore must be perfect, as your heavenly Father is perfect. (Matt 5:43–45, 48)

The attributes and virtues of God, and of Christ, are used metaphorically, and in the light of these, believers become children of them. God is light, and so those who do God's will and walk in the light become children, or sons, of light, as we can read in the following texts:

> For at one time you were darkness, but now you are light in the Lord. Walk as children of light. (Eph 5:8)

> For you are all children of light, children of the day. We are not of the night or of the darkness. (1 Thess 5:5)

Jesus came as the light of the world (John 1:4, 9), and those who believe in Him become children of light. Jesus Himself taught this to His followers and to the Jews, as we read in the following verses:

> So Jesus said to them, "The light is among you for a little while longer. Walk while you have the light, lest darkness overtake you. While you have the light, believe in the light, that you may become sons of light." I have come into the world as light, so that whoever believes in me may not remain in darkness. (John 12:35–36,46)

Jesus called His followers, "children," as expressed in one of His most gracious, caring, and endearing moments of His earthly ministry:

> Just as day was breaking, Jesus stood on the shore; yet the disciples did not know that it was Jesus. Jesus said to them, "Children, do you have any fish?" They answered him, "No." (John 21:4–5)

This truth had already been prophesied before Jesus came into the world, as the writer of Hebrews quotes for us in the following text:

> For he who sanctifies and those who are sanctified all have one source. That is why he is not ashamed to call them brothers, saying, "I will tell of your name to my brothers; in the midst of the congregation I will sing your praise." And again, "I will put my trust in him." And again, "Behold, I and the children God has given me." (Heb 2:11–13)

Jesus Christ is our brother through adoption, and in the mystery of God, we believers become His children. And as Jesus clearly said in His teaching, all that belongs to the Father is equally His, so those who believe in Him and become God's children also become

Christ's children. It is in light of this truth that Christians, followers of Christ, are called "children of Christ" in the Bafut church.

Since God is King and Jesus came as King to proclaim the kingdom of God, those who are called to live kingdom life and to inherit the kingdom of God are called "children of the kingdom," as in the following verse:

> I tell you, many will come from east and west and recline at table with Abraham, Isaac, and Jacob in the kingdom of heaven, while the sons of the kingdom will be thrown into the outer darkness. In that place there will be weeping and gnashing of teeth. (Matt 8:11–12)

"Sons of the kingdom" is a Semitic term used among the Jews to designate the nationals of Israel, as they were ruled by the Davidic kings.

The familial term "son," as used in the Bible, acquires more significance when its meaning is extended to include God the Father and His special relationship with Jesus Christ, His Son. The Jews mistakenly saw Jesus merely as the son of Mary and Joseph, and so they missed seeing him as the Messiah. Jesus Christ, as the Son of God, takes on a pivotal role, which is preeminent in Salvation history, as Matthew highlights this right at the beginning of his gospel, as follows:

> The book of the genealogy of Jesus Christ, the son of David, the son of Abraham. (Matt 1:1)

John the apostle says very clearly that inclusion in the family of God is predicated on confessing Jesus as the Messiah, Son of God:

> Everyone who believes that Jesus is the Christ has been born of God. Whoever confesses that Jesus is the Son of God, God abides in him, and he in God. (1 John 5:1; 4:15)

The motifs of the familial terms are used extensively in the

Scriptures. God is a relational being, relating with the Son and Holy Spirit in a profound way, as they are in union one with another. The relationship that exists within the Godhead determines that which should exist between us, his children, and among the members of His household. The unity within the Godhead defines our unity, the unity of the church (John 17:20–21). The love that God and Jesus Christ have for us as individuals, and as the church, should be the same love that we have for one another. It should be steadfast and unconditional:

> The LORD appeared to him from far away. I have loved you with an everlasting love; therefore I have continued my faithfulness to you. For the mountains may depart and the hills be removed, but my steadfast love shall not depart from you, and my covenant of peace shall not be removed," says the LORD, who has compassion on you. (Jer 31:3; Is 54:10)

And the love that believers, members of the household of God, have for one another should be the same as the one that God and His Christ have for us:

> A new commandment I give to you, that you love one another: just as I have loved you, you also are to love one another. By this all people will know that you are my disciples, if you have love for one another. (John 13:34–35)

The teaching that God is Father and believers are members of His family is very important in Christianity. This is what defines the identity, roles, and functions of each member of the family. The character traits and behaviour in the family are governed by the concept of family. Hence, in God's family, God the Father is loving, gracious, compassionate, and merciful while His children fear and honour Him in loving obedience, as can be read in the following verse:

> By steadfast love and faithfulness iniquity is atoned for, and by the fear of the LORD one turns away from evil. (Prov 16:6)

The love of God makes Him forgive us, and because we, His children, fear and honour him, we obey His Word and turn away from evil.

It should be borne in mind that this is a description of a situation where members of the family pattern their lives after the Father and Son, empowered by the Holy Spirit. Since we are not perfect beings, there will still be failures and problems in Christian families. The difference lies in the fact that with the help of the Holy Spirit and of Christ, all members of a Christ-centred family always support one another and turn to God for help when they have problems in the family. Each failure enables us to look to the Lord for help, and we grow in our family and Christian life as we walk closer to the Lord, seeking His will and glory in our relationships.

Family relationships and loyalties are the strongest and most important, and so we have the proverb "Blood is thicker than water."[61] If Christians see themselves as family; if, in business, partners see themselves as family; if, in politics, parties see themselves as family; and if, in the world, people see themselves as family, things will work well and efficiently; there will be enough for all and there will be peace, because there will be justice, and so there will be no war. Wars will cease in the world if the practical lesson taught in 2 Samuel 2:26–27 is learnt and applied. The question posed by Abner to Joab still rings true today:

> How long will it be before you tell your people to turn from the pursuit of their brothers? (2 Sam 2:26)

---

[61] However, as Jesus said, He came to bring the sword and not peace (Matt 10:34–36). Faith in Jesus can separate families: "... a man against his father, a daughter against her mother, a person's enemies will be members of his household" (Matt 10:35). This is especially fierce because those who do not believe in Christ are pitted against those who believe, since they are of the world and are therefore controlled by Satan, the ruler of this world (John 12:31; 14:30; 1 John 5:19).

4.10.2. The Family of God

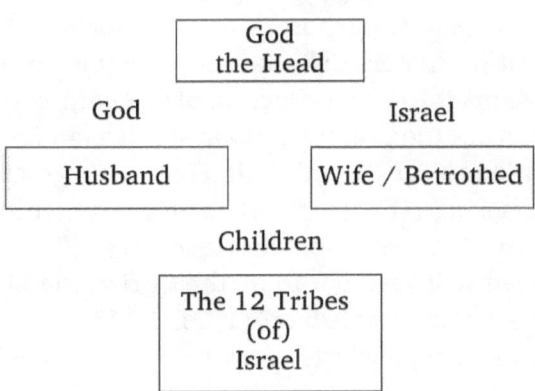

Fig. 1   The Family of God: Old Testament

The above diagram gives a picture of God's family. As we have seen before, God presents Himself as the Father of Israel and as her husband, Israel being the betrothed and the wife, while the people of Israel (the twelve tribes) are the children. And this is why we say that the family is founded on God, the Father, just as Paul intimates in his prayer for the Ephesians:

> For this reason I bow my knees before the Father, from whom every family in heaven and on earth is named. (Eph 3:14–15)

Paul, by this statement, affirms the redemption act of the Father through the Son. God the Father is the one who names *every* family in heaven and on earth. And this act of naming indicates His sovereignty over every human being. First and foremost, biblically, to name someone is to define his identity. So the children of God find their identity in Him. It is the same in Bafut society; one is identified by his family background. Every child, everyone, is known by who his father is (i.e., one is the child of his or her father). In the same, way our identity as Christians is found in Christ.

4.10.3. **Marriage and the Family and God's Purposes**

As stated at the beginning of the treatise on marriage and the family, man was the focus of Creation because God intended to use man to fulfil and advance His purposes. The family was at the centre of God's creative purpose, since God foresaw its importance in all of salvation history. The family is important in God's plan because He wants it to be a reflection of the nature and function of the Godhead. After the Creation, Adam starts a family, and although Adam had failed to fulfil God's will, He, in His grace, foretold the rise of the offspring (Hb "*seed*") of the woman, who would bruise the head of the Serpent (i.e., the Adversary) (Gen 3:15). And of course this seed will turn out to be the Christ, the Messiah, whom Paul identifies as "the last Adam" (1 Cor 15:45). Actually Paul says that Adam was "a type of the one who was to come" (Rom 5:14). "Type" (Gk "*typos*") means "model" or "pattern." Adam is therefore a type of Christ, because Adam is the covenantal head of the human race, just as Christ Himself is head. And as Paul explains, people are either "in Adam" or "in Christ." And so he writes, "For as in Adam all die, so also in Christ shall all be made alive" (1 Cor 15:22).

The call of Abraham marks an important milestone in the history of salvation. Consequently, through the family line of this one man, Abraham, the world would be blessed. And so from the seed of Abraham the nation of Israel was born (Gen 32:28). Subsequently, Israel became the chosen people and a nation unto God (Exod 19:4–6; Deut 7:6, 8). And as stated previously, God is presented as husband, and Israel as the betrothed of the Lord God. God is also seen in the Old Testament as Father, exhibiting the qualities and character of a father with regard to His chosen people, Israel. And in some contexts He even plays the role of a caring and comforting mother (Isaiah 49:15; 66:13).[62] And Jesus will come and depict the mother figure when He weeps over the city of Jerusalem (Luke 13:34).

---

[62] This may explain why some unorthodox minds treat God as both man and woman. Various issues have arisen in modern-day debates among theologians such that gender issues are being debated more and more. Some extremists are thinking that the Bible should be rewritten to meet the concerns of people imbued with feminist ideas and agendas.

4.10.4. The Family Line of Jesus Christ the Saviour

The following diagram further illustrates how God, from the foundation of the world, made marriage and the family the strategic means of accomplishing His plan to save the world.

Fig. 2: Marriage and the Family in Salvation History

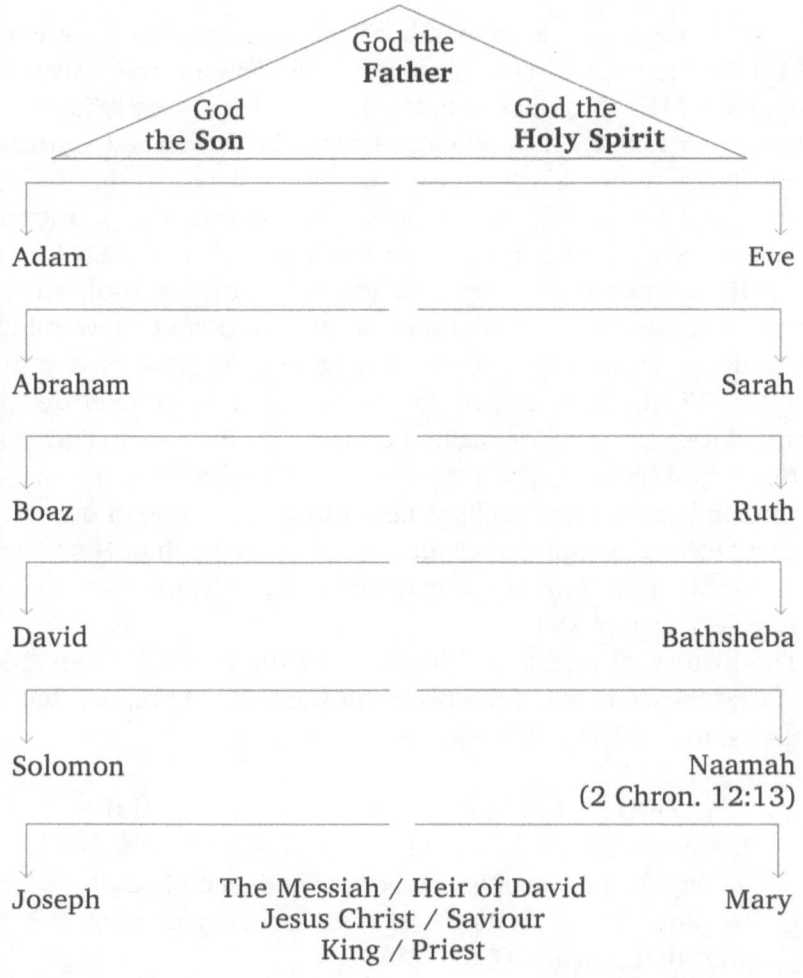

The diagram shows, in an abridged form, the family line (i.e., the genealogy of the Messiah/Saviour/King/Priest). God's plan of salvation was to be carried out by those He created, and so His purposes would be realized through the seed of Adam, Abraham, and David, the king and priest.

4.10.5. Priesthood and the Family

Right at Creation, God gave man both regal and priestly functions. The priestly functions were already foreshadowing the universal priesthood of His chosen people. We discussed the priestly function of man in section 1.9.2. In ancient Israel, the father had spiritual responsibility in his family and served as the priest in that he led worship and family prayers. As we see in Genesis, the patriarchs (Abraham, Isaac, and Jacob) made sacrifices to God (Gen 22:14; 31:54; 46:1). They started by building altars to the Lord, where they encountered God, and these served as places of worship, since before the tabernacle there was no central place of worship (Gen 12:7;13:18; 22:9; 26:25; 35:7). As stated in chapter 1, the priestly duties are very important because they have to do with our relationship with God. The primary call of God on our lives is to worship and enjoy Him. And the next thing in the line of our duty is to lead others to Him and ground them in the truth of His Word, beginning with our families, our households. This, in effect, is our priestly duty or ministry.

The history of priesthood began with the Exodus, when God asked that the firstborn of the people of Israel should be devoted to Him, as stated in the following text:

> The LORD said to Moses, "Consecrate to me all the firstborn. Whatever is the first to open the womb among the people of Israel, both of man and of beast, is mine." Every firstborn of man among your sons you shall redeem. (Exod 13:1–2, 13)

This is the foundation of the Levitical priesthood and the sacrificial system, which would be formalized later on. Prior to this, even before Moses was born, God had in His divine plan destined that Moses and his brother Aaron would be born into the family of Levi, as we read in the following text:

> Now a man from the house of Levi went and took as his wife a Levite woman. The woman conceived and bore a son, and when she saw that he was a fine child, she hid him three months. (Exod 2:1–2)

In God's plan, Moses would be adopted by the daughter of Pharaoh and would be brought up in the palace as a prince and would become learned in the wisdom of the court, in leadership, and in governance, as testified by Stephen:

> And Moses was instructed in all the wisdom of the Egyptians, and he was mighty in his words and deeds. (Acts 7:22)

He would in time be married to the daughter of Reul, a priest of Midian. And again this keeps him and his family in the priestly family and in the godly wisdom of priests, as is seen in the wise advice that his father-in-law gives Him as he judges the people (Exod 18:17–26).

While he went out visiting his people in Egypt one day, after the incident of the murder of an Egyptian, he sought to settle a dispute between two fellow Hebrews who were fighting. The one in the wrong rejected his intervention. This rejection by one of his Jewish brothers ironically affirmed his position—that is, what Moses would be to the people of Israel. This man queried, "Who made you a prince and a judge over us?" (Exod 2:14). And just as this fellow Hebrew rejected Moses, the man who would be sent by God to deliver them, the Jews would reject Christ, their Saviour. Paradoxically, this rejection that led Christ to His death would be the means of their salvation. While Moses later returned to save his people from the house of bondage, in the last day Jesus Christ will return for those who accept Him and to judge those who rejected Him.

The significance of Moses as a deliverer, lawgiver, prince, leader, and prophet of God will be seen in the narrative as we see signs and symbols of the hand of God on Him. These signs will point to his role in the history of salvation. Throughout the book of Exodus, each act performed by him accomplishes the purpose of God: to make people know who the Lord who had sent him is in His person, character, and deeds. And this is confirmed by the recognition formula, which is the chorus repeated over and over in the narrative:

> Know that I am the LORD. (Exod 6:7; 7:5, 17)

God's purpose was that the children of Israel who were then in bondage would know Him (their Deliverer) and His covenant identity; and that Pharaoh and the Egyptians would recognize who He is, the Lord God, and also know His sovereign judgment.

When Moses is born, the child is described in the following ways:

> He was a fine child. (Exod 2:2)
> He was beautiful in God's sight. (Acts 7:20)

This has led scholars to interpret this as an echo of the Creation narrative:

> And God saw everything that he had made, and behold, it was very good. (Gen 1:31)

And when we read Exodus 1:7 ("The people of Israel were fruitful and increased greatly; they multiplied and grew exceedingly strong, so that the land was filled with them"), we will see that this evokes the blessing of God at Creation (Gen 1:28). It has been said that the opening events of Exodus serve as the Creation-like account of the birth of the nation of Israel. So the birth of Moses marked the creation of the nation of Israel. And so we can see Moses as a sign of God's work and promises for His people and the symbol of Israel, the new nation that God is forming for Himself.

The way God protected Moses at birth from Pharaoh, enabling him to flee to Midian and then bringing him back, shows that God did all this in view of the important role he would play in the history of salvation. In the same way, He would protect the child Jesus from

Herod by advising His parents to flee with Him to Egypt. And God would speak to Moses in the same way, using almost the same words that He would use to assure Joseph, the father of Jesus:

> And the LORD said to Moses in Midian, "Go back to Egypt, for all the men who were seeking your life are dead." (Exod 4:19)

> But when Herod died, behold, an angel of the Lord appeared in a dream to Joseph in Egypt, saying, "Rise, take the child and his mother and go to the land of Israel, for those who sought the child's life are dead." (Matt 2:19–20)

So we see that there is a lot in Moses' life that reflects Christ and His mission. Looking into their lives and ministry, we note, for example, that both Moses and Jesus were servants, prophets, and mediators, that both were humble, and so on. God even tells Moses that he will be like God to Aaron (Exod 4:17), which tells us how highly God regarded Moses. The people of Israel would also come to hold him in high esteem, for disrespecting Moses would mean disrespecting God (Num 12:8–12; 16:11).

Moses and Jesus were important, and their ministries were very significant. Their mediating roles would be crucial in the history of salvation.

And given the fact that fallen man needs a mediator in order to be saved, the Lord established the Levitical priests and the Levites as mediators between the people of Israel and the Lord God. And so making this clear to the people of Israel was important. This became necessary and urgent because Korah, Datham, Abiram, and Non challenged the authority and position of Moses and Aaron. Korah, a Levite, had challenged Aaron about his status as high priest (Numbers 16:1–11). God then intervened in a dramatic way, consuming Korah and the 250 men who had teamed with him and presumptuously offered unauthorized incense. And so, by this dramatic act, God made it clear that it was He who had appointed Aaron as high priest to offer sacrifices (Num 16:1–35). And after this, He ordered that the Levites be cleansed and that, together with them, Aaron and his sons, the Levitical priests, be set apart to serve Him in the tabernacle. And therefore He told Moses, "Bring near to you Aaron your brother, and his sons with him, from among the people of Israel, to serve me as priests—Aaron and Aaron's sons, Nadab and Abihu, Eleazar and Ithamar" (Exod 28:1).

Having made it clear to the people of Israel that He had appointed Aaron and his sons to be the ones to burn incense to Him, He went on to instruct Aaron concerning their duties:

> So the LORD said to Aaron, "You and your sons and your father's house with you shall bear iniquity connected with the sanctuary, and you and your sons with you shall bear iniquity connected with your priesthood." (Num 18:1)

When the Lord slew the firstborn of Pharaoh and the Egyptians, the firstborn of both man and animal, He asked that the firstborn of the people of Israel should be dedicated to Him, and so He said to Moses:

> Consecrate to me all the firstborn. Whatever is the first to open the womb among the people of Israel, both of man and of beast, is mine.(Exod 13:2)

The firstborn sons of the people of Israel were redeemed, while the firstborn of animals were offered as sacrifice to the Lord. The Lord then asked the congregation of Israel to offer the Levites to Him in place of their firstborn, offering them to serve Him in the tabernacle:

> And the LORD spoke to Moses, saying,"Take the Levites from among the people of Israel and cleanse them. And you shall bring the Levites before the tent of meeting and assemble the whole congregation of the people of Israel. When you bring the Levites before the LORD, the people of Israel shall lay their hands on the Levites, and Aaron shall offer the Levites before the LORD as a wave offering from

the people of Israel, that they may do the service of the LORD. For they are wholly given to me from among the people of Israel. Instead of all who open the womb, the firstborn of all the people of Israel, I have taken them for myself." (Num 8:5–6, 10–11, 16)

It should be noted that the firstborn of the people of Israel were to be sacrificed to the Lord, and so in this act, the Levites were thus being given in sacrifice in place of the firstborn of the people. They would redeem the firstborn, foreshadowing the redemption that Christ would in history come to accomplish. And this is why the Lord said,

And I have given the Levites as a gift to Aaron and his sons from among the people of Israel, to do the service for the people of Israel at the tent of meeting and to make atonement for the people of Israel, that there may be no plague among the people of Israel when the people of Israel come near the sanctuary. (Num 8:19)

The Lord gives two main reasons for the offering of the Levites. The first is that the Levites would serve on behalf of the people. Everyone is to serve God—that is, to worship Him—but in this case, the service at the tabernacle was different, because this entailed coming near the presence of God, who was at the time terribly holy and separated from the people. And those who approached His presence would be slain immediately, as it was at the giving of the Ten Commandments (Exodus 19:9–21). That is why the Lord said that the Levites were there to protect the lives of the people. The next important thing was that they would make atonement for the people.

The implication of the offering of the Levites as an atoning sacrifice in the history of salvation is huge. Instead of offering their animals as blood sacrifices to God, the people of Israel offer the Levites as substitutes for both their firstborn children and animals. This already foreshadows Christ's substitutionary death, when God offered Jesus Christ, His One and only Son, to die in our place on the cross and atone for our sins. Jesus' sacrificial death established the new covenant and abolished the old covenant. And it is on this basis that Paul will exhort Christians in the new dispensation to offer their bodies "as a living sacrifice, holy and acceptable to God, which is your spiritual worship" (Rom 12:1). Thanks to Christ and the new covenant in His blood, we need to neither make physical animal sacrifices nor die because of our sins.

The contention of Korah and other rebels of the people (Num 16:3–38; 17:1–11) caused God to affirm Aaron as the high priest. The people of Israel had to learn that priesthood was a matter of appointment. This incident foreshadowed the appointment of Christ as the greater and ultimate High Priest and Mediator, as we read in the following text:

> And no one takes this honour for himself, but only when called by God, just as Aaron was. So also Christ did not exalt himself to be made a high priest, but was appointed by him who said to him, "You are my Son, today I have begotten you"; as he says also in another place, "You are a priest forever, after the order of Melchizedek." (Heb 5:4–6)

The Levites who were not priests were to serve the Levitical priests, in addition toot her duties (Num 3:21–26). They were to guard the Levitical priests and the exterior of the tabernacle to make sure that no one would approach the tent at the risk of his life. No ordinary Israelite could approach the sanctuary; even the Levites themselves were not allowed to approach the altar or touch the holy vessels, which were the responsibilities of the priests.

The Levites carried the tabernacle, its furnishings, when the people set out from the camp. Even so, specific clans of the Levites (the Korathites, Gershonites, and Merarites) were given specific tasks, as bearers of the tabernacle, which they had to strictly carry out (Num 4:15–33).[63]

---

[63] Gershon, Kohath, and Merari were the three sons of Levi (Gen 46:11). Levi was the founder of the Israelite tribe of Levi and the great-grandfather of Aaron, Moses, and Miriam.

The Levitical priests were responsible for service in the tabernacle and temple, guarding the inner sanctuary, leading worship, and mediating between the people and God.

Regarding the priests and their special and privileged position, the Lord gave this warning:

> And you and your sons with you shall guard your priesthood for all that concerns the altar and that is within the veil; and you shall serve. I give your priesthood as a gift, and any outsider who comes near shall be put to death. (Num 18:7)

Their special position also gave them special duties in addition to their service in the tabernacle, the sanctuary—they also served as judges:

> And you shall come to the Levitical priests and to the judge who is in office in those days, and you shall consult them, and they shall declare to you the decision. According to the instructions that they give you, and according to the decision which they pronounce to you, you shall do. You shall not turn aside from the verdict that they declare to you, either to the right hand or to the left. (Deut 17:9, 11)

They were responsible for teaching the people the law of the Lord, as we read here below:

> They shall teach Jacob your rules and Israel your law; they shall put incense before you and whole burnt offerings on your altar. (Deut 33:10)

They were to bless the people of Israel, as it was the desire of the Lord and the ultimate provision of the covenant that God made with Abraham:

> The LORD spoke to Moses, saying, "Speak to Aaron and his sons, saying, Thus you shall bless the people

of Israel: you shall say to them, The LORD bless you and keep you; the LORD make his face to shine upon you and be gracious to you; the LORD lift up his countenance upon you and give you peace. So shall they put my name upon the people of Israel, and I will bless them." (Num 6:22–27)

The coming of Christ and His sacrificial death transformed the whole Old Testament sacrificial system and the priesthood. His death on the cross tore down the curtain that kept the worshippers from approaching and worshipping God except through the high priest.

The Old Testament tabernacle and the whole sacrificial system were foreshadowing the real sanctuary where Christ went after His death and ascension:

> For Christ has entered, not into holy places made with hands, which are copies of the true things, but into heaven itself, now to appear in the presence of God on our behalf. (Heb 9:24)

Christ entered the heavenly sanctuary not with animal blood, as the Levitical priests, but with His own blood. And it is this blood that grants us access to the throne of grace. And so we are urged on:

> Therefore, brothers, since we have confidence to enter the holy places by the blood of Jesus, by the new and living way that he opened for us through the curtain, that is, through his flesh, and since we have a great priest over the house of God, let us draw near with a true heart in full assurance of faith, with our hearts sprinkled clean from an evil conscience and our bodies washed with pure water. Let us hold fast the confession of our hope without wavering, for he who promised is faithful. (Heb 10:19–23)

So we see the blood of Christ, which will seal the new covenant, which He announced during the last Supper (Matt 26:28; Lk 22:20).

And this covenant is not based on the law, as was the old covenant (Exod 24:7-8), but on the grace of God, since God, having seen the failure on people's part to keep the law, sent Christ to fulfil it. And consequently, Jesus Christ decided to come to do God's will. The following Scripture captures Christ's mind:

> Consequently, when Christ came into the world, he said, "Sacrifices and offerings you have not desired, but a body have you prepared for me. Then I said, 'Behold, I have come to do your will, O God, as it is written of me in the scroll of the book.'"
>
> And by that will we have been sanctified through the offering of the body of Jesus Christ once for all. (Heb 10:5, 7, 10)

The road that Christ travelled both physically and spiritually to the summit of God's will was long and hard. All his life on earth was focused on doing that will, and his face was set towards Jerusalem to be baptized with the baptism He had to be baptized with. And it was not an easy road. He Himself said, "I have a baptism to be baptized with, and how great is my distress until it is accomplished!" (Luke 12:50) And as Luke describes it, His soul was sorrowful unto death. And He prayed so hard that He sweated blood. And this led to the ultimate choice to do the supreme will of God. And kneeling down, He prayed:

> Father, if you are willing, remove this cup from me. Nevertheless, not my will, but yours, be done. (Luke 22:42)

And so the cross was the beginning and the inauguration of the new covenant, which God had promised in Jeremiah 31:33-34. Jesus' blood sanctified the believer, cleansing him and making him perfect, unlike the blood of animals of the old covenant. This covenant was a better one, as we read:

> But as it is, Christ has obtained a ministry that is much more excellent than the old, as the covenant

he mediates is better, since it is enacted on better promises. (Heb 8:6)

The best was yet to come! Better promises! For even after cleansing us and writing His laws on our hearts, we still wouldn't be able to obey them. And so God, in His grace, promised to cause us, through the Holy Spirit, who will teach us and enable us, to do it, as we read in the following Scripture:

> I will sprinkle clean water on you, and you shall be clean from all your uncleannesses, and from all your idols I will cleanse you. And I will give you a new heart and a new spirit I will put within you. And I will remove the heart of stone from your flesh and give you a heart of flesh. And I will put my Spirit within you, and cause you to walk in my statutes and be careful to obey my rules. (Ezek 36:25–27)

Another thing of significance in the priesthood of Jesus Christ that will change the nature of priesthood in the New Testament is the fact that Christ did not come from the family line of Levi. This was because the Levitical priesthood was not perfect because it was based on the law:

> For the law made nothing perfect); but on the other hand, a better hope is introduced, through which we draw near to God. (Heb 7:19)

So there was a need to change the order and go for one after Melchisedek rather than after the order of Aaron. Jesus descended from Judah, and so he belonged to the tribe of Judah, from whom no one had ever served at the altar. But Jesus became a priest after the order of Melchizedek:

> Not on the basis of a legal requirement concerning bodily descent, but by the power of an indestructible life. For it is witnessed of him, "You are a priest forever, after the order of Melchizedek." (Heb 7:16–17)

And unlike the former priests, Jesus was made priest with an oath of the Lord:

> And it was not without an oath. For those who formerly became priests were made such without an oath, but this one was made a priest with an oath by the one who said to him: "The Lord has sworn and will not change his mind, 'You are a priest forever.'" (Heb 7:20–21)

And by all accounts, Jesus' priesthood is unique for the following reasons:

1. The suffering He went through was unique:

   > Although he was a son, he learned obedience through what he suffered. In the days of his flesh, Jesus offered up prayers and supplications, with loud cries and tears, to him who was able to save him from death, and he was heard because of his reverence. And being found in human form, he humbled himself by becoming obedient to the point of death, even death on a cross. Therefore God has highly exalted him and bestowed on him the name that is above every name. (Heb 5:7–8; Phil 2:8–9)

2. He is the only mediator: Moses and the Levitical priests were not perfect and could not mediate an eternal redemption. And so, "For there is one God, and there is one mediator between God and men, the man Christ Jesus, who gave himself as a ransom for all, which is the testimony given at the proper time" (1 Tim 2:5–6).

3. He is the only way to God, in whom are the truth and eternal life:

Jesus said to him, "I am the way, and the truth, and the life. No one comes to the Father except through me. And there is salvation in no one else, for there is no other name under heaven given among men by which we must be saved." (John 14:6; Acts 4:12)

Whoever has the Son has life; whoever does not have the Son of God does not have life. (1 John 5:12)

4. He is priest (and king) forever. He lives eternally:

You are priest forever after the order of Melchizedek. One who has become a priest, by the power of an indestructible life. (Ps 104:4; Heb 7:5–6)

Jesus' resurrection from the dead proved that He was indestructible; therefore, his priesthood will last forever. He was not only priest but also king, like Melchizedek, who was King of Salem (Jerusalem) and "priest of God Most High" (Gen 13:18–20). So Jesus, the Davidic king, will be "after the order" (i.e., like Melchizedek, in the sense that He is both king (ruling in Zion) (Ps 104:2) and priest. The offices of priest and king were distinct in Israel, but the prophet Zechariah foresaw a merger between these two offices in Jesus the Messiah, the "Branch" who shall "bear royal honour and shall sit and rule on his throne. And there shall be a priest on his throne" (Zech 6:12–13). The continuation of the Davidic king and the Levitical priesthood are intertwined, and there will be peace between the two offices. This foresees the Messiah, the Davidic king who will come from the line of David. And Zechariah portrays Jesus as king in the following verse:

Rejoice greatly, O daughter of Zion! Shout aloud, O daughter of Jerusalem! Behold, your king is

> coming to you; righteous and having salvation is he, humble and mounted on a donkey, on a colt, the foal of a donkey. (Zech 9:9)

And so, Jesus is both priest and king.

5. He was a prophet: Prophets like Moses, and others, spoke the Word of God that revealed who God is, but Jesus was the final revelation of God (John 1:8) and so was a superior prophet.

   > Long ago, at many times and in many ways, God spoke to our fathers by the prophets, but in these last days, he has spoken to us by his Son, whom he appointed the heir of all things, through whom also he created the world. (Heb 1:1–2)

6. He is the firstborn of God, Sovereign Ruler/King: He is the firstborn in the sense that He is preeminent (Col 1:18), He has the right of inheritance (Rom 8:29, 16; Col 1:15). He is preeminent in family lineage (Gen 43:33) and rights of inheritance. The term "firstborn," although used of David, ultimately points to Jesus, the Davidic Messiah and Son of God, in view of His rights and privileges, which are those of the firstborn son of a monarch, who will inherit ruling sovereignty. This is the meaning of the expression used of David:

   > And I will make him the firstborn, the highest of the kings of the earth. (Ps 89:27)

   Jesus, the Davidic King and Messiah, "the firstborn of the dead," will be the ruler of the kings of the earth (Rev 1:5). That is, He will be King of Kings.

The priesthood of Jesus is remarkably different from the Levitical priesthood. Jesus is priest, King, Messiah, and Saviour.

He is fully man, the Son of Man, and God, and He gives life to those who believe in Him:

> Whoever has the Son has life; whoever does not have
> the Son of God does not have life. (1 John 5:12)

So the death of Christ opened the way for us to go direct to God, and because Christ has entered the sanctuary itself, He is better placed to minister on our behalf. And so "we have such a high priest, one who is seated at the right hand of the throne of the Majesty in heaven, a minister in the holy places, in the true tent that the Lord set up, not man" (Heb 8:1–2). He is now our high priest, interceding for us (Rom 8:32).

Though we are not descendants of the tribe of Levi, we can become priests, because in Christ we become His siblings, members of His family. And so we do not need to be descendants of Levi or be of the family lineage of Aaron to become priests; nor must we offer animal sacrifices, but rather, offer spiritual sacrifices to God (Heb 13:15–16; Phil 4:18; 1 Peter 2:5, 9). And so under the new covenant established by Christ, all believers become priests. And so the sacrificial death of Christ establishes the universal priesthood of believers. Jesus has now become our High Priest. Christ is now seated in heaven, at the right hand of the Father:

> Since then we have a great high priest who has
> passed through the heavens, Jesus, the Son of God,
> let us hold fast our confession. Let us then with
> confidence draw near to the throne of grace, that
> we may receive mercy and find grace to help in time
> of need. (Heb 4:14, 18)

The following diagram shows the generation of the priests and the history of salvation:

Fig. 3: The Priestly Family Tree

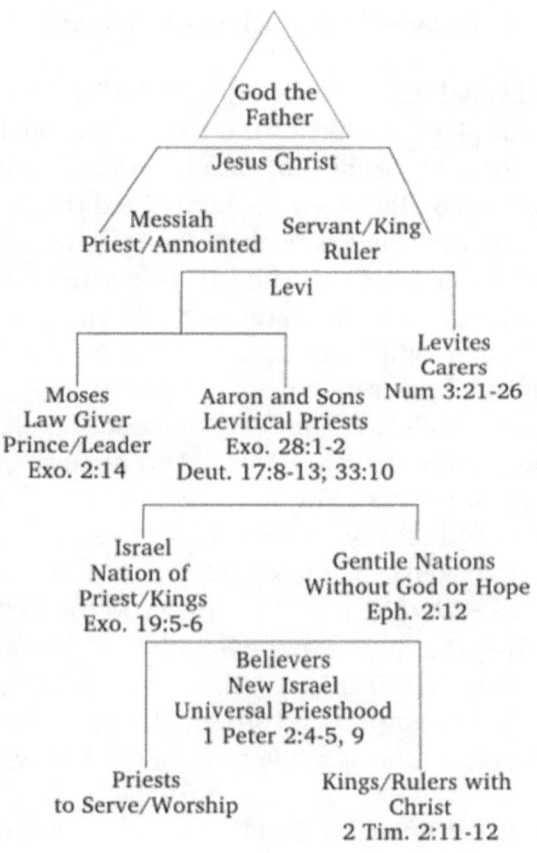

The priestly family tree starts with God the Father and Creator. Then comes Jesus Christ, the priest, Messiah, and king/ruler. Then comes Levi and his sons: Moses, Aaron and his sons (the Levitical priests), and the Levites.

Taking Israel as a nation, God had in His foreknowledge destined that the nation of Israel would be a kingdom and that the people would be priests:

> Now therefore, if you will indeed obey my voice and keep my covenant, you shall be my treasured possession among all peoples, for all the earth is

mine; and you shall be to me a kingdom of priests and a holy nation. These are the words that you shall speak to the people of Israel. (Exod 19:5–6)

God called Israel His firstborn son (Exod 4:22–23; Jer 31:9), and this, in the first place, speaks of the covenantal relationship that He had with Abraham, Isaac, and Jacob, and thus with the whole nation of Israel. Secondly, when the Lord killed the firstborn of the Egyptians and spared the firstborn of the Israelites, He then took those of Israel as offerings to Him. In this sense, spiritually the people of Israel will have the status of the Levites, of the house of Levi, some of whom will be priests. And this is why God said that Israel, His treasured possession would be priests. And given that the Davidic king was God's "son" and "firstborn son" (Ps 89:26–29), he embodied and represented the people. And because of King David and his lineage, Israel was a kingdom. The covenantal responsibility of the children of Israel was to mediate the presence of the Lord in the nations and make them know God.

Paul was called by the Lord to minister to the Gentiles, and so He saw himself as the apostle to the Gentiles. And he toiled to bring the gospel to them. In this ministry he functioned, so to speak, as a priest relative to the gospel. The offering he presented to God was the Gentile converts. This is made clear in the following quote:

> The grace given me by God to be a minister of Christ Jesus to the Gentiles in the priestly service of the gospel of God, so that the offering of the Gentiles may be acceptable, sanctified by the Holy Spirit. (Rom 15:15–16)

This offering was as pleasing and acceptable to the Lord as the Old Testament sacrifices because these Gentile believers were sanctified by the Holy Spirit. Paul championed the ministry of the gospel to the Gentile nations (Rom 15:18–20).

And when the Gentile nations got to know God through the gospel of Christ, they became the new Israel. And it is on this basis that Peter said that they were "a chosen race, a royal priesthood, a holy nation, a people for his own possession" (1 Peter 2:9). Here the church, now made of both Jews and Gentiles, takes on the role of Israel and is called to be witnesses, displaying the goodness—"excellencies"—of God, who called them from darkness (sin) into His light. As the chosen ones of God, Christians are to proclaim Christ, the light, and bring people who are in the world out of the dominion of the darkness of Satan, the ruler of this world system, and transfer them to the kingdom of Christ, God's beloved Son (Col 1:13). And as stated in section 1.9 of this book, the goal of every believer is to do everything in Christ in order to bring people to the faith, build them up, and establish them in Christ. Paul summed up the goal of his pastoral ministry in the following terms:

> Him we proclaim, warning everyone and teaching everyone with all wisdom, that we may present everyone mature in Christ. For this I toil, struggling with all his energy that he powerfully works within me. (Col 1:28–29)

The priestly functions fall on every believer, everyone who has been trained in Christ, and who will be seeking to minister to others, who will in turn train others. And this is just as Paul exhorts Timothy to do in 2 Tim 2:2. This is the foundation of the universal priesthood of believers. And since Christ came and inaugurated the kingdom of God and asked us to preach it, we are people of the kingdom. And what is our mandate? Christ tells us here:

> And this gospel of the kingdom will be proclaimed throughout the whole world as a testimony to all nations, and then the end will come. (Matt 24:14)

So Christians are kingdom people, living kingdom life, mediating God and His grace which He has lavished on us, and seeking wholeheartedly to bring those who do not know Christ into the kingdom of God.

The fallout of God's kingdom and Christ being King and Judge/Ruler is that we, too, will be kings and judges with Him. This sounds unbelievable and even presumptuous, but this is biblical truth! Believers are anointed (1 John 2:20, 27), and Paul says in several

Scriptures that we are seated with Christ (Eph 2:6; Col 3:1–3). He says that we shall judge even angels (1 Cor 6:2–3) and that we shall be kings and judge the world with Christ:

> The saying is trustworthy, for: If we have died with him, we will also live with him; if we endure, we will also reign with him. (2 Tim 2:11–12)

Christ Himself assures those who follow Him that they will sit on throne and rule with Him:

> Jesus said to them, "Truly, I say to you, in the new world, when the Son of Man will sit on his glorious throne, you who have followed me will also sit on twelve thrones, judging the twelve tribes of Israel. The one who conquers, I will grant him to sit with me on my throne, as I also conquered and sat down with my Father on his throne." (Matt 19:28; Rev 3:21)

This study of kings, the kingdom, and the priesthood, has highlighted the importance of the offices of the king and priest in the plan of God to save the world. I have cast these offices in the frames of the primary institutions of marriage and family. The Messiah Jesus Christ, King of the world, descended from the family of King David, and that is why He is called the "son of David." The high priest and the Levitical priests came from the family of Levi. And Christ, our High Priest, was from the family, or tribe, of Judah, the family being the microcosm of the church; that which is obtained in the family signals what will be obtained in the church.

4.10.6. God's Revelation as King: Ancient Israel and Traditional Bafut

In chapters 2 and 3, we saw that there were many similarities in the cultures of ancient Israel and traditional Bafut. And as stated previously, God put symbols and institutions in the two cultures that would enable the peoples to discover God, the Creator. God presented Himself to the people of Israel as King, and the people of Israel were ruled by Him. Christ came as the King of the Jews. Bafut is a kingdom and Bafut traditional religion reveres the Fon, their king. The king was the high priest in the traditional religious system. He led priests who made annual sacrifices at important shrines in the land. He was the mediator between people and the ancestors, whose spirits the Bafut people worship, even now. The ancestors, though dead, are present in, and control, the everyday lives of the people.

We are going to look at the attributes of the king in both Israel and Bafut so as to best appreciate the similarities and see why God made it so. We will also see how important it is that Jesus Christ, the Messiah, came as King among the Jews, the implications of this truth for the history of salvation, and how this is relevant for the Bafut people in their culture.

The royal family in Bafut is very influential, and members of the royal family enjoy a lot of privileges, particularly the princes, who are given principalities—territories over which they rule.

Families in Bafut are traced following roots that link them to some member of the monarchy that ruled the land in history. Although there are no family shrines, the Bafut people can talk about their family god, *nwì ǹdâ maà*, (the god of the house of my mother). It should be noted here that while the Jews will talk of the God of their fathers, the Bafut talk of the god of their mother.

Some of the questions I will be asking and trying to answer as regards the gospel and the purpose of God for the Bafut people are as follows: Given all that God has put in the culture, the institutions of marriage and the family, and the king and the kingdom, how can this help us in presenting the gospel to the people in a meaningful and relevant way? Given the power of the king and the influence and privileges of the royal family, how will this be exploited in the presentation of the gospel? How is this relevant in salvation History?

The centenary of the church in Bafut was celebrated in the year 2011. The king of Bafut was highly involved in the celebration. And it is worth noting that the church in Bafut started in the palace of the Fon, the traditional ruler. He provided a place where the Christians worshipped until the first church house was built, not far from the palace. And when the New Testament was translated and given to the Bafut people, the Fon (i.e., the king) said that he wanted me and him to make a covenant with God— that we would not die until we had given the whole Bible to the people. He said that giving the whole Bible (New Testament and Old Testament) to the people would make it easy for him to govern them. Given the attitude of the king, there is no doubt that he could be an agent in the accomplishment of God's will and advancement of the kingdom of God in his kingdom. Work on translating the Old Testament into the Bafut language for the Bafut people started in 2022, and the Fon has been very involved in the work, promoting it among the Bafut people.

Fig. 4: Ancient Israel and Bafut Traditional Society: Salvation History

King / Kingship

Israel	Bafut
God	The Fon
Attributes:	Attributes:
-Sovereign	-Sovereign
-Almighty	-Almighty
-Most High	-Most High
-King of kings	-King of kings
-Father of all	-Father of all
Chritianity	Bafut Traditional Religion
(the Gospel of Christ)	
Christ:	The Fon:
-God (the Father)	-Kwifor (Father of the Fon)
-God (the Son)	-Representing the gods
-God (the Holy Spirit)	-Spirits of the ancestors / Evil spirits
-Son of God	-Son of Kwifor
-Lord of lords	-Lord of lords
-Annointed / Messiah	-Annointed
-Mediator	-Mediator
-Elder brother / Firstborn	-Father of All

A look at the above diagram (Fig. 4) shows in an amazing way how God, in His foreknowledge, placed in both ancient Israel and Bafut traditional society concepts, symbols, and institutions which will reveal who He is so that these can be used as redemptive analogies. All these are pieces that, when connected together, tell the salvation history—the story of the God of the Bible reaching down and out to save all of mankind. And as Paul tells us, He is "God, our Saviour, who desires all people to be saved and to come to the knowledge of the truth" (1 Tim 2:4–5).

Jesus Christ is seen as God the Son. And the mission of Jesus in the world will be to save people and make them children of God. And so the family motif runs from God the Father down through Adam, Abraham, and David to Jesus Christ, the Incarnate Son of God, and then to us, children of God through Christ.

The divine kingship, as seen in ancient Israel, originates from the Creator God, who rules over His creation; and God is seen as the universal king (Exod 15:18; Ps 93; 97). He is called "the LORD of hosts, the God of the armies of Israel" (1 Sam 17:45). God is acknowledged as ruler over His people (1 Sam 8:7; 12:12–15), providing for them and protecting and delivering them from their enemies through mighty acts (Exod 9–17). The sovereign rule of God over nature, the nations, and His people is attested to by the attributes given to Him, as seen in Fig. 4 above. He is Almighty and the King of kings.

In ancient Israel, the king was given honour and respect, and the people looked to him, as to the Lord God, for protection and direction. And so the king was given some of the attributes of God. This is so because he went before the people in battle and was their protector, defender, and deliverer. As previously stated, the king was the anointed of the Lord. And so we read in the prayer of the pilgrim going up to Jerusalem:

> Behold our shield, O God; look on the face of your anointed! (Ps 84:9)

Here in this verse, the king is called the "anointed" of the Lord and "a shield." The shield is a metaphor often applied to the Lord. The king was called to represent Israel before God and to model faithfulness before the people in order to keep them serving God faithfully.

Traditional Bafut has the same worldview regarding kingship. The Fon has the same attributes as God Almighty: he is the sovereign ruler above all kings (*Tsyaà bɨ̀ fɔ̀*, which means he is king above all kings, or King of kings) and father of all.

When it comes to the kingdom of God in the New Testament, the focus is on how God ministers to His people and governs them through Jesus Christ, the heir of King David. This looks forward to when God, Creator of the universe, will in the end rule all nations (as seen in the psalms referenced above).

As regards Christianity and Bafut traditional religion (BTR), we also see correspondences as listed in fig. 4. God, the Father of Jesus, is matched with Kwifor, the Father of the Fon. Jesus, the Son of God, is marched with the Fon, Son of Kwifor. Just as Christ is Lord of lords, the Fon is also the Lord of lords. While we have the Holy Spirit in Christianity, in BTR we have the gods, spirits of the ancestor, and evil spirits. The Fon is the mediator between the people and the ancestors (gods). The Fon is also seen as the anointed. So, in a unique way, the spiritual worldview of BTR prepares the Bafut people for the gospel, since they already know what the concepts mean.

5

MARRIAGE IN THE NEW TESTAMENT

5.1. Foundation of Marriage and Family in the New Testament

The coming of Jesus, the Christ, Saviour, and the light of the world, is a fulfilment of prophecy foretold in the Scriptures as early as from the Creation in Genesis (Gen 3:15), in Isaiah (Isa 60:1–2), and in other Scriptures, to the last book of the Old Testament, Malachi (Mal 4:2). And at the birth of John the Baptist, the one to prepare the way of Christ the Messiah, Zachariah exuberantly praises God and declares,

> Blessed be the Lord God of Israel, for he has visited and redeemed his people and has raised up a horn of salvation for us in the house of his servant David. And you, child, will be called the prophet of the Most High; for you will go before the Lord to prepare his ways, because of the tender mercy of our God, whereby the sunrise shall visit us from on high to give light to those who sit in darkness and in the shadow of death, to guide our feet into the way of peace. (Luke 1:68–69, 76, 78–79)

It is important to note that whereas God could have chosen to have the Saviour come directly from heaven without any human agent, He chose a young woman promised in marriage to a man, thus giving value to marriage and the family. And when Jesus is born, the Gospel writers Matthew and Luke are keen to prove that Jesus is the Messiah predicted in the Old Testament. This is why Matthew, knowing the importance of genealogies in Jewish history and tradition, starts his Gospel with "the Genealogy of Jesus Christ, the son of David, the son of Abraham" (Matt 1:1). Jews used genealogies to establish a person's heritage, legitimacy, and inheritance rights. A person's ancestry also proves his inclusion in the covenant that God made with Israel. So it was important that Jesus' ancestry and mission be established. Jesus (GK "Iēsous"), Yeshua, or Yehoshua (Joshua) means in Hebrew "Yahweh saves." And Christ (Gk "Christos"), which is from the Hebrew word "mashiakh"(messiah [meaning "anointed"]) points back to David, the anointed king of Israel. Biblically, the designation "Messiah" has come to point to the promised "anointed one" who will rule the people of Israel in righteousness and justice (2 Sam 7:11–16); Isaiah 11:3–4). The *of* phrase "son of David" brings to mind the image of the Messiah and his royal lineage, who will, as predicted, establish his throne (in Jerusalem) and the kingdom of Israel and rule with righteousness and justice. The son of Abraham, on the other hand, evokes the covenant that God made with Abraham, which established Israel as His chosen people and affirmed that the people of all nations in the world would be blessed through his life (Gen 12:1–3; 22:18).

Matthew traces the lineage of Jesus from Abraham in order to underline His Jewish heritage, while Luke (Luke 3:23–38) traces it from Joseph back to Adam to show that Jesus came to fulfil the hopes of all men as the new or second Adam, who will accomplish the creative purposes of God and enable all men to seek and find God. Paul affirms this in the following text:

> The God who made the world and everything in it, being Lord of heaven and earth made from one man every nation of mankind to live on all the face of the

earth, having determined allotted periods and the boundaries of their dwelling place, that they should seek God, and perhaps feel their way towards him and find him. (Acts 17:24, 26–27)

In the genealogy provided in Fig. 2 (section 4.10.4) above, I have sought to reconcile both Matthew and Luke's perspectives. I have traced the genealogy of Jesus Christ from Adam to Joseph.

Matthew and Luke did a good job to prove that Jesus was the promised Messiah, because what had been promised in Old Testament prophecy was coming true before the eyes of the Jews, especially when Jesus started His public ministry. Matthew points this out when Jesus is forced by the action of Herod and the Jewish leaders in Judea to withdraw and go to Galilee. His presence in Galilee fulfilled the following prophecy:

> The land of Zebulun and the land of Naphtali,
> the way of the sea, beyond the Jordan, Galilee of the Gentiles—
> the people dwelling in darkness
> have seen a great light,
> and for those dwelling in the region and shadow of death,
> on them a light has dawned. (Matt 4:15–16)

The fact that Jesus was forced by circumstances to begin His ministry in Galilee proved the point made by Luke that Jesus, though a Jew, came not only for the Jews but also for the nations, the Gentiles.

5.2. The Family of Jesus

After giving us the family line of Jesus Christ, Matthew and Luke go on to introduce us to the family of Jesus, beginning with His birth.

5.2.1. The Birth of Jesus

Both Matthew and Luke report the birth of Jesus. Matthew tells us that Joseph is the husband of Mary, the mother of Jesus Christ (Matt 1:18–19). When Joseph realized that Mary was pregnant and was thinking of divorcing her, an angel of the Lord appeared to him in a dream and said, "Joseph, son of David, do not fear to take Mary as your wife, for that which is conceived in her is from the Holy Spirit" (Matt 1:20).

This assured Joseph of the origin of the child to be born. This child was from above, of God, and therefore the Son of God, born to a human father. The angel also tells us the lineage of Joseph; he is the son of David. The lineage and destiny of this child was prophesied by Isaiah. He would be a sign pointing to the Christ as the ultimate Messiah, who would bring God's presence into a broken world. He would be called Immanuel, meaning "God with us" (Isaiah 7:14). Such was the importance of the truth of this message that Matthew would make it abundantly clear (Matt 1:23). God being with someone means that God is with him to guide and help him fulfil his calling. Christ comes to help us do the will of God.

Luke, in his account, also brings this up when he explains why Joseph went up to Bethlehem, the city of David, to register with his wife for the census ordered by Quirinius. He went there "because he was of the house and lineage of David" (Luke 2:4). Luke goes on to report the birth of Jesus in Bethlehem. When this child is born, in the humblest of places, in the obscurity of the night, in an obscure environment, God Himself announces it to humble shepherds, but in a spectacular and glorious way. The angel of the Lord appears in the glory of the Lord to the shepherds, who are struck by fear. And at the same time, a host of heavenly angels appear, forming a glorious mass choir, singing the first Christmas carol:

> Glory to God in the highest, and on earth peace
> among those with whom he is pleased! (Luke 2:14)

The shepherds then hasten to go and see the baby Jesus and tell Mary and Joseph what the Lord has shown them. These revelations impress and assure the parents of this special baby that they are caught up in the gracious and glorious work of the Lord. Mary, in particular, is highly impacted by the weight of the revelations. The text goes on to state that she "treasured up all these things, pondering them in her heart" (v. 19).

The birth of this child was also revealed far afield, as Matthew reports it: A star appeared to wise men in the east and led them first to Herod, to announce to him that this child was the King of the Jews and that they had come to worship him (Matt 2:1–2). The star then led them to the child. And

> they saw the child with Mary his mother, and fell down and worshiped him. Then, opening their treasures, they offered him gifts, gold and frankincense and myrrh. (Matt 2:13)

In their accounts of the birth of Christ, Matthew and Luke bring up a number of things about the "holy family." First, concerning the child Jesus, He is the Son of God, though born to human parents Mary and Joseph. This child comes from the Father through the Holy Spirit. And suddenly, now and here, the Trinity that was active at Creation is working at the Incarnation.[64] God has indeed come down to humans, taking on a human form, becoming human, and yet still exhibiting all his glory:

> And the Word became flesh and dwelt among us, and we have seen his glory, glory as of the only Son from the Father, full of grace and truth. (John 1:14)

This means that the tabernacle, which was a shadow of what is now its reality, is here among people: First of all, God makes His dwelling in a human body! This took on flesh in Mary's womb! This is well expressed by Lisé and Mascaras (2013:36) in the following quote:

---

[64] The Incarnation was not an act of creation; neither was it recreation, such as the new creation or regeneration, which is akin to believers being made new in Christ through the work of the Holy Spirit. The Incarnation is God entering and coming into the world He created.

> The flesh of Christ was not some heavenly substance, it was as real and as human as our own bodies, and hence Jesus, in his human nature, was one of us. He was not some third sort of being, between God and man, but true God and true man.[65]

Secondly, God has come to dwell in a family, among other members of His family. This also means that He has come to a particular people, the Jews, and in their culture. Jesus was not an Arab, European, or African. All these peoples are related to him as peoples because they have their origin in God their Creator. So all attempts to represent Jesus, whether in the colour and shape of any of these other peoples, are misrepresentations. Jesus, of course, is different from all humans because He is God and was not created.

Thirdly, Jesus has come to dwell, or tabernacle, in the heart of whoever believes in Him and opens his heart to receive Him. And He does not come alone; together with the Father and Holy Spirit does He also find a home in the believer.

Fourthly, Jesus has come to also dwell in the church, the body of those who believe in Him and are baptized in His name. And these become members of His body; and He becomes the head of the body. He will become the Bridegroom, and the church, His bride.

The accounts of the birth of Jesus bring out important truths about the parents of Jesus, Mary and Joseph. Though humble country people, they were chosen firstly because they were prepared and set apart for a purpose. As for Joseph, Matthew tells us that he was "a just man" (Matt 1:19). And of Mary, it had been determined and foretold long ago what kind of a lady she would be—the one to carry the God child. Matthew refers to this in the quote from Isaiah, the prophet, "The virgin shall conceive and bear son" (Matt 1:23). So she was not just a virgin, as we have seen in ancient Israeli culture (2.4). She was specially consecrated even before she was born. So

---

[65] The word "consubstantial," found in the Nicene Creed, was used by the fourth ecumenical council, the Council of Chalcedon, held in 451, to describe the true divinity and the true humanity of Christ. It taught that Christ is "consubstantial with the Father, as regards his divinity, and consubstantial with us as regards his humanity."

Mary and Joseph were special vessels, consecrated; and they would be made truly holy by the Incarnation. The Lord in Mary, the divine presence, makes her markedly holy.

5.2.2. The Siblings of Jesus

Did Jesus have brothers and sisters? If yes, how many? The question of Jesus' siblings has been in dispute since the early days of Christianity. An objective and unbiased discussion of the question has been hindered because it has been coloured by doctrinal and denominational leanings. However, the accounts of the gospel writers and also the epistles talk about the brothers and sisters of Jesus. Matthew says the following about the matter:

> Is not this the carpenter's son? Is not his mother called Mary? And are not his brothers James and Joseph and Simon and Judas? And are not all his sisters with us? (Matt 13:55–56)

Mark, in his account, gives the same list of the four brothers:

> James and Joses and Judas and Simon. (Mark 6:3)

"Joses" is the same name as "Joseph," while Judas is called "Jude" elsewhere in New Testament, as we read at the beginning of the epistle of Jude:

> Jude, a servant of Jesus Christ and brother of James. (Jude 1:1)

Jude, the writer of the epistle, is seen by biblical scholars as the brother of Jesus. In a solemn declaration, Paul names James as the brother of Jesus Christ:

> But I saw none of the other apostles except James the Lord's brother. (In what I am writing to you, before God, I do not lie!) (Gal 1:19–20)

From the Scriptures, we read that Jesus had several sisters (at the very least, two sisters). The question, "And are not all his sisters with us?" suggests that the sisters were more than two.

We notice that in all the references that are made to the siblings of Jesus, they are called "brothers" and "sisters" and not "cousins" or simply "relatives" or "kinsmen." And according to the ESV footnote to Acts 1:14, the possessive phrase "his brothers" has the alternative reading of "his brothers and sisters," and the plural form of the Greek word "*adelphoi,*" translated as "brothers," refers to siblings in a family. And in New Testament usage, depending on the context, "adelphoi" may refer either to men or to both men and women who are siblings.

God picked people of humble beginnings to be members of the family of His Son. However, though Mary and Joseph were special instruments providentially picked, they had personal responsibilities, as they had to be available, trusting, willing, and obedient. The other children born to Joseph and Mary were ordinary, and typical of any family. They were not to suddenly become holy and consecrated, although Paul intimates that children of believers are consecrated because of their parents. He means that they are more likely to be brought to faith because of parental position and influence (1 Cor 7:14). These other children of Joseph and Mary had their doubts and questions regarding the faith. They initially did not believe the person and mission of their elder brother, Jesus. Was this person—who lived with them, did the same chores in the family, and helped in their father's trade—what He was telling the world that He was? Could it be that He was the expected Messiah, the Saviour of Israel? They, too, like a majority of the Jews, were not convinced about the person, the calling, and the Messianic claims of Jesus. This is what John the Gospel writer says about them:

For not even his brothers believed in him. (John 7:5)

However, they eventually became believers, most probably after the resurrection of Jesus. After the Ascension, just before Pentecost, the apostles and other followers of Christ, "with one accord were devoting themselves to prayer, together with the women and

Mary the mother of Jesus, and his brothers" (Acts 1:14). This is an indication that the brothers and sisters of Jesus at this point were believers. His brother James became one of the pillars of the church in Jerusalem (Gal 2:9). Actually he was the leader of the Jerusalem church (Acts 15:13; 21:18). It is he who wrote the epistle of James, while his other brother, Jude, wrote the epistle of Jude.

5.2.3. The Family in the New Testament

We have treated the family of God as seen in the Old Testament (Fig. 1) and as presented in the New Testament (4.2.1). The family of God in the New Testament still starts with God as Father. Jesus Christ is the Son of God and the elder brother of those who believe in Him and become children of God by adoption. This is shown in the following diagram:

Fig. 5 Our Place in God's Family Tree

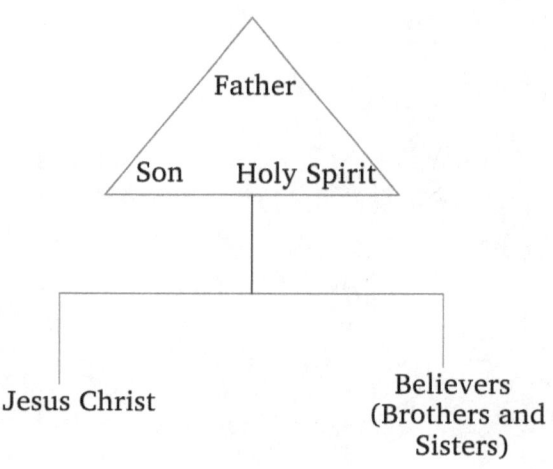

As the sketch in fig. 5 shows, God the Father, Son, and Holy Spirit work together, each playing His role, to make us born anew to become God's children. And through adoption we become brothers (and sisters) of Jesus and coheirs with Him.

Jesus is the centrepiece of marriage and the family. Here the family boils down to Christ and the members of His church, which is His body. The following diagram (Fig. 6) is a representation of the New Testament family and marriage structure:

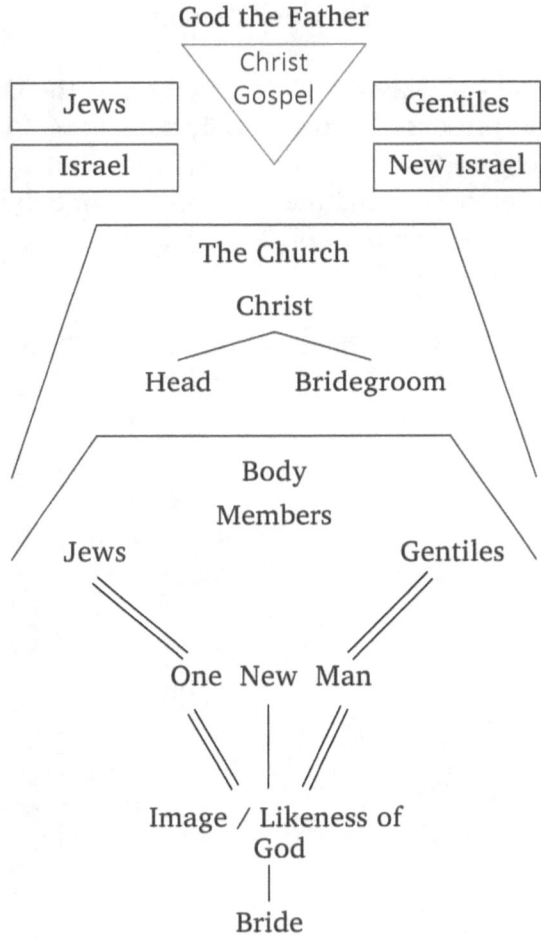

Fig. 6: Marriage and the Family
New Testament

The New Testament is the fulfilment of the Old Testament prophecies (Jer 31:31–34), the inauguration of the Christian era, and the establishment of the new covenant. Jesus, the seed of Abraham, son of David, and the Incarnate Son of God, comes with the good news of salvation, grace, and glory. He transforms both the Jews and Gentiles, making them new beings, and reconciles both peoples, making peace (Eph 2:8–14):

> But now in Christ Jesus you who once were far off have been brought near by the blood of Christ. For he himself is our peace, who has made us both one and has broken down in his flesh the dividing wall of hostility (Eph 2:13–14)

Both Jews and Gentiles have sinned without distinction, and so Christ proclaims the kingdom of God in the gospel of salvation, the Word of truth, to both Jews and Gentiles. The Holy Spirit effects a transformation and cleansing by the sacrificial blood of Christ. Paul describes this transformation in the following Scripture:

> And such were some of you. But you were washed, you were sanctified, you were justified in the name of the Lord Jesus Christ and by the Spirit of our God. (1Cor 6:11)

After being justified, Jew and Gentile believers will continue to be sanctified and transformed progressively into the image and glory of God (2 Cor 3:18) for the end-times presentation as the bride of Christ, blameless and irreproachable, as described in the following verses:

> Husbands, love your wives, as Christ loved the church and gave himself up for her, that he might sanctify her, having cleansed her by the washing of water with the word, so that he might present the church to himself in splendour, without spot or wrinkle or any such thing, that she might be holy and without blemish. (Eph 5:25–27)

The redeemed become the splendid bride of Christ, bearing his image and that of God.

God's ultimate purpose for His children is His glory. We can see from Scripture that the goal of salvation is that our Father be glorified. This is why, after Israel had rebelled against Him even after the redemption from Egypt, He, remembering His covenant with the patriarchs, had compassion on the children of Israel; and for the sake of His name and glory, He decided to gather His sons and daughters back to their homeland. This is what He said:

> I will say to the north, Give up, and to the south,
> Do not withhold; bring my sons from afar and my
> daughters from the end of the earth, everyone who
> is called by my name, whom I created for my glory,
> whom I formed and made. (Isa 43:6–7)

So, in order to see the ultimate fulfilment of this goal, God in His love, mercy and grace, sent His Son, Jesus Christ, our elder brother, head of the body, His Church, to gather all the people of God, wherever they may be, to Himself. And Jesus, who was fully conscious of this goal, would work faithfully to realize it. And consequently He says in the gospel of John,

> I am the good shepherd. I lay down my life for the
> sheep. And I have other sheep that are not of this
> fold. I must bring them also, and they will listen to
> my voice. So there will be one flock, one shepherd.
> (John 10:14–16)

It was the will of the Father that the Son should come and redeem all of humanity—not only the Jews, the chosen people of God, but also the Gentiles. And so the cross was the means of accomplishing the goal and also the ultimate price, for His utmost glory. And again, He said,

> "Now is my soul troubled. And what shall I say?
> 'Father, save me from this hour?' But for this purpose
> I have come to this hour. Father, glorify your name."

Then a voice came from heaven: "I have glorified it, and I will glorify it again. And I, when I am lifted up from the earth, will draw all people to myself." (John 12:27–28, 32)

The cross has then become the means of accomplishing the ultimate goal of God. Through the cross Jesus saved the world, breaking down the dividing wall between Jews and Gentiles and uniting both as one new man, the children of God the Father. Through suffering and dying, Jesus was exalted and also glorified through the cross, as Paul explains in Philippians 2:5–11.

So the saved people of God do not only bear His image and glory; they become the glorious bride of Christ and a display of the glory of God.

5.3. Reaffirmation and Consolidation of Marriage and the Family

In the New Testament, Christ and Paul built on what God had said and done at Creation. There was no further attempt made at changing what God had established.

5.3.1. Jesus' Affirmation

When the Pharisees came to test Jesus on the nature of marriage, Jesus seized the opportunity to nail down what God had said about marriage and the family. Marriage establishes a union that is lifelong and should not be dissolved. Marriage brings two individuals, a man and woman, to become one in nature, purpose, and function. And so He told the Pharisees:

> Have you not read that he who created them from the beginning made them male and female, and said, "Therefore a man shall leave his father and his mother and hold fast to his wife, and the two shall

become one flesh?" So they are no longer two but one flesh. What therefore God has joined together, let not man separate. (Matt 19:4–6)

Here in this declaration, Jesus affirms that (1) God created man and woman, (2) He created them male and female, (3) marriage is between a man (husband) and woman (wife),[66] (4) this presupposes procreation (fruitfulness), and so the family unit will be made of father, mother, and children (5), the bonding between husband and wife will be inseparable since they form one body, (6) the man will leave his father and mother and be bonded to his wife, which means that his faithfulness and responsibility to his wife, meeting her needs, will come before his responsibilities to his parents (though in no way does this suggest that he should no longer take care of his parents), and (7) the underlying truth is that the established form of marriage is monogamy.

5.3.2. Paul's Affirmation

Paul affirms the basic truths about marriage and the family, as instituted at Creation. He in several of his epistles, explains and highlights some of the truths about marriage and family.

5.3.2.1. *Leaving, Cleaving, and One Flesh*

The first thing that Paul affirms is the nature and form of marriage, as stated below:

> "Therefore a man shall leave his father and mother and hold fast to his wife, and the two shall become one flesh." This mystery is profound, and I am saying that it refers to Christ and the church. (Eph 5:31–32)

---

[66] There is no room for gay or lesbian marriage (i.e., same-sex marriage [homosexuality]).

Paul, just like Jesus, affirms what is at the core of marriage. He affirms what God stated when He instituted marriage at Creation—that is, the nature and form of marriage, bonding in marriage as husband and wife, bonding to form a family (bearing fruit of the womb), and bonding within the family.[67] When a man enters into a marriage relation with a woman, the strong bond that tied him to his parents is loosened, and the man is let loose and becomes bonded to his wife, and so the two become one flesh.

Walter Trobisch (1971) gives a very dynamic, practical, and meaningful description of marriage in terms of leaving, cleaving, and becoming one flesh. These three steps in the process are represented in the following diagram:

Fig. 7: The Marriage Triangle
Leaving, Cleaving, and One Flesh

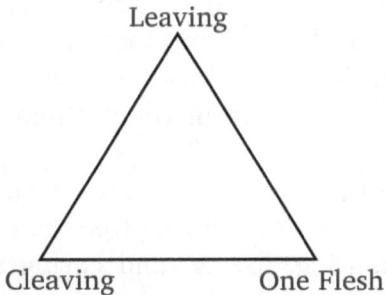

5.3.2.1.1. *Leaving (The Top Angle)*

According to Trobisch, marriage begins with leaving. However, leaving is here conceived of both literally and metaphorically. Although the Bible talks of the man leaving his father and mother, Trobisch focuses on physical leaving when the bride leaves her

---

[67] As stated earlier, the ideal form of marriage, per the reading of Genesis 2:24 (quoted above by Paul in Ephesians 5:31), is monogamy; and the nature of marriage is between a man and a woman, thus excluding same-sex marriage and all other perversions as we see being promoted today.

father's house and is taken to her husband's home and people. As previously shown, both in ancient Israel and Bafut traditional society, the bride was escorted to her marriage home in a public occasion. Leaving is what serves as a testimony of alegal act, because it occurs in public, witnessed by both curious onlookers and the people taking part in the procession. Since leaving is the first act and thus what sanctions marriage as such, it is placed at the top of the triangle. Leaving as a legal act is sanctioned either in a religious service at church, where the couple is married by a minister and declared husband and wife, or in a civil status office where the marriage ceremony is conducted by a government official, and the couple is given a licence or a marriage certificate. Thus the public act of leaving makes marriage legal.

Leaving gives the couple space to develop and form their own family, free from parents' interference. Leaving is likened to cutting an umbilical cord so that a baby can develop and grow as a separate human being. In marriage ceremonies, parents have been exhorted to leave their children alone, because many problems in the marital home have been caused by mothers-in-law, who have sought to control couples and have destabilized their marriages.

Leaving does not imply that the parents can no longer advise or help a couple; neither does leaving free the children from their obligations of honouring, loving, and caring for their parents. Leaving is not only an outward act but also an inward one, and both the man and the woman have to leave and cleave together.

5.3.2.1.2. *Cleaving (Left Angle)*

While leaving describes the public and legal aspect of marriage, cleaving describes the personal and relational aspect of marriage. Cleaving means sticking together or being glued together. The husband and wife are glued together and are thus close to each other. There can therefore not be separation without tearing and injury. This is why divorce is difficult and harmful. Since in a deep sense only two people can be glued together, this speaks against polygamy.

Cleaving means deciding to love—to specially love. Cleaving boils down to mature love; it is love in which one has decided to remain faithful to one person and to share one's whole life with this one person.

5.3.2.1.3. *Becoming One Flesh (Right Angle)*

Becoming one flesh describes the physical aspect of marriage. This aspect is as essential for marriage as the legal and personal aspects. This is the physical union between husband and wife, which is God's will for marriage. The consummation of a marriage occurs in their sexual union. And this is followed by the blessings of children. The physical union of husband and wife is as important to God as their being legally married and staying faithful. Paul considers this as a duty that the couple owe to each other.

Trobisch (1971:27–28) describes what becoming one flesh means in the following quote:

> It means that two persons share everything they have, not only their bodies, not only their material possessions, but also their thinking and their feeling, their joy and their suffering, their hopes and their fears, their successes and their failures. To become one flesh means that two persons become completely one with body, soul, and spirit and yet they remain two different persons. This is the innermost mystery of marriage.

The three steps—leaving, cleaving, and becoming one flesh—are necessary for there to be marriage. These, as we have seen, are

1. the upper angle (the public legal act, or wedding),
2. the left angle (love or faithfulness), and
3. the right angle (physical union, or sex).

Since a triangle is not a triangle if one of the angles is lacking, so too marriage is no marriage if one of the three aspects in the process is lacking.

Trobisch makes the interesting point that marriage does not necessarily require children to make it marriage. While it is the desire of most couples to have children, children are an added blessing in marriage. "Children are a blessing, but they are an additional blessing to marriage ... Even if there are no children, the one-flesh union does not become meaningless. Barrenness is no reason for divorce."

5.3.2.1.4. *The Cohabitation of a Man and Woman Is Not Marriage*

It is common nowadays that a man and a woman would come to live together but avoid getting married for one reason or another. Because of material reasons, for example, they may not want to get married officially. This could be because of inheritance purposes—because they want to avoid the joint property option (matrimonial property). And so, for selfish reasons, they or their children do not want their property to be owned by the other partner. In some countries—for example, Switzerland—some partners do not want to marry because putting their income together would entail paying a higher tax on the total amount, and so they see marriage as punishment. Some couples just want to avoid the responsibilities and commitment of the marriage contract and so will not want to make a life-commitment to the other partner. And so the term "partners" has come to describe such couples. In this context, the term "partners" has come to acquire a new sense, making it the synonym of "married" or "spouses." However, Jesus teaches us in John 4:16–20 that such a relationship is not marriage, as we read in the following verse:

> For you have had five husbands, and the one you now have is not your husband. What you have said is true.(John 4:18)

By saying this to the woman, Jesus implied that merely living together does not constitute a marriage. For, as previously stated, marriage requires some kind of official sanction and a public ceremony during which the man and woman commit themselves to the obligations of marriage.

5.3.2.2. *The Mystery of Marriage*

Walter Trobisch calls the marriage union that makes a man and woman one flesh "the innermost mystery of marriage."

Paul, the rabbi of the Torah and interpreter of the New Testament teachings of Christ and the church, affirms the basic truths of marriage as stated by God at Creation and reinterprets these with regard to the relation of Christ to the church. In doing so, he brings out something about the meaning of marriage that is deeper and yet more revealing. He says, "This mystery is profound, and I am saying that it refers to Christ and the church." The mystery of the church will be explained in the next section.

Paul was a sharp and deep thinker, a reputable theologian unrivalled in his generation.[68] Here he brings up the term "mystery," which he has used in various contexts in a number of his epistles. He says that the fact that the man and woman become one flesh is a mystery, and this mystery will reflect the nature of the church and the relationship that exists between Christ and the church.

According to Paul, marriage is part of the mystery of God's will. As a result of the abundant grace which God lavishes on believers in all wisdom, He makes known to them "the mystery of his will, according to his purpose, which he set forth in Christ, as a plan for the fullness of time, to unite all things in Him, things in heaven and things on earth" (Eph 1:9–10). Here Paul wraps up the whole purpose of marriage, as the beginning of the fulfilment of the will of God, planned in eternity, to be realized fully at the end time. This

---

[68] Paul's writings on some matters were so deep and hard to understand that simpletons and false teachers, out of ignorance, would distort and so be teaching a false gospel or a distorted version of Paul's message (2 Peter 3:16).

plan was to unite the Jews and Gentiles to form one body in Christ. This is elaborated on by Paul in his epistles to the Ephesians and, partly, the Colossians. The marriage bond, as we shall see, will be an illustration of the unity of the body of Christ becoming one with Him, the Head of the church. And this union will be consummated at the end times when the church, purified and made perfect and splendid, is presented as the bride to Christ, the Bridegroom.

"Mystery" in this context means something that was hidden before but has now been revealed, made known clearly, thanks to the teachings of Christ, the inspiration of the Holy Spirit, and the instruction of inspired teachers and men of God.

Paul's use of the word "mystery" is most revealing in Ephesians and Colossians. In Ephesians (3:3–5) and Colossians (1:26–27), he tells us the content of the mystery—first the mystery of the church and then the mystery of Christ. It is God who revealed this mystery to him through Christ (on the road to Damascus and on various occasions) and by the Spirit. This mystery was not made known to people prior to when Paul was writing. Even though Moses and the prophets had written about Christ and His salvation to the nations of the world (the Gentiles), and although God had even promised to Abraham that the nations would be blessed through him (Gen 12:3), the full realization of who Christ was and the extent of the salvation that would come to the Gentiles was not fully understood until after the giving of the Holy Spirit, who enables God's people to understand spiritual things, including the truths about Christ (1 Cor 2:8–12). This mystery had been revealed to the holy apostles and prophets by the Spirit:

> This mystery is that the Gentiles are fellow heirs, members of the same body, and partakers of the promise in Christ Jesus through the gospel. (Eph 3:6)

And so in the above verse Paul gives us the content of the mystery concerning the Gentiles' inclusion as full partakers of the promises in Christ Jesus. He further gives the content of the mystery relating to Christ in the following teaching to the Colossian believers:

> The mystery hidden for ages and generations but now revealed to his saints. To them God chose to make known how great among the Gentiles are the riches of the glory of this mystery, which is Christ in you, the hope of glory. (Col 1:26–27)

The glorious riches hidden in this mystery are embodied in Christ, and so when He comes into the lives of believers, and when the Holy Spirit gives them understanding, they will have hope and be assured that they will be glorified on the day of His return.

Another word for "mystery" is "secret," which can refer to the secrets of God, as we read in the following verse:

> The secret things belong to the LORD our God, but the things that are revealed belong to us and to our children forever, that we may do all the words of this law. (Deut 29:29)

The above quoted verses tell us not only what "mystery" means but also the raison d'etre of mysteries (i.e., why God reveals his mysteries or secrets to his covenant people). He reveals His secrets to us and our children so that we may obey Him as we enjoy the covenantal relationship with Him. It is important to know that God chooses to reveal his secrets generally to those who fear Him (Ps 25:14). The friendship ("the secret counsel") of the Lord is with the faithful, those who fear him and keep the covenant. The more people obey, putting into practice what they know, the more God will teach them and reveal further truths to them (John 7:17). Jesus revealed important truths or secrets to His disciples while He was with them, and the Holy Spirit continued to reveal more things to them after He returned to the Father (John 14:15–17; 15:15; 16:13).

The following verse will shed more light on the important riches and blessings of our knowledge of God and relationship with Him with regard to His revealed truths:

> There is a God in heaven who reveals mysteries, and he has made known to King Nebuchadnezzar what will be in the latter days. (Dan 2:28)

When we live in communion with God and listen to Him, He reveals things to us: things as they are and those that will happen in the future. God uses the word "mystery" in various other contexts to refer to His plan of redemption and salvation, which is set forth in His Word and revealed progressively to His servants—first to the prophets, then to the apostles and the other gospel writers, and also to Paul. Paul testifies in various places that He was given stewardship of the truth of the Word revealed to Him personally by the Lord Jesus Christ, as we read in the following verses:

> The mystery hidden for ages and generations but now revealed to his saints. To them God chose to make known how great among the Gentiles are the riches of the glory of this mystery, which is Christ in you, the hope of glory. (Col 1:26–27)

Given that the man and woman were created in the image of God, God breathing the spirit of life into them, there was immediately a connection created between God and the human being. This is when the mystery of the union between God and man began—right at Creation. Jesus will mention this in the gospels when He talks about church unity (John 17) and the special relationship and union between Him and His followers. He likewise talks of our union in the Godhead. Let us take, for example, this statement of His:

> Because I live, you also will live. In that day, you will know that I am in my Father, and you in me, and I in you. (John 14:19–20)

From a human and logical perspective, it is incomprehensible that Christ can be in the Father and the Father in Him. Neither can we easily see how Christ can be in us and we in Him. However, these truths will become clear when we dig deeper and grow into them, as we experience the reality of God in our life with time. First of all, Paul uses the expression "in Christ" to explain the deep union we have with Christ. For example:

> If anyone is in Christ, he is a new creation. (2 Cor 5:17)

The other prepositional phrase regarding the Holy Spirit also shows a close relationship with the Spirit. For example:

> I was in the Spirit [i.e., surrounded by the presence of the Spirit]. (Rev 1:10)

As for the Godhead being in one another, this is understood first in the sense of the Trinity, the Three-in-One. For example:

> And Jesus, full of the Holy Spirit, returned from the Jordan and was led by the Spirit in the wilderness ... And Jesus returned in the power of the Spirit to Galilee.(Luke 4:1, 14)

As regards our being in God, it speaks of the redemption and our deliverance from the dominion of the world and Satan into the kingdom of God:

> He has delivered us from the domain of darkness and transferred us to the kingdom of his beloved Son, in whom we have redemption, the forgiveness of sins. (Col 1:1–140)

God takes us into His life. The initiative comes from Him. And as we live and work in communion with Him, His life and power flow into ours, and He lives in us and works in us and through us. His Spirit in us empowers and directs us, such that we would live and move in Him, as we read and have examples in the Scriptures. Simeon, a man who was so devoted to the Lord and communed with Him through the Spirit, lived virtually with God and in Him, as we read in Luke's gospel:

> And it had been revealed to him by the Holy Spirit that he would not see death before he had seen the Lord's Christ. And he came in the Spirit into the

temple, and when the parents brought in the child Jesus. (Luke 2:26–27)

Simeon was in such a close relationship with God that the redemptive and messianic plan had been revealed to Him.

Paul's closeness to the Lord, as seen in his close walk with Him and his total surrender to Him, opened the door for the Lord to come and take over his life, working in and through him, and progressively drawing him into Himself. So it is that Paul says towards the end of his ministry,

> I have been crucified with Christ. It is no longer I who live, but Christ who lives in me. (Gal 2:20)

Having experienced what it means to live in God, Paul found it easy to tell his audience that this reality could be the experience of all who turn from false gods and the darkness of sin to the living God:

> The God, who made the world and everything in it, being Lord of heaven and earth, does not live in temples made by man. [He is actually not far from each one of us, for]'In him we live and move and have our being;'as even some of your own poets have said. (Acts 17: 24 & 28)

Paul will declare to the believers in Corinth that God lived in them, as we read in the following verses:

> Do you not know that you are God's temple and that God's Spirit dwells in you?

> Or do you not know that your body is a temple of the Holy Spirit within you, whom you have from God? You are not your own. (1 Cor 3:16; 6:19)

On the other hand, God, who put His Spirit in us, longs to have us in His heart so that we will be irresistibly drawn into Him in love.

To this effect, James asks, "Or do you suppose it is to no purpose that the Scripture says, 'He yearns jealously over the spirit that he has made to dwell in us?'" (Jas 4:5).

Our spirits also cry to be connected with Him through the Word and the Spirit. We are born with a yearning for fellowship and communion with God. This is borne out by what Augustine said—that man is restless until he finds rest in God. Henri Nouwen echoes this truth when he says that God has given us a deep hunger for communion with Him, and that this yearning is a precious gift because it becomes a driving force in our spiritual journeys of faith. Nouwen (2011:21–22) defines communion in an experiential way:

> To believe in Jesus is to believe in Jesus as the one who is sent by God and in whom God's fullness becomes visible ... To believe in Jesus means to believe in the intimate, full total communion between the Father and the Son, that seeing Jesus is seeing the Father, touching Jesus is touching God ... And Jesus wants to include us in this intimate communion by giving us the holy Spirit ... In and through the Spirit we become full participants in the communion of love that Jesus shares with His Father. This is the mystery of redemption and the promise of the spiritual life.

Eldredge (2020:123) echoes what Nouwen says above in the following quote:

> Unity with God is the ultimate goal of human existence-a united life with God. Sadly, most believers have been given the impression that the sum total of the Christian life is faith, obedience, and service. Jesus invites us into something far more thrilling and beautiful and intimate than a life of Christian service. The intimacy that we can experience with God is absolutely wonderful.

Jesus' gentle rebuke to Martha, one of His dear friends, teaches us about the primacy of communion and fellowship with God. He told Martha, who placed service over being with the Master, that Mary had chosen the one thing needed. He told her,

> Martha, Martha, you are anxious and troubled about many things, but one thing is necessary. Mary has chosen the good portion, which will not be taken away from her. (Luke 10:41–42)

Fellowship with the Lord should be placed over service. The good portion that Mary had chosen was Jesus—being with Him. Jesus here is echoing what Scripture had taught to be treasured—that the greatest possession is close fellowship with the Lord, taken as one's "portion" in life (Ps 16:5; 27:4; 119:57). This is best expressed in the following Scripture:

> Whom have I in heaven but you? And there is nothing on earth that I desire besides you. My flesh and my heart may fail, but God is the strength of my heart and my portion forever. But for me it is good to be near God. (Ps 73:25–26, 28)

God had demonstrated this when He established the Levitical priesthood. He said the Levites would not have any portion as inheritance. The Lord God Himself would be their portion. This was repeated and emphasized by Joshua when he gave the tribes of Israel their portions:

> The Levites have no portion among you, for the priesthood of the LORD is their heritage. (Josh 18:7)

Being in communion with the Godhead is a journey of faith, where we see and get to know and experience the presence Jesus and the Father through the eyes of faith. This is why Jesus queried Philip as follows:

> Have I been with you so long, and you still do not know me, Philip? Whoever has seen me has seen the Father. How can you say, "Show us the Father?"

> Believe me that I am in the Father and the Father is
> in me. (John 14:9, 11)

Being in communion with the Lord is abiding in Him. Abiding in Christ is becoming closely connected to Him in fellowship as we dwell in His Word, meditating on it, taking it in, laying it on our hearts, and living continually in the presence of the Father and in obedience to Him and praying at all times in the Spirit. The Word of God puts us in union with the Father, Son, and Holy Spirit. We have to remember that the Word is God and Christ is the living word. And the Spirit works through the Word to produce spiritual life. We can obviously connect this to what Jesus told His disciples after the hard teaching about His flesh and blood. He said, "The words that I have spoken to you are spirit and life" (John 6:63). The Spirit works through the Word, teaching us and giving us understanding and enabling us to live through it, by it, and in it. This is why Jesus asks us to abide in His Word (John 8:31; 15:7). Abiding in Jesus and abiding in His Word mean the same thing, and this enables us to accomplish untold things in life as we see in the following Word:

> Abide in me, and I in you. As the branch cannot bear
> fruit by itself, unless it abides in the vine, neither can
> you, unless you abide in me. If you abide in me, and
> my words abide in you, ask whatever you wish, and
> it will be done for you. (John 15:4, 7)

When the Word abides in us, we will also abide in God and in Christ, as we can read from the following verse:

> Let what you heard from the beginning abide in you.
> If what you heard from the beginning abides in you,
> then you too will abide in the Son and in the Father.
> (1John 2:24)

What is heard from the beginning is the original gospel message of salvation, which Paul describes as "the power of God for salvation" (Rom 1:16). And of course, as we have seen so far, when the Word of Christ abides in us, we also abide in Christ, and consequently

God and the Spirit abide in us. When we are saved, salvation experientially brings us into the family of God. And henceforth we live in Him and in Christ and are changed and renewed, and we are continually transformed into the image of God (2 Cor 5:17; 3:18).

Our abiding in God, and He in us, therefore speaks of the closest relation we can have with the Father, Son, and Holy Spirit. And so we live in fellowship with the God head by being in the Word, in prayer, and living in obedience, as John spells out in his epistle:

> Whoever keeps his commandments abides in God, and God in him. And by this we know that he abides in us, by the Spirit whom he has given us. (1 John 3:23–24)

Jesus told His disciples that at His departure from them into glory, He would send the Spirit, who would be with them and in them. So with the Spirit living with us and in us, we abide in God, and He in us. And when in doubt, the Spirit who dwells in us will testify to our spirits not only that we are God's children (Rom 8:14) but also that God actually dwells in us. And by faith, we experience this mystery in answer to Paul's prayer:

> That according to the riches of his glory he may grant you to be strengthened with power through his Spirit in your inner being, so that Christ may dwell in your hearts through faith (Eph 3:16–17)

Unbelievable, yet true! Christ actually dwells in us, with all the benefits and accompanying power! And what the Godhead can accomplish through us is mind-boggling! Believe it or not, this is the heritage of every believer—everyone who trusts in God, every child of God! And all that we need to do, if still in doubt, is pray the prayer of the apostles of old: "Increase our faith" (Luke 17:5). And we will hear Jesus telling us of the incredible power and effectiveness of genuine faith:

> If you had faith like a grain of mustard seed, you could say to this mulberry tree, "Be uprooted and

planted in the sea," and it would obey you. (Luke 17:6)

The picture of marriage and the family that Paul gives reflects the full and abundant life that God intended for us in Christ to enjoy. The gospel that Christ brought us is one that seeks us out and brings us together in fellowship with the Godhead and with one another. This life is portrayed in the Old Testament (Ezek 34:12-15, 25-31) and the New Testament (John 10:10, 14-16; 1 John 1:1-4). John describes this life in the prologue of his first epistle: Jesus came to show us the quality of life and the fellowship that existed between the Father and Himself, the Son. John and the other disciples saw and experienced this life and proclaimed it, not just that those who heard it should experience salvation, but, more importantly, that they would have fellowship with them, with the Father and the Son, so that their joy would be complete:

> That which we have seen and heard we proclaim also to you, so that you too may have fellowship with us; and indeed our fellowship is with the Father and with his Son Jesus Christ. And we are writing these things so that our joy may be complete. (1 John 1:3-4)

The institutions of marriage and the family, though physical and earthly realities, when perceived as they were meant to be, should point us to the spiritual reality: We have been adopted into the family of God. We are heirs with the Son. We are the bride of Christ and are looking forward to the marriage of the Lamb. The Christian marriage and the relationship of the man and woman with the Godhead is a mystery, but it is a mystery that has been revealed. This is the joy of believers, the children of God.

5.3.2.2.1. *Marriage Reflects the Mystery of the Church*

The final paragraph of the above section leads us to what Paul says in his description of the church. He says that this mystery refers to Christ and the church:

> This mystery is profound, and I am saying that it refers to Christ and the church. (Eph 5:32)

Paul links the institution of marriage at Creation to the Church and Christ. Just as in marriage the two, husband and wife, become one flesh, in the same way, Christ, the Bridegroom, and the church, His bride, become one body. This is the foundation of the doctrine of the body of Christ. Also, relationship in marriage should reflect the perfect relationship that exists in the Godhead and between God and His people. Allender and Longman III (1995: xvii) describes this for us in the following quote:

> First and foremost, marriage is a mirror of the divine-human relationship. Every marriage is meant to represent God: his perfect relationship; with himself-Father, Son, and the Holy Spirit-as well as his relationship with his people.

Paul wraps up the truth of the family of God by showing that we, who believe in Christ and have become the children of God and form the church, are built on the firm foundation that is the Word of God, which has come to us through the prophets and the teachings of Christ and the apostles. And so he writes:

> So then you are no longer strangers and aliens, but you are fellow citizens with the saints and members of the household of God, built on the foundation of the apostles and prophets, Christ Jesus himself being the cornerstone, in whom the whole structure, being joined together, grows into a holy temple in the Lord. In him you also are being built together into a dwelling place for God by the Spirit. (Eph 2:19–22)

Paul is thus unravelling the mystery of the church: we, both Gentiles and Jews, through faith in Christ, have been brought together to form the children of one family, the church, which is indwelt by the Spirit. The church isa family and a body. As a family, it recognizes God as the Father; and as a body, Christ is the head as well as the Bridegroom.

In the family, the most important members are the father (husband) and mother (wife). Paul, in his metaphorical analogy, describes the relationships and authority in the family as follows: God the Father is the head of Christ; Christ is the head of the man (husband), and the husband is head of his wife (1 Cor 11:3). This analogy refers to the authority of Christ over the church and that of the husband over his wife. This authority is not a self-centred exercise of power but is such as Christ exercises over the church by serving it and taking care of the spiritual, emotional, and physical needs of the church (Mark 10:44–45; Eph 5:25–30). And this is how the husband is to treat his wife.

When Paul says that the head of Christ is God, he means that within the Trinity, though Christ and God are equal in deity and attributes, God exercises the role of authority and leadership. And with respect to the man and woman, though they both were made in the image of God and are therefore equal in nature, the husband has a leadership function and so exercises authority over her.

And continuing the relational and positional aspects of the family down to the children, Paul intimates that children are under their parents' authority. And parents are responsible for the instruction of the children in the Lord, teaching them to be submissive to them. Since young people are more and more often rebelling against authority, parents should prayerfully and practically teach and model authority in the family. The teaching of Thomas Aquinas is very clear about this, as we can see in the following quote:

> Authority is the key. This means, that we as parents must make a concerted effort to teach our children about authority in the family. Since the family is a microcosm of the Church, what the children learn about authority in the family they will automatically transfer over to their understanding of authority in the Church.[69]

---

[69] https://www.artoffatherhood.ca/aquinas-and-the-family

And when children are instructed in the fear of the Lord, they will honour and serve the Lord and live in obedience to Him. A good understanding of authority in the family is very important for a healthy life, contentment, and peace in the family and as well as in society. Authority is best modelled in the Godhead; Christ knowing His position as Son and subjecting Himself to the Father, and the Holy Spirit recognizing His own position, being subject to both the Father and Son; and the Father and Son exercising authority over the church and the world makes for harmony and effective carrying out of the mission of God on earth. If in the family, the children, see their father subjecting himself to the authority of God and the leadership of Christ, and if they see how their mother is submitting to their father and also living in a godly way, the children will learn submission and find it easy and natural to respect authority and live in the fear of the Lord. A godly family is not only a blessing to the church but more so a blessing to society as a whole.

Paul ties the running of the family and discipline in the family to that of the church. And so he says the following, concerning the work of the overseer:

> He must manage his own household well, with all dignity keeping his children submissive, for if someone does not know how to manage his own household, how will he care for God's church? (1 Tim 3:4–5)

This confirms the fact that the family is the basic unit of the church, just as Thomas Aquinas will agree that "the family is a microcosm of the Church."[70] This goes as far back as the time of Joshua, when he distinguished himself and his family from the faltering Israelites and challenged them to make a choice between serving other gods and serving God. He declared, "But as for me and my house, we will serve the LORD" (Josh 24:15). Here Joshua was setting up his family not just as a godly and God-fearing family but as the basic unit and the foundation of the godly nation, the nation

---

[70] Ibid.

of Israel, the holy nation, as pictured by Peter (1 Peter 2:9). In this light, the family is the basic unit and the foundation of a nation.

And in the New Testament, because of the political situation at the time under the Roman Emperors, the church met in the homes of Christians, where they held worship services. And so it was that at Colossae, the family of Philemon, which included Apphia (probably his wife) and Archippus, (most likely his son) formed the nucleus of the church (Phlm 1–2). In order to make the analogy clear, Paul goes on to say that what the husband did for the welfare and spiritual growth of his wife should necessarily reflect what Christ did for the church. And so he exhorts husbands:

> Husbands, love your wives, as Christ loved the church
> and gave himself up for her. (Eph 5:25)

Unity and harmony in the family will also reflect what the church should be. Christ says that where two or three come together in His name and agree about anything they ask the Lord, this will be done for them. Thus Philemon, his wife, and his child formed a unity, and the degree to which they would impact society would point to what the church can do when there is agreement in mind, heart, and action. A loving family will point to a loving church, and a loving church will make loving and caring families. This is borne out by what Paul writes concerning the family of Philemon and the church in Colossae. Archippus had received an important ministry from the Lord in the church at Colossae, which he fulfilled effectively (Col 4:17). The church in in Colossae was therefore a model. And so, writing to Philemon, Paul testifies, "I thank my God always when I remember you in my prayers, because I hear of your love and of the faith that you have towards the Lord Jesus and for all the saints" (vv. 4 and 5). Given how godly Philemon and his family were, this surely must have contributed to what the church in Colossae became. And because the family of Philemon lived in love and harmony and ministered well as a family, their life and ministry impacted the church. And so having observed and seen that the church was modelled after the family of Philemon, Paul writes, "We always thank God, the Father of our Lord Jesus Christ, when we pray for you, since we heard of your faith in Christ Jesus and of the love that you have for all the saints" (Col 1:3–4).

And therefore, given the important role of the family in the mission of the church, there is no doubt that the spiritual health and vitality of a church depends a lot on the wholeness and vitality of the family. It will also follow that a loving and growing church will reflect the family life of its members. And so it is no surprise that the family is the church and the church is the family. And this is why Paul was able to affirm that the mystery of marriage and the family was a picture and mirror of Christ and the church.

5.4. Roles and Relations in Marriage and the Family

Jesus did not say much about marriage and family, especially about roles and relations. He surprised people when he was told that His mother, brothers, and sisters were looking for Him. He asked,

> "Who are my mother and my brothers?" And looking about at those who sat around him, he said, "Here are my mother and my brothers! For whoever does the will of God, he is my brother and sister and mother." (Mark 3:33–35)

As we have seen already, Jesus grew up with His siblings as a normal child respecting his parents. And it will be assumed that He had a good relationship with his brothers and sisters. People regarded him as the son of Joseph, the carpenter, and his wife, Mary. Although He was raised in his earthly family, He knew where He came from and why He came (i.e., He knew that He came from the Father and that His mission was to do the will of His Father). He placed the kingdom of God at the forefront of His life and ministry. And this is why he taught His disciples to pray, "Our Father, who art in heaven ... Thy kingdom come. Thy will be done on earth, as it is in heaven."

When He asked, "Who are my mother and my brothers," He did not mean to disregard or disown His earthly family. He wanted to make a point: *He came to do His Father's will* by making those who believed in Him become children of God, thus bringing about the kingdom of God on earth. His siblings had not yet believed in Him, and so His point to them was that they should be part of the heavenly Father's family and kingdom, doing His will. That is when they will truly be His brothers and sisters. And as Paul taught, God's will was that those who believed would "be conformed to the image of his Son, in order that he might be the firstborn among many brothers" (Rom 8:29). And so Jesus was doing the will of God by seriously seeking to make his own family children of God, getting them to the point where they would also be doing His heavenly Father's will. It is then and only then that they would truly become His siblings. Here we learn from Jesus that our mission is also first to our families. The family is our first mission field.

Jesus did not only change the perspective of roles in the family; He also changed the focus of relationships by declaring, "Whoever loves father or mother more than me is not worthy of me, and whoever loves son or daughter more than me is not worthy of me" (Matt 10:37).

Jesus shifts the focus from the biological or earthly family and makes all to focus more on the spiritual and heavenly. Once one has become a child of God and member of God's household, his focus will be on God and on His kingdom, where His will is done. His first loyalty will be to God, and so Jesus says, "Seek first the kingdom of God" and "love God first, with all of your being."

Paul's view of the family is based on the established norms and customs found in ancient Israel. However, he, like Jesus, gave more value to women and children than ever before. His definition of roles in the family aims at promoting the health and joy of the whole family. Family for him also included those of one's household, and so he included servants and bondservants or slaves in the family.

5.4.1. Husband and Wife

5.4.1.1. *Husband*

The husband is the head of the wife, even as Christ is the head of the church, His body. The husband and father is leader in his home. The husband is to love his wife as he loves his own body. He compares the love of the husband to that of Christ, as we read in the following verse:

> Husbands, love your wives, as Christ loved the church and gave himself up for her, that he might sanctify her, having cleansed her by the washing of water with the word, so that he might present the church to himself in splendour, without spot or wrinkle or any such thing, that she might be holy and without blemish. (Eph 5:25–27)

Paul gives the most difficult responsibility to the husband. This is because leadership goes with responsibility and love is sacrificial. Although love does not come easily with the husband because of his distraction with work and other business-related affairs, he has to lead by loving patiently and truly in the Lord. The husband is responsible not only for the material daily needs of his wife (and children); he is also responsible for the spiritual growth and godly life of his wife. He must see to it that in the end his wife is presented to God in "splendour, holy and without blemish." Paul describes here the work of God through Jesus Christ—that is, what the husband is to do for his wife is the very thing that God, in His role as Husband, does for His people. And it is exactly what Christ, the Bridegroom, will do for the church, His body and bride. The life of believers is secure to the end, given that both God and Jesus are working together to keep them from falling. This is stated in Jude, as we can read in the following text:

> Now to him who is able to keep you from stumbling and to present you blameless before the presence of his glory with great joy, to the only God, our Saviour,

through Jesus Christ our Lord, be glory, majesty, dominion, and authority, before all time and now and forever. Amen. (Jude 1:24–25)

Peter, the elder, loved Christ in a unique way, and so his love for Christ moved him to love and care for the church, as we see in His writings. Just as he urged pastors to gracefully care for the church, he was adamant that husbands should show the same care to their wives. After all, the church begins at home. And so he gives the following advice to husbands:

> Likewise, husbands, live with your wives in an understanding way, showing honour to the woman as the weaker vessel, since they are heirs with you of the grace of life, so that your prayers may not be hindered. (1 Peter 3:7)

Here again, Peter places on the husband the greater spiritual responsibility. He is to treat his wife with care, grace, and consideration, knowing that she is more vulnerable. Here Peter urges the husband to add value to his wife by honouring her. This is a good leadership quality, giving value to those we lead, making them feel appreciated. Jesus and God the Father place a high value on each of us, and so the husband and every leader must value those under their authority. The other important point that Peter makes reminds husbands of their priestly responsibility. The husband, just like the priest, is to intercede for the members of his family, including his wife. This is in accordance with the role that God gave man at Creation, as stated in section 1.9.2. God changes lives through prayer, and so Peter wants the husbands to treat their wives with grace and consideration so that their prayers would be effective.

As stated previously, the husband, viewed from God's perspective, should reflect His character and should be the most desirable person before his wife. This should not basically be the slavish desire that was the result of the fall (Gen 3:16) but a desire after the one loved and valued. A picture of such a man is painted for us in the following verses from the Song of Songs:

> His arms are rods of gold, set with jewels. His body is polished ivory, bedecked with sapphires.
>
> His legs are alabaster columns, set on bases of gold. His appearance is like Lebanon, choice as the cedars.
>
> His mouth is most sweet, and he is altogether desirable. This is my beloved and this is my friend, O daughters of Jerusalem. (Song 5:14–16)

These verses give us a picture of an attractive man of value. The description speaks of precious materials used in the statutes of important people or those used in the construction or furnishing of the temple (gold, jewels, ivory, alabaster, and cedars from Lebanon). The description "His mouth is most sweet" speaks of a gentle tongue that characterizes the wisdom and grace of God and the Lord, the Bridegroom of the church, as we see in the following Scripture:

> And all spoke well of him and marveled at the gracious words that were coming from his mouth. And they said, "Is not this Joseph's son?" (Luke 4:22)

The description also speaks of the anointed of the Lord or of a wise king, as we read in the following verses:

> My heart overflows with a pleasing theme; I address my verses to the king; my tongue is like the pen of a ready scribe.
>
> You are the most handsome of the sons of men; grace is poured upon your lips; therefore God has blessed you forever. (Ps 45:1–2)

A wise and compassionate mouth bespeaks the man whose tongue the Lord has touched, such as that of the prophet Isaiah, who said,

> The Lord GOD has given me the tongue of those who are taught, that I may know how to sustain with a

> word him who is weary. Morning by morning he awakens; he awakens my ear to hear as those who are taught. (Isa 50:4)

Isaiah's words as described here are words of compassion, encouragement, and comfort to the people of God.

Our words can either be destructive or build up. They can indeed be devastating, especially in marriage. How many times have I spoken words that have hurt my wife and made me ashamed because of the vileness of my mouth? Many marriages die because of verbal abuse. So the prayer of a caring husband should be such as David prayed—that God would touch his tongue, set a guard over his mouth, and keep watch over the door of our lips (Ps 141:3).

Paul also cautions us regarding the use of our mouths in the following Scripture:

> Let no corrupting talk come out of your mouths, but only such as is good for building up, as fits the occasion, that it may give grace to those who hear. (Eph 4:29)

The man described in the Song of Solomon has qualities that make him desirable. So a husband should, by all means, make himself desirable. It has been the common expectation that it is the woman who should make herself attractive and desirable. I say that the man should also make himself desirable. The first and most important demand is that the husband should be like the Lord, modelling the character of Christ before his wife. These are the virtues described in Galatians 5:22–23, qualities that make Christ desirable. We admire the woman described in in Proverb 31. She is virtuous, caring, and hardworking and so makes her husband proud when he sits with other men at the gate. So, too, the man should not only make himself attractive and desirable to his wife but should also make her and his children proud of him because he is godly, hardworking, caring, and respected in the community.

Although the man cannot change his physical form or colour, it is important how he treats his body in order to make it fit and desirable. Paul says that training the body is of value, and so the man should take care of his physical body and make it attractive. Body hygiene should be of particular importance to the man too. This is more so when it comes to the intimate relationship in marriage. Some men do not care about this aspect of their lives and so make themselves repulsive to their wives. A man's wife should feel the freshness of his body in his intimate relation with her. There is a lot that the Song of Songs teaches us about men. For example, see the following:

> My beloved is to me a sachet of myrrh that lies between my breasts. (Song 1:13)

It should be mentioned here that an important way for a man to make himself attractive to his wife is to watch his weight, which is good for health and physical appearance. Paul says in 1 Timothy 4:8 that bodily training is of value. Men should exercise and mind what they eat and drink, so as to be in good physical shape. There are men who drink and eat uncontrollably, and this affects their bodies, making them less attractive.

Another important quality in marriage that the woman in Song of Songs brings out is that of friendship. She presents her beloved to the women of Israel in the following words:

> This is my beloved and this is my friend.

How many men find in their wives friends? Or, to put it the other way round, how many women can find in their husbands friends? The culmination of the relationship of Jesus to His disciples occurred when He said, "I no longer call you servants, but I have called you friends, for all that I have heard from my Father I have made known to you" (John 15:15). The culmination of a marriage relationship is reached when husband and wife are friends. There should be such mutual trust and confidentiality between husband and wife that they can freely share with each other and support each other. As it is the Lord who initiates love and friendship in our relationship with Him, so it is the duty of the man to initiate friendship in marriage.

5.4.1.2. *Wife*

The biblical wife is virtuous and loving and brings tenderness and attention to every situation in the home. And this is attested to by Scripture, as we read in the following verse:

> Charm is deceitful, and beauty is vain, but a woman who fears the LORD is to be praised. (Prov 31:30)

A virtuous wife exercises what is called soft power. A loving wife captures the heart of her husband, while a caring mother captures the hearts of her children. She has the advantage of being with the children more often than the husband, having carried them from the womb, and she keeps them at home till they are ready to leave home. And because of this special relationship, the children get more attached to her than to their father. It is because of this bond that children, even adult children, call their mother when in trouble or in life-threatening situations.

Finding the wife of one's life is the most rewarding and precious gift of God. This is affirmed by the Scriptures:

> He who finds a wife finds a good thing and obtains favour from the LORD. An excellent wife who can find? She is far more precious than jewels. (Prov 18:22; 31:10)

Given the value that God attaches to the wife, it is foolish for a woman to want to be a man or compete with her husband. If women were conscious of the powers and abilities that God has endowed womanhood with, the absurdity of the clamour of the women's liberation movement would be silenced.

Regarding the wife, Peter makes other important points, as we read in the following text:

> Likewise, wives, be subject to your own husbands, so that even if some do not obey the word, they may be won without a word by the conduct of their wives, when they see your respectful and pure conduct.

> Do not let your adorning be external—the braiding of hair and the putting on of gold jewellery, or the clothing you wear—but let your adorning be the hidden person of the heart with the imperishable beauty of a gentle and quiet spirit, which in God's sight is very precious. (1 Peter 1–4)

In the above text, Peter brings up another important point regarding the character of the wife: A wife's virtuous character can win her husband to God. Paul also makes this point when he says that a godly wife could impact the life of her husband, and that he could even be saved through his wife (1 Cor 7:14, 16).

Next Peter brings up another point concerning dressing and adornment. Some women spend a lot of time and money on their outward appearance. Peter cautions moderation and places more value on inner beauty, character, and "the hidden person of the heart with the imperishable beauty" than on outward beauty. Yes, gentle and quiet character traits reflect the character of the Lord. As Jesus Himself testified, "… for I am gentle and lowly of heart" (Matt 11:29).

Paul, in his letter to Titus, addresses the role of older women (wives who are older in marriage) in training younger women to be good wives and mothers, as we read in the following instructions:

> Older women likewise are to be reverent in behaviour, not slanderers or slaves to much wine. They are to teach what is good, and so train the young women to love their husbands and children, to be self-controlled, pure, working at home, kind, and submissive to their own husbands, that the word of God may not be reviled. (Titus 2:3–5)

This text shows how important it was for women to be trained to fulfil their homemaking duties. Both Peter and Paul stress the desired results of gospel living. Such living attacts peple to the gospel. We can see how important this was for the gospel and the need to protect and uphold the Word of God and godly values for the purpose of wining souls to the Lord. This fact points to the symbolism and image of the church as the bride of Christ. It calls to mind the mystery of marriage: the man or husband representing Christ, the head of the church; and the wife representing the woman as the bride (Rev 19:7).

Paul makes a very important point concerning women, which might be overlooked by today's society. Enumerating the virtues of godly women, he adds that women should be "working at home." In the modern world, most women want to work in jobs for the value of it. Biblically, the primary responsibility of a wife and mother is at home. Even if for economic reasons she has to work, this should not compromise her primary responsibilities as wife and mother. One of the things our children appreciate my wife for is the fact that she was there for them each day when they came home from school. She interrupted her training to work at home until all the children had left home. She then pursued her theological studies and subsequently the pastoral ministry.

5.4.1.3. *Balance, Harmony, and Healthy Authority: A Beautiful Attraction*

The wife is under the authority of her husband, and so her primary duty is to submit to her husband, respecting him. This was already foretold by God in the Garden of Eden after the Fall. God told the woman, "Your desire shall be for your husband, and he shall rule over you" (Gen 3:15). Although this declaration came as punishment for the rebellion of Adam and Eve, this should be the ethical behavioural expectation in a functional marriage, where the husband asserts his leadership role and the woman accepts the authority of the man over her and over the children. With regard to the adverse effect of members of the family not accepting their biblical roles, Gangel (1979:36–37) says,

> In Christian homes today one of the biggest pitfalls on the path to happy family living is the distortion of Biblical roles for family members. Society, of course, has hopelessly distorted the Biblical view through equalisation of the sexes (a perverted role of the

wife), television situation comedies (a perverted role of the husband) and an extreme overemphasis and almost glorification of youth (a perverted role for children). The issue of role breakdown is viewed as a significant factor in the family breakdown.

In order to assume proper relationships, each person must accept the biblical roles in the family structure. The biblical order of subjection is as follows: the husband is in subjection to Christ, the wife subjects herself to her husband, and the children subject themselves to their parents. It is therefore important to respect the biblical roles for order and well-being in the family. If the husband and wife carry out their assigned roles, the husband leading well and loving his wife, while the wife accepts his leadership by submitting to him and honouring him, the children will consequently subject themselves to parental authority, and there will be harmony, peace, and happiness in the family.

In a Christian marriage, the husband does not lord it over his wife but will show respect for his wife by the way he leads in modelling a Christlike caring and loving attitude. Husbands who rule their families with love and gentleness succeed best when they work to make their wives and children good learners and followers. This is the way Christ taught, as we read in this cardinal pedagogical statement:

> Take my yoke upon you, and learn from me, for I am gentle and lowly in heart, and you will find rest for your souls. (Matt 11:29)

The Lord Jesus describes for us here the heart of the leader who rules effectively and influences those under his authority by his compassion and his gentle, loving, and caring character. Being in authority does not exclude humility and gentleness. Neither is being soft weakness; rather, it shows strength of character and winsome leadership. Anyone under such leadership and authority will not find any task or duty a burden.

Leadership is a huge responsibility, and it can be very demanding and exhausting. Just as elders in the church were expected to rule their families well, in the same way, all Christian husbands are expected to rule their households well. The family is a foundational unit of the church, and so running a family has burdens of its own, similar to those carried by church leaders. And this is not an easy task, as we can see in the case of Paul, from what he tells us regarding the churches he leads:

> And, apart from other things, there is the daily pressure on me of my anxiety for all the churches. Who is weak, and I am not weak? Who is made to fall, and I am not indignant? (2 Cor 11:28–29)

It should be noted that Paul considered believers in the churches he ministered to as his children, members of his family. And since he treated the Corinthian Christians as his children, the pressures of that church weighed heavily on him as its father. These pressures were such as parents are under, and so he would bear the burden rather than the children (2 Cor 12:14–15). And since Paul was the student of Christ par excellence, he would have learned from Christ, the burden-bearer. So the best way to deal with family issues is to give these to Christ, who will teach us how best to effectively play our roles in our families, making it possible to have functional and happy families, carrying out the purposes of God. This means that a husband will strive to do his best as leader and a wife to do her best to submit and honour her husband and to love her children. This is why all burdens that are borne in the Lord are nothing but light and easy.

The most dysfunctional family is one in which the wife does not respect her husband and wants instead to act as the rival of her husband—or, worse still, where the wife takes over the leadership role and appropriates the authority of the man. Paul, talking about the humility of Christ, states the following important truth:

> Have this mind among yourselves, which is yours in Christ Jesus, who, though he was in the form of God, did not count equality with God a thing to be grasped. (Phil 2:5–6)

Over and over, we see the comparison that is made between the relationship that exists in the Godhead and that which is in marriage. Though God the Father, God the Son, and God the Spirit are equal in essence, there is submission regarding the exercise of authority. And as stated previously, although the Son is equal to the Father, He submits to the Father's authority, as Paul says in the following Scripture:

> When all things are subjected to him, then the Son himself will also be subjected to him who put all things in subjection under him, that God may be all in all. (1 Cor 15:28)

On the other hand, there are husbands who have neglected their authority and position as heads in their families, and in such cases, their wives find themselves playing roles they were never meant to take on. When this happens, there is an authority vacuum in the families and the wives and children suffer. Again this gives room for a dysfunctional family, which leads to wayward children and juvenile delinquency. Even in a case where a husband neglects his leadership position and duty, the wife should constantly be asking herself why this is so. It may well be that the man was made insecure in one way or another. The wife, for the health of the family, should always seek to be humble and submissive. It could be that the wife is either more educated or has a more lucrative job, or it may be that she is more articulate. All these, or even one of these, may give rise to an unhealthy complex. In such a case, humility on the part of both parties ends up being a remedy. If a husband and wife have the attitude of Christ and heed the exhortation of Paul to be giving "thanks always and for everything to God the Father in the name of our Lord Jesus Christ, submitting to one another out of reverence for Christ" (Eph 5:20–21), this will surely lead to a healthy and happy life in their marriage.

An important area where both the husband and wife are expected to submit to one another is the area of their body. When they are joined together as husband and wife, they "become one flesh." It is from this perspective that Paul exhorts husbands to love their wives as themselves. As stated in section 5.3.2.1.3, becoming one flesh, in a sense, means having intimate sexual relationship in marriage. Allender and Longman III (1995:230) support this and go even further by relating this to our intimacy with God:

> The oneness that married couples experience in the act of sexual intercourse becomes a biblical symbol for the oneness we experience in our deeply intimate relationship with God.

The wife shows her love for her husband in the sexual part of marriage. Here Paul also exhorts the husband to show his love for his wife by giving himself to her in the sexual part of marriage. He says,

> The husband should give to his wife her conjugal rights, and likewise the wife to her husband. For the wife does not have authority over her own body, but the husband does. Likewise the husband does not have authority over his own body, but the wife does. Do not deprive one another, except perhaps by agreement for a limited time. (1 Cor 7:3–5)

It may be the case that couples have difficulty in the area of sex and therefore are not able to derive the desired satisfaction from it. Gangel (1972:42) makes this important point which should be taken into consideration while trying to find another reason for unfulfilled sex:

> Most sexual difficulties in marriage are psychological in origin and a willingness on the part of marriage partners to give of themselves in love to one another physically and emotional is the only response to the [Scripture] passage above.

Another view that supports this assertion is what Miles (1967:447) says in the following quote:

> In the infinite wisdom of God, He wilfully planned human life so that husband and wife could regularly express their love and commitment to each other through satisfying sexual experiences. These are designed to support, cultivate, nourish, fortify and keep fresh personal love and devotion between husband and wife.

This means that sex was ordained by God to be enjoyed by couples and so deepen their relationships. They owe it to God and to each other. Given that this is meant to be enjoyed by both partners, there should be great expectation as each of them looks forward to the act. This therefore means that none should be forced into it. In the case where one partner is hurting or where there is disagreement resulting in bitterness, or when there has been an offence, time should be taken to pray and make peace. Sex is a gift from God, and it should be had with thankfulness to the Lord. The couple should be grateful to each other, for they are giving of themselves to each other. And so, after having sex, each partner should thank the other, for this is the will of God for them.

5.4.1.4. *Family Worship*

The family altar is very important for the spiritual health of the family. The family should set a time when all members of the family come together to worship regularly. This grows out of a situation where the couple, even before they have children, have made it a practice to set times to read the Word and pray together. During this time, they share the treasures that they have gleaned from the Bible and other inspiring devotionals in their personal time in the Word and prayer with each other. It is during this time that they can also bring their concerns and joys before the Lord. It goes without saying, and we take this as a promise, that where two or three come together in the name of the Lord, they are guaranteed the presence, and thus the blessing, of the Lord (Ps 133:1–3; Matt 18:18–20). The Lord promises to hear them and grant them whatever they ask of Him in prayer.

It is also important to stress that the Christian family is the foundation and fundamental unit of the church; this is where the church begins. So the unity and fervour that we find in individual families, put together when families come to form the local church, create strength and a ripple effect that gathers momentum and creates a dynamic and vibrant church. It is taken as a given that as long as family members live in the same house, they are to worship together. This also means that the whole family should attend the same church and worship there together. It is unhealthy for the couple not to worship in the same church. If parents worship in separate churches, this will place the children in a difficult situation. The children will be confused, or even feel frustrated, if father and mother worship in different churches. There might be exceptions. It may be the case that one member of the family has to leave the place where they have been worshipping for personal and understandable reasons. For example, if the church is not Christ-centred or does not faithfully preach and teach the gospel, a believer will certainly not be satisfied, and so will want to go where he or she will grow spiritually. If both husband and wife are believers, they should look for a Bible-believing and teaching church and attend it together. Parents should be on their guard against division, which gives the devil a foothold, thus bringing about a strain in their relationship. This will weaken their marriage and place the growth and welfare of the children at risk.

Marriage is a school a couple gains admission when they are declared husband and wife and are given a certificate of entrance into the state of holy matrimony. It should be regarded as an institution with many disciplines and departments. And because they are many disciplines and departments, the marriage institution of high education is difficult and demands a lot of work, time, commitment, patient endurance, and devotion. It is a lifelong institution, and so one is a student for life, and learning is ongoing. The most important discipline in this institution is character formation, which is under the subject or discipline of spiritual formation. This is a discipline that will help the couple to build themselves up and also prepare them to train and build up their children and members of their household.

When the couple enrol and enter the marriage institution,

they come in as freshmen. Their freshman years may appear very romantic and idyllic, but as the years pass, the realities of married life become more and more evident, and so difficulties begin to surface. The love that each was hoping would keep burning in their hearts begins to die and so becomes an illusion. Some mistakenly begin to question themselves regarding whether they really loved each other. The happiness and joy they were envisaging begins to fade. At worst, they begin to look down the road of divorce.

If we go into marriage to seek happiness, we will fail. Happiness is only found in the Lord, and it is appropriated and sustained by doing the will of God. God gives wisdom, knowledge, and joy to those who please Him, as the Preacher says, "For to the one who pleases him God has given wisdom and knowledge and joy" (Eccl 2:26). Wisdom demands that we choose to do the will of God, doing what is right out of reverential fear. James defines wisdom in very practical terms, as we can read in the following text:

> Who is wise and understanding among you? By his good conduct let him show his works in the meekness of wisdom. But the wisdom from above is first pure, then peaceable, gentle, open to reason, full of mercy and good fruits, impartial and sincere. (Jas 3:13, 17)

James proves our point and tells us how to be wise—by being humble and doing what is right. And as the Bible says, "My son, if your heart is wise, my heart too will be glad" (Prov 23:15). The wise son does the will of his father, and this makes both him and his father happy. So our happiness comes from having a godly attitude and choosing to do the right thing before God. This is where the saying "Happiness is a choice" becomes relevant. If we chose to do the right thing, we will definitely be happy. If we see marriage as an institution that will help us grow spiritually and grow further into the image of Christ, we will succeed and graduate as joyful people because we have been in the school where Christ is the teacher, the model, and our end.

The difficulties and challenges we encounter in marriage should challenge us to examine our character traits. Prayerfully taking a hard look at our attitudes, actions, and reactions will enable us, through the help of the Holy Spirit, to rid ourselves of those traits that don't reflect a Christian character and Christ. Thomas (200:86) puts it this way:

> Marriage forces me to face myself honestly and consider my character flaws, selfishness, and anti-Christian attitudes, encouraging me to grow in godliness.

When we realize our failings, our hurts, this should make us look up to God, for the Scriptures say, "The LORD is near to the brokenhearted and saves the crushed in spirit" (Ps 34:18). Marriage is a humbling institution where our pride and stubbornness bring us low so God can raise us up from dust and ashes. If our hearts are broken and our spirits crushed, and we turn to God in trust and hope, He will surely heal us and strengthen us to keep on keeping on. Again, brokenness and contrition bring God into our lives, as we read in the following Scripture:

> For thus says the One who is high and lifted up, who inhabits eternity, whose name is Holy: "I dwell in the high and holy place, and also with him who is of a contrite and lowly spirit, to revive the spirit of the lowly, and to revive the heart of the contrite." (Isa 57:15)

The above verse is very reassuring in that, although God is so holy and exalted high in heaven, He will come to dwell with the contrite in heart. This is good news for the hurting in marriage and the family. This should therefore encourage us to continually seek his presence and strength.

Therefore, the problems we face in marriage and family should not make us discouraged. They should show us how needy and weak we are, and consequently draw us closer to God as we seek Him in prayer and struggle to find solutions. As we turn to God in desperation, earnestly seeking His face and help, we will discover that it is not by might or in our own power but by the help of His Spirit. And as the Spirit in us produces the fruit of love, joy, patience, kindness, faithfulness, gentleness, and self-control in increasing measure, we will be daily equipped for marriage and family life. These qualities make us reflect the character of God in Christ. And when we linger in the glorious presence of God, we behold His glory, and the more we experience Him, the more we "are being transformed into the same image from one degree of glory to another" (2 Cor 3:18). It was because Moses dwelled long in the presence of God that he emerged with his face reflecting the brilliance and glory of the Lord that he had experienced (Exod 34:29–30).

In a wedding ceremony, a pastor or priest may say, for example, "I, a minister of ...pronounce/declare you united in holy matrimony." The question that one may ask is, Why is marriage regarded as holy? Is it because this institution is set apart or because the couple is set apart? In light of that stated above, it is because marriage is of God and therefore holy; and because it is holy, those entering this state would rightly seek to be holy. Practically speaking, when the couple is just being enrolled in the school of marriage, they are not holy; although justified, they are gradually being sanctified as they yield themselves to the Holy Spirit. Holiness in marriage is the end, not the beginning. People in marriage learn as they grow and advance in years and knowledge. Their graduation occurs in the end, when they leave this earth and go to meet their Lord and Bridegroom in heaven. At this point, they are presented to Christ, as described by Paul, "in splendor, without spot or wrinkle or any such thing, that she might be holy and without blemish" (Eph 5:27).

5.4.2. **Parents and Children**

Children, the fruit of the womb, are a special blessing from the Lord, who created the man and woman and called them to be fruitful. And bearing fruit is a primary purpose of God, spelt out at Creation (Gen 1:11–12, 22, 28) and in His redemption plan (Gen 22:17; 28:14; John 15:8, 16).

Bringing up children is one of the most sacred duties of parents. Children are entrusted to parents and they are therefore stewards.

And as stewards, they will give an account to God concerning them in the same way as pastors or overseers to whom God has entrusted the souls of the wider church family to shepherd will be called upon to give an account to Him (Heb 13:17; 1 Peter 5:1–4). Parents have the joint responsibility of bringing up their children in the fear of the Lord, thus fulfilling this important responsibility that God gave them right at the time when they were created.

The Bible teaches us that the home is the most important school of Christian education, as we read from the words of Paul to Timothy, who had been well taught at home:

> [Remember] how from childhood you have been acquainted with the sacred writings, which are able to make you wise for salvation through faith in Christ Jesus. (2 Tim 3:15)

Given the importance of instructing children in the home, and mindful that this is a sacred duty, parents ought to seek the face of God, who gave them the children. To be successful in their task of parenting, they should dig deep in His Word to discover the precious gems hidden in this minefield in order to share them with their children. The Bible is the best manual for child rearing. In addition to what they learn from sacred Scripture, parents should also seek the counsel of those inspired and experienced in this art. Reading what others have garnered over years of seeking is helpful.

Margaret Anderson, one who has written books on children's devotionals, underscores the importance of teaching children and advises parents and teachers on how to effectively train and bring up children in the Lord. She intimates that bringing up children in the Lord is, in effect, bringing them to the Lord. And by bringing up children to know the Lord, we are indeed obeying His command. He commanded His disciples, "Let the children come to me." This command was not given only to the disciples; it now goes to every parent and Christian educator. With regard to this, Anderson (1975:5) says,

> To you, parents, teachers, pastor, missionary, Jesus reiterates this admonition: Let the children come to

me. To facilitate this coming you will spend time with children. You will listen to them. You will guide and teach them. According to God's Word, they will never be more receptive to Bible truths than they are now. Be assured, too, that faith established in childhood will not, in the final analysis, be discarded at an older age.

This perspective of parenting is in full accord with biblical teaching. Our primary task in child rearing is to train them to grow up in the knowledge and love of the Lord. St Thomas Aquinas' teaching on the family also focuses on the knowledge of the Word and God. He says that all that we do and teach to the children should lead them to God, as we can read from the following quote:

> All our acts should lead us to God. EVERYTHING we do and say and see and touch and think and smell points us to God. In Him we live, and move and have our being (Acts 17:28). This again is a hint to us parents that we need to, unabashedly, point out God in our daily lives. He is the centre of our home, our family, our existence.[71]

Kenton Biffert summarizes the practical teaching of Thomas Aquinas and suggests ways in which parents can integrate his teaching into family life. Presented below are some of Aquinas' teachings that we find very practical:

1. Spend time in the mountains with your children. The mountain that is firm and unmovable and sustaining ecosystems and life is a great metaphor for God.
2. Garden with your children. The metaphors that come about when you begin to weed are numerous. Weeds (sins), if we let them take root in our hearts, are very difficult to get out—especially dandelions.

---

[71] Kenton Biffert, "The Domestic Aquinas Project," Kenton E. Biffert: Catholic Fatherhood, 2016, https://www.artoffatherhood.ca/aquinas-and-the-family.

3. Read stories from Scripture. During the story reading, establish the literal sense and then apply it to your lives using the moral sense. Sometimes you can connect an allegorical sense, and it is fun to look for ways in which the Old Testament foreshadows the New Testament.
4. Have your children memorize passages. A good place to begin is Matthew 5 and 6—the Sermon on the Mount.
5. Learn to pray the psalms together, knowing that somewhere out there, someone is needing the words of this psalm prayed on his or her behalf.

Mother Teresa, addressing the blessings of a godly family life, says the following:

> A family that prays together stays together. And if you stay together, you will love one another, as God loves each one of you. Today in the world there is so much suffering because of the want of prayer, of unity in the family. So today when we are together, let us make one strong resolution. That we will bring prayer in the family. That we will teach our children to pray and pray with them. And you will see the joy and the love and peace that will come into your heart. Because the fruit of prayer is the deepening of faith. And the fruit of faith is love.[72]

All these methods of parenting are meant to bring God into all facets of life. These are practical ways recommended by God to the people of Israel, as explained in other sections. This is what Moses reminded the Israelites to do when they were about to be led into the Promised Land:

---

[72] **The Family that Prays Together Stays Together #Mother Teresa, produce 3 years ago, during the corona lockdown, to make family stay together prayerful and meaningful.**
From a YouTube video produced by *Live to Inspire*
https://youtu.be/2ULxJVLAkFg?si=S5IGgajBxUVRDOFW1.44 minutes, accessed 23/01/24

> You shall therefore lay up these words of mine in your heart and in your soul, and you shall bind them as a sign on your hand, and they shall be as frontlets between your eyes. You shall teach them to your children, talking of them when you are sitting in your house, and when you are walking by the way, and when you lie down, and when you rise. You shall write them on the doorposts of your house and on your gates. (Deut 11:18–20)

If the church succeeded in bringing up children in the fear of God, making every aspect of life a means of knowing God and living according to the principles so learned, the world would be a better place, much different from what it is today. This is supported by the following quote:

> It remains true that the welfare of the world in which we live is dependent upon families founded upon the teaching and practice of the Christian faith. (Gangel, 1979)

However, with God's purposes for the world in mind, there is always hope. Our prayer is that the church will keep the family as its primary purpose in the mission of God. God's plan is to use us as His people to build His kingdom even here on earth so that His will shall be done on earth even as it is in heaven. This is what Christ Himself taught us to pray and believe. Oh, that it will be done according to our faith!

Good parenting not only benefits the children; most especially, it benefits the parents, teachers, and spiritual leaders who dutifully and wholeheartedly do this as a God-given mission. This is attested to in the following Scripture:

> My son, if your heart is wise, my heart too will be glad. My inmost being will exult when your lips speak what is right. (Prov 23:15–16)

The end result of good parenting is blessings and joy both to the children and the parents. Seeing our children grow and follow the truth of the gospel, as they follow Christ faithfully, gives us joy and satisfaction. This is the joy that St John the Elder experienced when he saw that his spiritual children had followed his teaching and were walking in the faith. The joy he expressed will surely be ours:

> I rejoiced greatly when the brothers came and testified to your truth, as indeed you are walking in the truth. I have no greater joy than to hear that my children are walking in the truth. (3 John 1:3–4)

5.4.2.1. *Father*

Paul addresses the father and places on him the responsibility of the spiritual and emotional welfare of the children. He says, in particular:

> Fathers, do not provoke your children to anger, but bring them up in the discipline and instruction of the Lord. (Eph 6:4)

The father figure, according to Jesus, is one who reflects the love and compassion of the Father, as we read in the story of the prodigal son in Luke 15. The father is thus reflecting the same compassion and forgiveness described in Psalm 103:8–13, which describes the character of God as given in Exodus 34:6, where the Lord comes and declares His name to Moses. As for the apostle John, he emphasizes the love of the Father. He says that God is love, and this is the love which moves Him to make us His children (1John 4:16; 3:1). And the measure of love that the Father has for the Son is the same that earthly fathers should have for members of their families.

Paul's picture of a father is one who loves and cares so much as to sacrifice for the children. A father should spend and be spent in order to meet the needs of his children. And so he challenges the Christians in Corinth by his life:

> Here for the third time I am ready to come to you. And I will not be a burden, for I seek not what is yours but you. For children are not obligated to save up for their parents, but parents for their children. I will most gladly spend and be spent for your souls. If I love you more, am I to be loved less? (2 Cor 12:14–15)

A combination of Paul's concern for the material as well as the spiritual well-being of his children models healthy parental care for children. The spiritual father should, as a result of his embracing the covenant and walking faithfully with his God, be blessed materially and so leave an inheritance for his children. This is in line with wisdom literature and Old Testament teaching, as we read in the following Scriptures:

> Blessed is the man who fears the LORD, who greatly delights in his commandments! His offspring will be mighty in the land; the generation of the upright will be blessed. Wealth and riches are in his house, and his righteousness endures forever. (Ps 112:1–3)

> A good man leaves an inheritance to his children's children, but the sinner's wealth is laid up for the righteous. (Prov 13:22)

The character of the godly man influences and benefits his offspring, for he does instruct his children in the faith and in holy living. The children not only listen to his instructions to learn; they learn more by observing the life of their father. As we have seen repeatedly in Paul's life, he often tells those he is teaching to watch him and imitate what they see him do. This is how, as the quoted Scripture says, "his righteousness endures forever."[73] So the godly father's righteous character passes unto his offspring, and even when they die, they, too, enter into glory with it, and that is how it endures forever. And so the righteous father leaves not only

---

[73] Eemphasis mine

material wealth to be inherited by his children but also, and more importantly, a spiritual legacy.

Paul's fatherly sacrificial love and care stood out in the way in which he treated the Christians in Thessalonica, as captured in the following verses:

> But we were gentle among you, like a nursing mother taking care of her own children. So, being affectionately desirous of you, we were ready to share with you not only the gospel of God but also our own selves, because you had become very dear to us. (1 Thess 2:7–8)

Here we again see Paul as the father who cares for the emotional, material, and, especially, the spiritual needs of his children. This again reiterates the fact that the ultimate aim of parenting should be to lead the children to God and train them in the Lord. This stands out in the following text:

> You are witnesses, and God also, how holy and righteous and blameless was our conduct towards you believers. For you know how, like a father with his children, we exhorted each one of you and encouraged you and charged you to walk in a manner worthy of God, who calls you into his own kingdom and glory. (1Thess 2:10–12)

It is clear here that Paul is the father who models godliness before his children. He is eager not only to lead his children to the Father but also to help them grow up and live worthy of the Lord. He is the father who will, in the end, stand before God without reproach and present his children and their mother with joy to the Father on the last Day. This is what Jesus calls husbands to do for their wives (Eph 5:25–27). So according to Paul, fatherhood is best seen where the father is one who reflects the character of God the Father and models godliness before his family.

5.4.2.2. *Mother*

Mothers can have even a greater responsibility to influence the lives of their children. Even from the womb, a child is sensitive and can respond to and be impacted by what happens around him, particularly by the attitudes, words, and actions of the mother and, to a certain extent, those of his father. Studies have shown that babies learn language from the womb. Behavioural scientists have established experimental methods to prove that foetuses can and do learn.[74] Also, it has been shown that a child can grow up speaking a foreign language he did not learn just because during pregnancy the mother was working with that language. John the Baptist reacted joyfully to the greeting of Mary, underpinning the reason why child rearing begins in the womb. The Lord called and equipped some of His servants from the womb, as in the cases of Jeremiah, Isaiah, and Samson, as well as Israel, who were called collectively to serve the Lord:

> Listen to me, O house of Jacob, all the remnant of
> the house of Israel, who have been borne by me from
> before your birth, carried from the womb. (Isa 46:3)

Even as regards a whole people, the people of Israel, the servant of God (Isa 41:8), God called them before they even came to be. He called them, chose them, and formed plans for them while they were not yet in the womb of their ancestors—their fathers, Abraham, Isaac, and Jacob—as we read in the verse quoted above. This is reminiscent of the legacy we inherit from our parents and ancestors, especially our spiritual inheritance.

The spiritual influence of the grandmother and mother of

---

[74] Beth Skwarecki. 26 August 2013. Babies Learn to Recognize Words from the womb, article https://www.science.org/content/article/babies-learn-recognize-words-womb
Gina Kolata. 20 July 1984. Studying Learning in the Womb, scientific article. Science, Vol 225, Issue 4659, pp. 302-303
https://www.science.org/doi/10.1126/science.6740312
Accessed 30/01/24

Timothy on his life is very revealing, as Paul testifies here in the following verses:

> As I remember your tears, I long to see you, that I may be filled with joy. I am reminded of your sincere faith, a faith that dwelt first in your grandmother Lois and your mother Eunice and now, I am sure, dwells in you as well. (2 Tim 1:4–5)

Given the lasting blessings on children and society when they are well brought up, it is important to invest more in training our children and in setting good examples for them so they can learn from us in all aspects of life.

5.4.2.3. *Children*

Paul recognizes the duties of children, as we saw in the section on ancient Israel. Children are to honour and respect their parents, as we read here:

> Children, obey your parents in the Lord, for this is right. "Honour your father and mother" (this is the first commandment with a promise). (Eph 6:1–2)

What section 2.9.5 states about children in ancient Israel will be true in the New Testament for the most part since the Old Testament Scriptures formed the foundation of the teaching about children.

Paul teaches that the primary role of children is to obey their parents. They honour their parents by listening to them, obeying them, and respecting them.

Jesus and Paul looked at children in light of the redemption and their covenant relationship with the Father. Both Jesus and Paul added value to the child. Contrary to Old Testament thinking, Jesus said that adults should turn and be like children because the kingdom of God belongs to children.

Jesus obeyed His parents though even in his teens, He was fully aware of His divine nature and the position He had in heaven with His Father before the Incarnation. He humbled Himself to obey, respect, and honour his earthly parents, even as He humbled himself to obey His heavenly Father. This attitude is seen in the following verse:

> And he went down with them and came to Nazareth and was submissive to them. And his mother treasured up all these things in her heart. (Luke 2:51)

In honouring His parents by obeying them, He also acknowledged the responsibility of taking care of His parents, as we read in the following verses:

> When Jesus saw his mother and the disciple whom he loved standing nearby, he said to his mother, "Woman, behold, your son!" Then he said to the disciple, "Behold, your mother!" And from that hour the disciple took her to his own home. (John 19:26–27)

Jesus expected children to honour their parents by caring for them and providing for them, as required by the Law. That is why he rebuked the Pharisees and Scribes who sought to circumvent what the law required of children, as seen in the following Scripture:

> He answered them, "And why do you break the commandment of God for the sake of your tradition? For God commanded, 'Honour your father and your mother,' and, 'Whoever reviles father or mother must surely die.' But you say, 'If anyone tells his father or his mother, "What you would have gained from me is given to God," he need not honour his father.' So for the sake of your tradition you have made void the word of God. (Matt 15:3-6)

And as Christ obeyed and honoured his parents, so would He expect children to honour and give value to their parents. Paul also taught that children should look to Jesus as the ultimate example and copy the same attitude that He exhibited, as we read in the following text:

> Therefore be imitators of God, as beloved children. And walk in love, as Christ loved us and gave himself up for us, a fragrant offering and sacrifice to God. (Eph 5:1–2)

The members of the family that is founded on God and Christ find their joy in the Lord. And if they depend on one another, as they serve one another in love, they will live happily, enjoying the blessings of God. In this situation, both the young and old will cherish one another and their intergenerational relationships. This is what we read in the following Scripture:

> Grandchildren are the crown of the aged, and the glory of children is their fathers. (Prov 17:6)

5.4.2.4. *Masters and Servants*

The family extends to servants, since in some cases, servants formed part of the household. In ancient Israel, as depicted in the Old Testament, a man's household included his biological children, his bondslaves, and their children, as we see in the case of the patriarchs.

Paul's teaching on the family, masters, and servants and slaves in his Epistles is based on what existed in ancient Israel and in the Old Testament Scriptures. Onesimus, for example, was the slave of Philemon. And even when Onesimus became a Christian Paul still considered him a bondservant. This shows that Paul still respected the Old Testament system. However, Paul teaches in his his epistles that whether slave or free, once people have become believers in Christ, they are bound together by their common faith. Masters and servants or slaves have now become bondservants of Christ, the Master. So when he restored Onesimus to his master, Philemon, he urged him to treat him graciously and to receive him back as he would Paul himself. And so he made the following appeal to Philemon:

> I appeal to you for my child, Onesimus, whose father I became in my imprisonment ... I am sending him back to you, sending my very heart ... no longer as a bondservant but more than a bondservant, as a beloved brother—especially to me, but how much more to you, both in the flesh and in the Lord. So if you consider me your partner, receive him as you would receive me. (Phlm 1:10, 16–17)

Nowhere else is the father heart of Paul so openly revealed, in his love and care, as in this epistle. He wants Philemon, who is also his child in the faith and partner in the gospel, to have his very nature and to be a good master.

Paul knew that his audience, both masters and servants, had become Christians. And when he writes to the Christians in Ephesus, he advises masters to treat their servants well because God is both their Master and that of their servants, and so will require them to treat those who serve them with justice and care.

> Masters, do the same to them, and stop your threatening, knowing that he who is both their Master and yours is in heaven, and that there is no partiality with him. (Eph 6:9)

On the other hand, servants who had become Christians were taught to treat their masters with more respect and loyalty, since their masters had become fellow believers, and thus brethren in the faith. With regard to this Paul wrote to Timothy:

> Those who have believing masters must not be disrespectful on the ground that they are brothers; rather they must serve all the better since those who benefit by their good service are believers and beloved. Teach and urge these things. (1 Tim 6:2)

Servants are to obey their earthly masters and work heartily and faithfully, as serving God. When we become Christians, we are first of all followers of Christ and are to serve faithfully, taking our cue from our Master, who came to serve. He is the servant par excellence. And so Paul admonished those who were called to work as bondservants in Ephesus as follows:

> Bondservants, obey your earthly masters with fear and trembling, with a sincere heart, as you would Christ, not by the way of eye-service, as people-pleasers, but as bondservants of Christ, doing the will of God from the heart. (Eph 6: 5–6)

He equally admonished servants in Colossae, telling them that when they served their masters heartily, they would receive even a greater reward than what their earthly masters would give them. They would receive the inheritance kept in heaven for God's children:

> Whatever you do, work heartily, as for the Lord and not for men, knowing that from the Lord you will receive the inheritance as your reward. You are serving the Lord Christ. (Col 3:23–24)

He told Timothy that servants should serve their masters well for the sake of the gospel, as we can see in the following verses:

> Bondservants are to be submissive to their own masters in everything; they are to be well-pleasing, not argumentative, not pilfering, but showing all good faith, so that in everything they may adorn the doctrine of God our Saviour. (Titus 2:9–10)

Since Paul's heart desire was to see that the gospel is preached in all circumstances, he wanted the servants whose lives had been transformed by the gospel to serve with a view to winning their masters to Christ. Paul wanted Timothy and those he was teaching to serve in such a way as to attract those they served to the gospel.

The gospel we preach is, as Paul describes it, the glorious gospel. It is the gospel of the glory of God and Jesus Christ (1 Tim 1:11; 2 Cor 4:4, 6). It is the gospel of life, which changes people and transforms them into the image of the glorious God, making them to also share the glory of God. It is therefore also the gospel of the glory of God's people. Jesus shared His glory with the disciple seven while He was still with them on earth, for He told God in His prayer, which was also His mission report,"The glory that you have given me I have given to them" (John 17:22). The glory here is presumably the manifestation of the excellent and entire character of God in the life of Jesus; and it is this glory that Jesus has given to the disciples, and of course to believers who came after them (John 17:20). The gospel we preach is indeed the glorious gospel. There is no better way to attract unbelievers to the gospel than to let them see it working out from the inside (i.e. their character). "The hidden person of the heart with the imperishable beauty of a gentle and quiet spirit, which in God's sight is very precious" (1 Peter 3:4).

Peter had the same perspective on mission as Paul. He wanted every Christian, no matter the difficult circumstances he or she faced, to honour Christ by the way he lived. If we live godly and contented lives in the world, those who watch us will be challenged to ask why we are so different (1 Peter 3:15). That is why he exhorted servants to submit to their masters, and even to those who treated them unjustly:

> Servants, be subject to your masters with all respect, not only to the good and gentle but also to the unjust. For this is a gracious thing, when, mindful of God, one endures sorrows while suffering unjustly. (1 Pet 2:18–19)

Unbelieving people of the world are without hope, while believers are people of hope. Even when the servants are mistreated, they should live faithful lives in obedience to the Lord because of the hope of the inheritance that awaits them in the life to come. They would simply be following the example of Christ, following in His footsteps and fixing their eyes on Him so as not to lose heart.

Whatever hardship and suffering they face would pale when they consider the glory that awaits them in the end. Christ also suffered shame, but because of "the joy that was set before him endured the cross, despising the shame, and is seated at the right hand of the throne of God" (Heb 12:2).

In the family of God, the overriding calling is to serve faithfully wherever He has placed us to serve. We are on mission, and so we should seek to do His will, doing whatever He has called us to do wherever He has placed us. And wherever God has placed us is our mission field. Christ, our Master, was pleased to serve no matter the difficulties He faced, even on the cross. He declared that when He would be lifted up, he would draw people to Him. And so His primary purpose was to glorify the Father by drawing people into the Father's kingdom. So Peter, in the text quoted above, is exhorting Christians under the yokes of harsh and unjust masters to serve well, mindful of how Christ bore suffering in order to save us. He did not resist or threaten those who mistreated Him but instead entrusted Himself to the Father, who judges justly (1 Peter 2:23). And so believing servants who patiently endured injustice by the power of God and the Holy Spirit (2 Tim 1:7, 8) would receive a reward from God the Father. This is the best way to be the light and a witness in a dark world, displaying the grace of God—His goodness and beauty. The gospel, the glorious message that brings life and immortality (2 Tim 1:8–10) is worth suffering for (Dan 12:3; Mt 13:43).

5.4.3. Marriage Boundaries

The first couple was of God, and they were made in the image of God, and the marriage was of God, by God, and for God. And God made the woman fit for the man. That is to say, she was tailored to fit the man so that the two would best serve God's purposes. As husband and wife, they would be playing different roles, which would still lead to the main goal of serving God as a team, the woman complementing the man and filling up what was lacking in him.

Given that the primary calling of the husband and wife is to serve God and be effectively fulfilling their God-given ministry, it will be important that in looking for a partner, each person—young man or woman—should make sure that the one he or she is seeking to marry is one who knows the Lord in a personal way and has a Christian testimony.

And as we have seen before (cf. 2.1) in ancient Israel, marriage occurred preferentially within the group. And God came to affirm this by ruling that the children of Israel should not make alliances with the nations or marry foreigners. So in God's plan, there is normally no room for mixed marriages. The primary reason for this was to prevent Jews from being attracted by the gods of the nations and be drawn away to worship them. However, foreigners who had become proselytes and therefore had converted to Judaism could be married to Jews. Also, a Gentile born into a Jewish household, slave or servant, could become heir and inherit the property of his master if his master did not have a son (Gen 15:2–3).

In the New Testament, when Christ came and broke down the dividing wall between Jews and Gentiles, the in-group now became the church, the new Israel made of both Jews and Gentiles. And so the boundary line was now between believers in Christ—those who were baptized and had become members of the church—and non-believers. From this point on, marriage would be only between two people—a man and a woman. This was already mentioned regarding the institution of marriage when it was underlined that the marriage of the man, Adam, and the woman, Eve, established the blueprint of this divinely ordained institution.

Marriage would henceforth also be only between two people separated and set apart to be holy unto the Lord. God had chosen Israel to be a holy nation of priests, and so he gave command that they not make themselves unclean and abominable by marrying into and mingling with the Gentile nations that were being driven out of the Promised Land. So getting married to one who is not of the fold is a flagrant violation of the statutes of God, as Ezra decried and bemoaned in the following Scripture:

> "The people of Israel and the priests and the Levites have not separated themselves from the peoples of the lands with their abominations, from the Canaanites, the Hittites, the Perizzites, the Jebusites, the Ammonites, the Moabites, the Egyptians, and the Amorites. For they have taken some of their daughters to be wives for themselves and for their sons, so that the holy race has mixed itself with the peoples of the lands." As soon as I heard this, I tore my garment and my cloak and pulled hair from my head and beard and sat appalled. (Ezra 9:1–3)

Christians are now the new Israel, a race and priest, and so getting married to an unbeliever is a violation of God's will and is thus appalling.

So Christians were to marry only Christians. And so Paul, writing to the Corinthians, gave these instructions:

> Do not be unequally yoked with unbelievers. For what partnership has righteousness with lawlessness? Or what fellowship has light with darkness? What accord has Christ with Belial? Or what portion does a believer share with an unbeliever? What agreement has the temple of God with idols? For we are the temple of the living God; as God said, "I will make my dwelling among them and walk among them, and I will be their God, and they shall be my people." (2 Cor 6:14–16)

Paul reinforces this rule when he talks about a woman who loses her husband and becomes a widow:

> A wife is bound to her husband as long as he lives. But if her husband dies, she is free to be married to whom she wishes, *only in the Lord*.[75] (1 Cor 7:39)

---

[75] Emphasis mine

In the case where the husband or wife dies, the believer who wants to remarry has only one choice—to be married **in the Lord** (i.e., marriage in this case will only be to a fellow Christian; someone who believes in Christ as his or her Saviour and Lord and is thus to obey Him as his or her Master).

The other key boundary that God set from the beginning, at the institution of marriage, reaffirmed by Christ and now by Paul, was the law of inviolability of the marriage vow. Paul states it here in no uncertain terms:

> To the married I give this charge (not I, but the Lord): the wife should not separate from her husband (but if she does, she should remain unmarried or else be reconciled to her husband), and the husband should not divorce his wife. (1 Cor 7:10–11)

Marriage is a sacred institution because it was sanctioned by God, our Father. The decision to get married and pick a life partner is an important life decision. Friesen (1980:284) says, "In terms of impact on the course of one's life, the determination concerning marriage probably ranks second only to one's decision to accept or reject Jesus Chris as Saviour and Lord."

What Friesen is saying is basically true, but I would rank this differently: The two things of highest importance in the life of a person have to do with choosing to know the Lord and then finding one's ministry calling. The next in line after these is finding a spouse. I have always advised young people who have known the Lord to be careful about picking who they are thinking of getting married to. Praying for the right partner is an important responsibility of both parents and the young people seeking to be married. Parents should start praying for their children regarding whether it is God's calling on their lives to be married. If it is God's calling, they should be praying for the partners that God is preparing for them to get married to. As stated previously, while the general will of God for man and woman is that they be married, the Scriptures also state that God has called some to be celibate.

God took time to create a woman fit for Adam, and so this is the way we should go about picking a partner. We must follow this pattern, because it will be a partner for life in every sense. Marrying the wrong partner can mean missing the mark and could lead to hell on earth. This will mean a hindrance to the ministry God has called one to—or, at worst, missing the call of God on one. This might even mean missing one's ministry. That is why Paul asked the serious rhetorical questions in 2 Cor 6:14–16, pointing to the fact that Christians should never be yoked to unbelievers. Life and death cannot go together, just as light and darkness, or Satan and God, cannot have any fellowship.

Sometimes a young person "falls in love" with an unbeliever thinking that they will marry and that he or she will make the one he or she marries a Christian. This is a grave mistake. Once a young man has got the girl who is his dream partner, he will have no incentive to think of the Lord, especially if he is driven by the desires of the flesh. Once you are married, you are stuck, because normatively divorce is not an option for a Christian, except under some of the circumstances and considerations mentioned previously regarding the subject. As for a believer who falls in love with an unbeliever and goes ahead to make marriage plans, this person is acting in flagrant disobedience to the Lord. This boils down to idolatry, as Friesen and Maxson (1980:303) describe in the following quote:

> Words cannot express the tragedy of this situation. The Christian is mocking God by reneging on his or her commitment to Him. A Christian is committing idolatry by falling down before someone other than God. And he or she is blatantly disobeying God, who said we are to marry only within the faith.

Hudson Taylor was the founder of the China Inland Mission (CIM, now OMF International, previously Overseas Missionary Fellowship). He married, Maria Jane, "Mother" of the China Inland Mission. Taylor spent 54 years in China and lived there longer than Maria, who died early at the age of 33. The society that Taylor began brought over 800 missionaries to the country, and started 125 schools and trained 499 local helpers. Their hard work resulted in 20,000 Christian conversions. The story of the dating and marriage of Hudson Taylor to Maria illustrates the influence of God and Christ in the seeking of a marriage partner. It is said of Hudson Taylor that at some point he was divided between God and his desire for Maria. He was so much in love with Maria that he tried to bargain with God on the matter. As he planned to go to India as a missionary, he would muse on how wonderful it would be if he had Maria. His love bordered on idolatry. One day when he was praying to God and telling Him (in the words of Ps 73:25) that there was nothing on earth that he desired more than God, he heard God say to him, "You, liar, what of Maria?" Hudson quickly confessed and gave up the idea of wanting to marry Maria. And having surrendered to God, he was released to go to India with the peace of the Lord. After this release, he was liberated and was fully committed to follow the will of God, thus acknowledging the lordship of God in a major decision of his life. Eventually, when God saw his surrender to Him, He worked in circumstances to grant Hudson's desire of wanting to marry Maria. This thus confirmed the word of the Lord, which says, "Delight yourself in the LORD, and he will give you the desires of your heart" (Ps 37:4). It is in view of the previously discussed circumstances and how they lived and worked so well together as partners in marriage and mission that it has been said that their marriage was "A match made in heaven" (Pollock 1996).

Marriage being a family institution, it is good for parents to be involved with their children as they seek partners in marriage. And young people should avail themselves of the wisdom of their parents and family members when they are seeking to get married. In ancient Israel and in New Testament times, when Jesus and Paul taught about the choice of marriage partners, their teaching involved the family, especially the father. The father was the key decision maker. But in today's culture, especially from the perspective of Western culture, it is thought that marriage decisions are more a matter of the individuals considering marriage. However, biblical and conventional wisdom teaches that parents know their children better and know much more about life and marriage than the young people wanting to get married. Also, parents have the best interests of their children at heart. With regard to this, Friesen and Maxson (1980:301) say,

> The primary advantage of such an approach is that parents, who have the best interests of their children at heart, are able to bring maturity and good judgment to bear upon the decision. A father is not so vulnerable to the distorting effects of romantic involvement.

Mature Christians, the church, and other wise people in the lives of young people are human and spiritual resources at their disposal, and valuable advice can be had from these.

Finding the right spouse takes time. Young people should not hurry to get married. Those intending to marry should take time to get to know themselves. The expressions "falling in love" and "love at first sight" can be misleading and therefore very deceptive. These concern emotions and, as we have seen previously in this study (4.4.2.), marriage should not only be based on emotions but on true love, which is loyal to and seeks the good and welfare of the object of love. True love waits; it is considerate. And as the Bible says, "Love is patient." Making a wise choice takes time and knowledge. We can learn from the following Scripture:

> Desire without knowledge is not good, and whoever makes haste with his feet misses his way. (Prov 19:2)

And as we have seen earlier (cf. 1.9.2), John Wesley fell in love and got married in a very short time, making him to regret having married Mary. This is why the wisdom of the proverbial saying, "Marry in haste, repent at leisure," should be taken seriously. Couples should not rush into marriage only to later on regret that they got married.

5.5. The Corporate Family

5.5.1. Becoming Members

The priority of churches and mission organizations is to make sure that members are children of God. It is not necessary that people attending a local church already be Christians, but it is important to make sure that they will be truly converted and be instructed in the faith. And as such, they will have been prepared to do the will of God, alongside the rest of the body. As for mission organizations, they must make sure that those who are accepted as members are truly born-again Christians. However, most mission organizations have set up mechanisms to ensure that those they recruit are believers. For example, candidates are asked to write a doctrinal statement in addition to a salvation testimony following an interview.

5.5.2. Working as a Family

As we have seen so far, God's purposes are most effectively carried out in the context of the family. Also, as previously stated, Jesus changed the perspective of the family from the restricted biological family to the wider spiritual and kingdom family. This already places people in a body where the Spirit has room to work in the lives of members, changing them and drawing them together in fellowship with Him and with one another, infusing them with love, and thus equipping them to do God's will. And that is why members of the family of God are those who do His will, as Jesus pointed out to His followers.

As partners in the mission of God, we have an identity: we are children of the Father. Our identity and authority come from God the father through Christ. We, both the leaders and members, have the responsibility of building one another up, taking care of one another as brothers and sisters of the family of God, using our various gifts for the good of others so that together we become a family of grace, effectively accomplishing His purposes because we are a caring and growing family.

The dynamics in the church, or any Christian institution or mission organization, will change remarkably if members see themselves as one family, brothers and sisters of Jesus, the Elder Brother, working together with Him to accomplish the purposes of God. The love which is from the Spirit (Gal 5:22; Rom 5:5) and the sacrificial love of Christ will be the controlling force, just as Paul testifies in 2 Corinthians 5:14–15. In this environment, it will be easy for members seek the interests and welfare of the others because, marked by humility, they consider others as significant as, or even better than, themselves. And as everyone in this family is in communion with God, Christ, and the Holy Spirit, the Spirit is at work distributing gifts among them and enabling them to be fruitful. The members of this family use their varied gifts to support and strengthen one another to the glory of God. The corporate family can be diagrammed as follows:

Fig. 7 Corporate Family

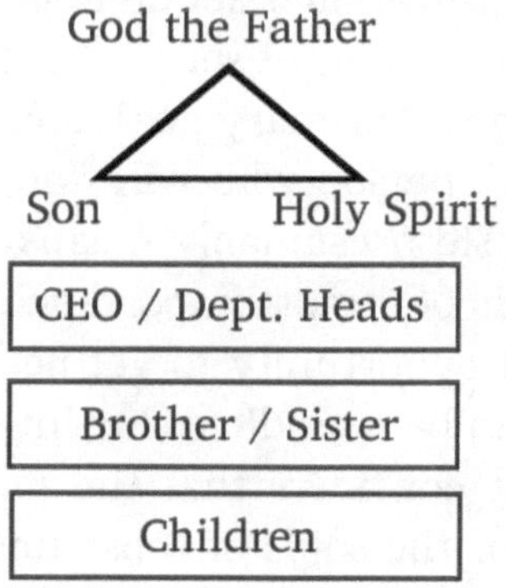

God the Father

Son   Holy Spirit

| CEO / Dept. Heads |
| Brother / Sister |
| Children |

The diagram above shows the roles and relationships in the corporate family. The Triune God (i.e., the Trinity [Father Son and Holy Spirit]) figure in the angles of the triangle. God the Father, as a matter of course, appears at the top angle, the Son at the left angle, and the Holy Spirit at the right angle. The roles and relations of the Triune God play into the roles and relations of the organizational body, as described above. The organizational body is made up of the CEO, his leadership team, and the rest of the membership. The identity of the whole organizational body is from God, each person of the Godhead playing His role in the redemptive plan which made them children of God. They became children in the family of God through adoption. We have already looked at the roles and relations within the body. We will now look at the role of the CEO and the leadership team in the following section.

5.5.3. The Role of the CEO and the Leadership Team

The title of a chief executive officer (CEO) depends on the organization; it could be "director," "president," "moderator," "bishop," or the like. The primary aim of the CEO and his leadership team should be to take care of the membership so that they are healthy, in body, mind, soul and spirit. Ministry to the body of the membership should be holistic. If the body is well ministered to, the members will be able to glorify God by carrying out the duties assigned them. Although each Christian organization is set up to produce results that lead to an overall accomplishment of set goals, these goals are secondary when compared to the primary goal. John Piper has said that the missionary is a sick person who will find healing while serving in the mission field. He presumably means that the spiritual health of the missionary is of utmost importance and service in a mission organization is an opportunity to get healing. So mission-minded organization should be a cradle of healing for healthy service. The writer of Hebrews considers that the main responsibility of the leader is to care for the souls of those under his authority, and he will be called to give an account to God (Heb 13:17). Jesus, in His mission report, said the following to the Father:

> While I was with them, I kept them in your name, which you have given me. I have guarded them, and not one of them has been lost except the son of destruction, that the Scripture might be fulfilled. (John 17:12)

It was because of His concern for the welfare of the apostles and those who would believe following their testimonies that Jesus prayed that Peter would be kept safe and strong so as to be able to strengthen the others (Luke 22:31–32).

It has been heartbreaking to see that churches and mission organizations have often prioritized programmes and accomplishment of projects over the care of their personnel. I have witnessed, with dismay and grief, cases where organizational leaders have not only vilified and made fellow members suffer but have also caused them to leave the organization because they have opposed the unbiblical ways and methods used in order to accomplish organizational or departmental goals. Leaders of Christian institutions should be mindful of what Paul taught within the context of family in Ephesians 5:15–21. May these verses speak to all as they are read with a humble and teachable spirit, mindful of the purpose of the family—to do the will of God and glorify Him.

> Look carefully then how you walk, not as unwise but as wise, making the best use of the time understand what the will of the Lord is. Be filled with the Spirit, addressing one another in psalms and hymns and spiritual songs, singing and making melody to the Lord with your heart, submitting to one another out of reverence for Christ. (Eph 5:15–16, 19, 21)

CONCLUSION

The problems young people face in choosing whom to marry are the same problems parents face when their children present to them the one they think is the right person to marry. How are we guided when faced with these practical problems? It was in view of all these questions that I decided to look at marriage from Creation, determined to find out the purpose of God regarding marriage and the family. Studying marriage in ancient Israel and in traditional Bafut society enables us to see how marriage and family were viewed in the past.

This study of marriage and the family enables us to see more clearly the purposes of God in Creation.

The fact that man was created in the image of God prepared him for the duties he would carry out as God's vice regent. God is the sovereign ruler of the earth, and men and women are called to rule as God's representatives and so should rule wisely and justly.

Good governance results in a just management of resources and people so that there is well-being.

Of all the created living beings, it is to man alone that God gave a royal and priestly status, because he was made in His image.

God commanded man to work at the time of the Creation. This work involved doing productive activity to meet his needs. This included agricultural exploitation, food production, tending of livestock, and nursing plants for vegetables and for fruits.

Just as God intended the Garden of Eden to be a sanctuary, we can make the world a sanctuary of the Lord by our devotion and service to Him.

The institution of marriage and family functioned basically in the same way in ancient Israel and in Bafut traditional society. It has been very revealing to see how close the worldview of Bafut traditional society was to that of ancient Israel. In both communities, marriage was honoured and upheld. The values and customs of both societies worked towards forging and solidifying marriage and the family. That is why divorce was not as widespread and frequent then as it is in our present world.

Both in ancient Israel and in traditional Bafut, marriage was a family transaction. It was not a matter between just two individuals. The parents and siblings were involved, and the negotiations and decisions arrived at were made by the parents. Even though the parents and siblings took the decision regarding the marriage, the young girl to be married was informed of everything, and her views were taken into consideration. Marriage within the group was preferred, though there were cases of marriage outside the group.

Marriage was a family celebration. The two families and even the community joined in celebrating the marriage of the young people.

This study of marriage and the family in the New Testament shows that while the same values that existed in ancient Israel and in the Old Testament were upheld, some were changed by Christ in view of the new covenant. Women and children were given more value than they had ever had. Marriage between two people was determined more by their salvation experience than their ethnic group affiliation. Marriage would be strictly within the community of believers. So the expectation was that both the young man and the young woman be believers belonging to the church.

Though there were cases of polygamy in ancient Israel and in traditional Bafut, monogamy was the ideal form of marriage.

Throughout Scripture, we see the importance of marriage. Marriage and family started at Creation, when the man and woman were created male and female. We also see that marriage will end in heaven with the marriage of the Lamb.

APPENDIX I

Wedding Message: Marriage is a family celebration
"And bring the fattened calf and kill it, and let us eat and celebrate"(Luke 15:23).

Bible Readings

> Psalm 128:1–6
> 1st Reading: Genesis 24:56–61
> 2nd Reading: Revelation 19:6–8

Message of Parents

Dear Ruth and Val,

> This is the day that the LORD has made; let us rejoice and be glad in it. (Ps 118:24)

Yes, this is the day that the Lord, in His foreknowledge, has made. Our joy is great and full!

What a contrast, when we think back and recall the night, 20 years ago, when you, Ruth, called and told me that you wanted to inform me that you were already married! That was a terrible night for me and your mother. You would recall my reaction.

However, with time, God did a work both in our lives and yours. The comforting thing in all this was that, though you had moved away from us your parents, you had not turned away from the Lord. The Lord was still faithful and He, for sure, had allowed what had happened to happen. And as Paul says,

> And we know that for those who love God all things work together for good, for those who are called according to his purpose. (Rom 8:28)

I am also reminded of what Ruth told me once when I was anxious about a choice that they had made. She said that God would not allow them or any of her siblings to go overboard, because of our love for Him and faith in Him. This was reassuring, given the fact that this accords with God's redemptive plan in our lives, as we read in the following verse:

> Are they not all ministering spirits sent out to serve for the sake of those who are to inherit salvation? (Heb 1:14)

The lesson for us here is that we should learn to leave the protection of our children in the hands of God, the Good Shepherd. There is a time to let go, even when we do not totally agree with the choice any of our children makes. And there is a time to withhold when prompted by the wisdom of experience and foresight.

God can redeem every situation in the lives of His people. The fiery serpent that brought death in the desert became the bronze serpent that ministered life, as we read in this Scripture:

> And the LORD said to Moses, "Make a fiery serpent and set it on a pole, and everyone who is bitten, when he sees it, shall live. (Num 21:8)

Jesus Christ, our Redeemer, would come to make reference to this in order to teach us that His death on the cross would be the means of our Salvation, as we read here:

> And as Moses lifted up the serpent in the wilderness, so must the Son of Man be lifted up, that whoever believes in him may have eternal life (John 3:14–15)

The story of Ruth and Val fits into God's redemption history. God the Father loves us, His children, so much that He is prepared to have us back once we realize that we have taken the wrong course of action in rebellion from Him. This was taught by our Redeemer Himself in the parable of the Prodigal Son. The return of the son, who had gone away from home, was a time of great joy and celebration. His father said,

> 'Bring quickly the best robe, and put it on him, and put a ring on his hand, and shoes on his feet. And bring the fattened calf and kill it, and let us eat and celebrate. (Luke 15:22–23)

Ruth and Val, today is the day of celebration. Our joy is full. The wedding attire you have today: the robe, the rings on your fingers, the shoes on your feet, do not speak only of the celebration feast offered by the father for his son, but also of the joy and happiness of the Marriage Supper of the Lamb. The Lord, the Bridegroom, has invited us all today; and so,

> Let us rejoice and exult and give him the glory, for the marriage of the Lamb has come, and his Bride has made herself ready; it was granted her to clothe herself with fine linen, bright and pure. (Rev 19:7–8)

Val and Ruth, today you have been clothed by the Lord with "fine linen, bright and pure." The fine linen, as it is said, "is the righteous deeds of the saints." You are forgiven, and it has been given you to cloth yourselves with the righteousness of the Lord.

Val, when we discussed your story and how this day would be, you said you were waiting for your own fattened calf. Well, there is a big party organized for you. All of us are here in attendance because of you. We will celebrate with you. Your mother and I, your siblings and all the guests are thankful you came back to us.

Yes, marriage is a family feast! It is a time for celebration! So let us celebrate the love, grace and redemption plan of the Lord; the plan that has been accomplished in your lives and ours today. Let us celebrate and sing:

> "Hallelujah!
> For the Lord our God
> the Almighty reigns" (Rev 19:6)

APPENDIX II: TESTIMONIES

Testimony of Val

First, I want to welcome you to our wedding. It is truly an honour to have you with us to celebrate this great day. My hope is that we would have a great time together. In Psalms 68 verse 6, the psalmist says that *"God settles the solitary in a home; he leads out the prisoners to prosperity, but the rebellious dwell in a parched land."* The heavenly Father places us in a family. He puts us in a place where we can prosper. We do not choose our family, but God does. I am glad that He has brought my wife and me together into this family. The intent of this testimony is to tell you a little bit about my journey, hoping that you will get to know me a bit. We all have a story. The Christian story is a story of redemption. It is the story of how the Lord in His great mercy extends His grace toward us. God is the one who brings us together and uses us as a conduit to fulfill His will in our lives.

I was born in a small Island called Guadeloupe. My mother and father migrated to the Island of Haiti. When I was two years old, my mother left the Island to migrate to America. Since I was too young, my mother decided to leave me with my family in Haiti and continued alone. I grew up in a pagan society where voodoo was and still is the prominent religion (Christianity is well adopted as a form of religion but voodooism is deeply rooted in the minds and culture of Haitians). The only person in my family who encouraged my siblings and me to go to church was my Uncle Rogèst.[76] And this only happened when we visited with him during the summer. He was a real Christian in every sense of the word. I say that because during those days I did not know any true Christians. Yes, I knew

---

[76] My uncle Rogèst was a great influence in my family because he and his wife practised what they believed.

people who had been baptized into the Roman Catholic Church; but for Haitians, this is just a ritual that everyone feels like they had to observe. In Haiti, it does not matter whether you are a Christian or not, once you attain a certain age you are baptized in the Church (Christianity and voodooism are institutionalized within the society). I did what everyone was doing. I was baptized in the Catholic Church and went to a Catholic school. I did not know what it meant to be a Christian.

I grew up believing that both religions (voodooism and Christianity) needed to be respected so that things can go well with me. The way that worked out practically was that I attended the Voodoo ceremonies and acknowledged the spirits just as I went to mass on Sunday morning. At that time, this was what people did (and some are still doing the same thing today). However, when I was about ten years old, I had a friend whose family were real Christians. His mother used to hold regular prayer meetings at her house. One day, my friend invited me to attend one of the meetings. I remember that day I stood at the farthest back of the room I could find. The people were praying non-stop. While they were praying, I started to cry. I could not explain it. I was not sad. I was not happy, yet I knew something was going on within me. When my friend saw me crying, he quickly alerted his mother to see what was going on. I got so scared that before she could reach me, I ran out of her house and never came back. This was the first spiritual encounter in my life.

Conversion

My day of deliverance came in 1999. I had just moved to Charlotte, N.C. area. It was a place that was far away from friends and my family. I did not know anyone in the area so therefore my life revolved around work. I was not there for long when suddenly I felt like I was missing something. I was not lonely (I had moved from N.Y. to Charlotte with a good friend that I had met). It was something that I could not describe. I felt a sudden urge to go to church. I had never been to church in Charlotte so I did not know where to start. I was living in a hotel and I woke up one Sunday and drove down the street from where I was living until I found the first church. As I was about to go in, the usher informed me that the preacher had already begun his sermon and that it was better to come next Sunday. I quickly apologized and went home. I did not think anything of it; I was not planning to come back.

Shortly thereafter a co-worker who was struggling with drug addiction spontaneously invited me to come and visit his mother's church.[77] The church was an African American congregation. It was the second time I went to an African American church. After the sermon, there was an altar call and so I went forward. The preacher prayed for me and asked me whether I wanted to receive the Lord as my Saviour. The question caught me off guard. I did not expect to make such a big decision on one Sunday. I stood there wrestling with the question in my mind. I wanted to be saved (what did that mean?) Who in his right mind does not want to be saved? The problem is, being saved comes with a cost. Was I prepared to leave everything behind and follow Jesus Christ? I did not think I could do it.[78] I said to myself I don't want to be a hypocrite, if I have to be a Christian I have to be one all the way. So that day, I accepted Jesus as my Lord and Saviour and was baptized in the church the very same day (these folks were not playing around). However, I always considered my conversion into the faith a two-part story. There was the public confession and baptism. Then there was the time when I was baptized with the Holy Spirit and fire. This literally happened to me. On one Wednesday night the church prayed for me and God poured out His Spirit on me. After that experience, I felt the very presence of the Lord with me. And from that time on, the Lord used some of the grandmothers in the church to pray and encourage me in the faith. That period of time was pivotal in my spiritual life. They taught me that the Christian faith is not a set of rules that I must follow but it was a personal relationship with the Lord. I knew my conversion was real when people who knew me, started to tell me that I had changed.

---

[77] It is funny that after this friend came to church with me, it was the last time I saw him in church. Later, he confessed that he had been struggling with drugs and was very ashamed of his addiction.

[78] I was thinking living a righteous life was something that I had to do in my flesh.

Meeting my Wife
I met my wife while I was taking classes in a small community school in Charlotte. She had just transferred from a college in Tennessee. I had met her sister Esther while playing soccer (we were playing for the same team). She introduced me to her sister Ruth. She was very different from any girl I had met. She was funny, loyal, and generous. She loved her family. I loved all those qualities about her but what attracted me to her the most was that she was pure (blameless). You could see it by the way she carried herself, the way she talked, walked. I was the total opposite. To say that I was rough around the edge would be an understatement. Yes, I was saved but we all come to faith at different points in life. Some are born in the faith. They are sheltered by the wisdom of God. But others have different life experiences which influence their actions.

Once I got to spend some time with Ruth and got to know her, I fell in love with her. But I never asked her if she would go out with me. I wanted to ask her but I did not know what she would say.[79] So, I did not say anything. One day, when we were in the parking lot, she asked me why I had never asked her out. That night I got on my knees and asked her out and she agreed. We were two young people who fell in love with each other. I can say that after my conversion my wife was the best thing that happened in my life. Before I met her I was a young man without purpose in life. But she challenged me in a positive way. My wife is the one who taught me what it meant to be a spiritual leader.

One day, my wife, who was my girlfriend at that time, called me to break up with me. I can't remember what she said exactly but she said something to the effect that things weren't going right. She had been convicted spiritually and wanted to change course. I was serving in the US Navy at that time. I did not ask any questions. I did not believe that she was going to break up with me. How could she break up with me? We talked over the phone twice that night. It was still the same thing. Then that was the time that I asked her to marry me. I did think that she was going to say yes. I had always wanted to marry her but again I knew I had to do a lot of asking. I

---

[79] At that time, I had a hard time asking for anything. I didn't know what it was. I knew that I had to ask but it never could come out.

had to go through a lot of loopholes. And I knew that there was no chance on earth that her parents would agree to this foolish idea.[80] I knew I was not the ideal person for their daughter. I was not ready. But I was madly in love with her. So I robbed you, her parents and family this wonderful time of celebration. For this I want you to forgive us.

Ministry
I have been serving the Lord for many years now. I did not choose the Lord; rather, the Lord chose me. The Lord alone knows how to restore broken pieces. He has done it in my life. I hope He will do it for you. Jesus said, "Those who are well have no need of a physician, but those who are sick. I came not to call the righteous, but sinners." God has given me a heart for the sick, for those who are lost, for those who hunger for the Word of God. I love God's word. I have been a pastor for 15 years. I have served in various capacities in the church. But what I love the most is teaching the word of God. I believe this is my calling and I am going to pursue this for the rest of my life. Thank you for welcoming me in your life. Thank you for welcoming me in to the Mfonyam clan. I love you. May God bless you!

Testimony of Ruth

My Beginnings
I was born in Yaoundé the capital city of Cameroon and in the first 3 years of my life we travelled a lot as a family, as my father just started his call into Bible translation. I have had the privilege of always knowing the Lord and His goodness. This started even before I was born with my grandfather. He literally changed the course and legacy of his family by rejecting pagan worship and embracing Christianity. I am a direct beneficiary of this significant decision. I came to know the Lord at a very young age. We were in Nigeria

---

[80] I thank God for giving Mummy and Daddy the heart to forgive us. I am sorry for hurting you and the family. And thank you for giving us another chance.

at the time and my mother was reading a book about Christian martyrs and at the end of the book, I told my Mom that I too would like to serve God like the people she had just read to me about. And then we prayed the sinner's prayer. I was around 3 years old. My mother did not believe at first that I knew what I was doing. So, when we moved back to Cameroon to our village, Bafut, several months later, she asked me if I had received Christ and I said yes. She asked me where and I told her in Nigeria. The things of the Lord are spiritual and often baffle our understanding.

My Early Years to Adulthood
I had a very happy and stable childhood. Looking back now I do feel that the Lord's hedge of protection was around me and my parents were very intentional about surrounding us with only things that were good for our soul. We had family devotions morning and evening every day. We memorized scripture weekly. We learned disciplines of fasting and prayer. Our parents also had us start praying for our spouses from a young age. We were not allowed to spend the night at others homes. We went to Christian schools. We did not have a TV growing up (Dad and Mom did get one after we were out of the home). And so we did not have many outside influences. We also listened mainly to Christian music except my Dad, who had and still has a weakness for American country music. I remember as a teenager not knowing many of the things that went on in the secular world and at times, I would be frustrated but as a parent now I see how those boundaries kept me innocent till I was mature enough in my faith to handle the temptations.

Adulthood and Moving to America
When I was 17, after high School, I got accepted to go to college in the US to further my studies. I went to a Christian school in Tennessee for a year and then, in my second year, I moved to Charlotte to a community college with a more diverse and international community. I started at Central Piedmont Community College in August 2000. That is where I met my husband Val. I remember the first time I met him at a picnic table before class started in the evening. I asked him what his name was and where he was from. He told me his name and

that he was from heaven. I was immediately irritated (dude, who is from heaven? That's a stupid answer. I thought he was cocky). I had no more meaningful conversation with him after that. However, a week or so later, my sister was on the phone and in the middle of the conversation she paused and asked me if I would accompany her to go watch a movie with some guy on her soccer team. At the time she had a boyfriend and refused the invitation unless she could go with me. After she got off the phone, she said that this guy played soccer with her and she had gifted him with a necklace she had brought with her from Cameroon (my sister is generous like that, always giving). She explained to me that the guy was taken aback by her act of kindness and wanted to reciprocate the kindness. She told him kindly that she could not go out with him as she already had a boyfriend, but she agreed to go as long as she brought her sister. I guess she was trying to play match maker, I don't know, or she was trying to be nice and not say no outright. The following Saturday he came and picked us both up for dinner and a movie. From that night on we were inseparable. It did not take me long to fall in love with this handsome skinny guy from "heaven" with dreads who was a little rough on the edges.

Our Relationship
Our relationship was exciting yet challenging. For me it was really my first relationship. My husband at the time was a brand-new Christian and I found myself having to really help encourage him. There were many things about the discipline of being a Christian that he did not know. Through the months he would see me practise many things that I did naturally as part of my walk with God, but that were new to him, for instance, daily devotions, prayer and fasting, and intentional discipleship and mentorship were new to him. Another one of our challenges was our cultural differences. He was a very free-spirited young man and did not like cultural limitations (really very few limitations) and he would be very outspoken about it. For instance, when my Dad first came to visit, I told him that in our culture you call him Dad. He said he was not doing that and he proceeded to call my Dad, Joseph not even Mr Mfonyam. After a talk with some Pastors at Church he finally

started calling my Dad Mr Mfonyam. Still not culturally acceptable but it was respectful. Over the months, our spiritual maturity differences and many cultural differences became very strenuous to me and I decided that I just needed to break up with him. So, I called him up in September of 2001 and broke up with him. The break-up only lasted a few days ("the spirit was willing, but the flesh was weak") for we reconnected and when we talked again he asked me to marry him. I knew fully well that my parents would not allow us to get married as I was only 19 years old and just in my 3rd year of college. Being very young and foolish and seeking no one's counsel, we decided to get married at the courthouse and not tell anyone, especially not my parents. We decided that when we were ready to get married for real (for we knew we were going to be married to each other anyway why wait), he would go ask for my Dad's permission to marry me and they would never know that we were already married. Of course, 2 years later "our secret" leaked out. With that began a tumultuous journey of repentance and reconciliation between us and our family.

20 Years Later
Since our "court signing" on December 19th, 2001, we have had many challenges in marriage, parenting, ministry and professionally. The one thing promised to us is that in this world we shall have tribulation. God has also promised to never leave us or forsake us, and He has been there every step of the way. Over the years God has been merciful and the process of reconciliation and healing has been evident in our lives. He has also been faithful and blessed us with 5 children and dozens of spiritual children. We have been in ministry for over 15 years in many different capacities and I have enjoyed over a decade of serving the sick as a Registered Nurse. Today marks a culminating celebration of the journey from rebellion to unity and reconciliation. We robbed ourselves and our family by transgressing against our parents and our families of a wonderful celebration of the union of two people in the beginning. God has taught us many things in this 20-year journey and today we celebrate the miracle and gift of redemption, forgiveness and reconciliation. Thank you for coming to join us to celebrate this miraculous and joyous milestone.

STUDY QUESTIONS AND NOTES

Chapter 1: Divine Institution

> So God created man in his own image, in the image of God he created him; male and female he created them. (Gen 1:27)

1. What does it mean to be created in God's image? See Colossians 3:10.

> Therefore a man shall leave his father and his mother and hold fast to his wife, and they shall become one flesh. (Gen 2:24)

2. How do you understand the fact that a man leaves his father and mother to "hold fast to his wife? What responsibility does he still have towards his parents? What about his relationship with his other siblings? Does he have any responsibilities towards them?
3. In what sense do the man and woman become one flesh? How does Trobisch explain leaving, cleaving, and becoming one flesh, using the marriage triangle? (See section 5.3.2.1.2.)
4. What was God's purpose in creating the man and woman? What did He tell them to be doing in the garden? What were they to be doing in order to live?
5. What should be our attitude to work? What does Paul say about work? See 2 Thessalonians 3:7–12. What did Jesus say about work? See John 9:4.
6. What was God's purpose in marriage?

> And God blessed them. And God said to them, "Be fruitful and multiply and fill the earth and subdue it, and have dominion over every living thing that moves on the earth." (Gen 1:28)

7. What does it mean to subdue the earth?
8. What does it mean to have dominion over all things?
9. What are the regal duties that God gave man?
10. What do you understand by priestly duties? Are these duties exercised solely by pastors or priests? What does Peter mean when he says that believers are a royal priesthood? What were the sacred duties of the priests? In what way is every believer considered a priest? Why? Read 1 Peter 2:5, 9.
11. With regard to our work and worship of God, what was the primary purpose of God in Creation? When it is said in the catechism that the purpose of man is to glorify God and to enjoy Him forever, how do you understand this? How do you live it out? See Isaiah 43:7. Where does the joy of the Christian come from? And how does he enjoy the Lord? How does God take joy in us?
12. What was the woman's primary responsibility when God created her? Was Eve to be a helper just by working the ground or to help him in other ways? What about bearing children? Was it a helping job?
13. What does it mean to be fruitful? How do you understand what is said in Ps 128:1–6? Does it mean that if a couple does not have children they are not blessed? What should the couple do in the case that they do not have children? Study the case of Hannah and how she prayed to have a son (1 Sam 1:9–20).
14. Can God withhold children from a couple? How do you understand what Jacob tells Rachel in answer to her complaint that he had not given her children? See Genesis 30:1–2.
15. If even after praying children do not come, does this mean that God has not answered the prayers of the couple? Could it be that God wants the couple to consider other options? What options are open to the couple in this case? What of taking care of other children who need parents, especially the children of relatives?

> Read the story of Mordecai and his cousin Esther, whom he took care of and who became the queen of the king of Persia. Read Esther 2:5–7.
>
>> He was bringing up Hadassah, that is Esther, the daughter of his uncle, for she had neither father nor mother. When her father and her mother died, Mordecai took her as his own daughter. (Esther 2:7)

16. What of adopting children? Could it be that God wants the couple to think of adopting some of the children who are born by single girls who are not able to bring them up? How does this fit in the story of salvation? Those who believe in Christ become God's children by adoption; they have been adopted into the family of God (Rom 8:14–17). What joy have loving parents given children who had no future, and thus no inheritance, when they have gone out to adopt helpless and neglected children either from poor mothers or from orphanages?

Chapter 2: Marriage in Ancient Israel

1. How was betrothal done in Ancient Israel?
2. How binding was betrothal?
3. Why was it important to be married within the group?
4. Why was marriage considered a family event? Why was it that the parents had a strong say about whom their children should marry? What was then the role of the girl in decision-making? What role did the young man intending to marry play in the whole process?
5. Why was it important for the girl to be a virgin?
6. What did virginity represent in the Bible?
7. In ancient Israel, lamps were used. What is the significance of light (a) in the community and (b) in the Bible?
8. How did people view divorce? What was the process of divorce in Israel?
9. Why was it important for a couple to have children? What was the risk of not having children? Why was it important to have

a boy? What was the place of the girl child in the family? How were women treated in the community?
10. With regard to levirate marriage, why was it important for the brother-in-law to marry his late brother's wife? Is this practised in your community today? What do you think about this practice?
11. How was an unmarried woman viewed in ancient Israel? See Isaiah 4:1. Why was celibacy not viewed favourably? How did Jesus and Paul view celibacy?
12. What is special about those who have received the gift of celibacy? Will you encourage and support your children if they receive the call to live the monastic life? What difference does the monastic order make in the spiritual life of the church and society?
13. Should priests be obligatorily celibate? What are the advantages and disadvantages?

Chapters 3: Marriage in Traditional Bafut

1. How was betrothal done in traditional Bafut?
2. How binding was betrothal in Bafut as compared to betrothal in ancient Israel?
3. Regarding the marriage process in Bafut, why was it necessary to do all the things required? Could the number of things required from the young man be a hindrance, making it hard to get married traditionally? What is the advantage of such a system?
4. What was the purpose of (a) all the soups (ǹnù'û ǹjyà) and (b) the wines (mɨ̀lù'ù mî bɔrə̀, mɨ̀lù'ù mî wè)?
5. Did marriage in ancient Israel and in Bafut differ? In what ways?
6. Why was it important for the girl to be a virgin?
7. In Bafut, bamboo torches were used; while in ancient Israel, lamps were used. What is the significance of light (a) in each of the communities and (b) in the Bible?
8. How was Levirate marriage practised in Bafut? How did this practice help to cement relationships in the family? Did the practice of levirate marriage in Bafut differ from its practice in Israel? What do you think about the way it was practised in Bafut? What are the advantages of levirate marriage?

9. How was divorce viewed in Bafut? Under what condition was divorce allowed by Bafut traditional law? Was divorce viewed in the same way in ancient Israel and in Bafut traditional society? If not, what was the difference? Looking at the situation today, why is divorce more rampant than it was in these two communities?
10. Why was it important for a couple to have children? What was the risk of not having children? Why was it important to have a boy? Comparing the situation in ancient Israel and in Bafut traditional society, what was the place of the girl child in the family? How were women treated in both communities?

Chapter 4: Important Cultural Symbols and Virtues

1. What do you understand culture to be? Did God create culture? If not, where did it come from? Who put virtues like love, kindness, unity, and such in the cultures of people? How did Jesus live in Jewish culture or the culture of ancient Israel? Give some examples where Jesus subjected Himself to the Jewish culture and religion. Give examples of cultural aspects that Jesus rejected or transformed. Why is it easier for people to understand the gospel if it is brought in native cultural terms?
2. What customs and traditions of ancient Israel and traditional Bafut could be used in order to present the gospel?
3. How do you understand the term "enculturation?" Is it good or bad? Why is it often said that Christianity is a Western religion?
4. Why was unity important both in Israel and Bafut?
5. What does the Bible say about unity? How does unity reflect the Christian faith? How do we understand unity in the light of what Scripture says about it? Read Ephesians 4:4–6 and Philippians 2:1–6. Are there any bad things in your culture that could be used to present the gospel? Jesus was born in the Jewish culture at a time when the Romans were ruling the Jews and Roman culture and its system of governance could be seen in all of Israel, and so this affected the Jews and Christians. Crucifixion was the most shameful and harsh punishment used by the Romans, and only the worst offenders and criminals were

condemned to hanging. And yet this came not only to be used in presenting the gospel; the cross on which Christ was crucified became the centrepiece of the gospel. Death by hanging was a curse even according to the law of Moses. What does this teach us about the bad things that we find in our cultures? In Bafut, death by hanging is a curse; the place where the person hanged himself—the whole property and his family—needs to be ritually cleansed, which is very costly to the family. How does this compare with the Jewish culture and religion? How did Paul use this to explain the gospel? See Galatians 3:13. How could suicide by hanging be used to present the gospel in Bafut?

7. This book on marriage and the family can be described as a love book. Why do you think this is so? What kind of love is it about? What are the different types of love that have been described in the book? Which one best characterizes the book?
8. Why is light so important in the Bible? What does it stand for in the Christian faith? What does it mean to be the light of the world? Name the main objects of light as described in the Bible. For example, what does the following verse mean?

> Your word is a light to my path. (Ps 119:105)

9. What is the importance of oil both in ancient Israel and in Bafut traditional society? Why is it important in the Bible? Why is anointing significant in both communities?
10. Why are brides, successors, chiefs, and the Fon (king) anointed in Bafut?
11. Why was anointing of the king significant in ancient Israel? What was its significance?
12. In Israel, God was King and ruled His people Israel from heaven. How did it come about that the nation started to have kings? Why did the people of Israel want a king?
13. What does God require of kings of Israel? See the laws of kings as given in Deuteronomy 17:14–20.
14. Saul was the first king of Israel; how did it happen that David became the most important king in Israel?
15. Why is the line of David important in the history of salvation?

16. Why is Christ called the Son of David? Why is He called the Anointed?
17. Why is the office of the king, kingship, and the idea of kingdom important in the history of Salvation? In ancient Israel, what was the role of the king in fulfilling the purposes of God? How did God expect them to rule so that His rule would be seen in the nation?
18. What does God require of the kings of the nations? See what He said about King Cyrus, who was not of the people of God in Isaiah 44:28–45:1. Does this justify what Paul says about rulers in the following passage?

> There is no authority except from God, and those that exist have been instituted by God. Therefore whoever resists the authorities resists what God has appointed, for he [the one in authority] is God's servant for your good. (Rom 13:1–2, 4)

19. Study the titles and attributes of the Fon/king of Bafut and those attributed to God in ancient Israel. See Fig. 4 (section 4.10.6). Why do you think the Fon is given the attributes of God? Is this good or bad? Will it hinder or help in presenting the gospel to the Bafut people? How will what God has put in the culture help the people to easily understand God and Christ as king? How will this help the Bafut people understand the idea of the kingdom of God? What do you think when you compare the worldview of the Bafut people and the worldview of ancient Israel? What are the similarities and differences?
20. How are the similarities of divine titles and attributes in the worldviews of Bafut and ancient Israel speak to the truth that God is the King and ruler of the world and Jesus came as the King of the Jews and of the nations?
21. It is made clear in this book that the kings of Israel were chosen by God to serve as His representative. Looking at the crowning of the monarchs of England, what is it that points to the way the kings of Israel were chosen and consecrated?

22. The Lord told Samuel to fill his horn with oil and anoint the one whom He would choose as king. What kind of oil was used to anoint the king? How was this different from the holy oil that was used to anoint and consecrate priests for the service of God?
23. Why do you think British monarchs take great care in creating the holy oil used to anoint new monarchs? What is it that makes the oil special or holy?
24. Looking at the coronation ceremony, what is it that makes it so solemn? Why? Why is it that the Archbishop of Canterbury consecrates and crowns the monarch?
25. What do you think of the fact that Christianity is the state religion of Britain? The monarch, Queen or King, is the Supreme Governor of the Church of England, the Defender of the Faith. What do you think about this?
26. The monarch takes an oath before God to uphold the Church and rule with honour, wisdom, justice, and mercy. How does this fit into the role of the servant of God, as prophesied in Isaiah 11:1–5 and 42:1–4?
27. Regarding the coronation service and the reign of Queen Elizabeth II, how well did she fulfil the role of God's chosen monarch? How was she conscious of the fact that the role of a monarch is a sacred duty? How did her faith influence her life and the way she ruled? How did she influence the church, her nation, and the world?
28. What would you say is the spiritual legacy of Queen Elizabeth II, both in her family and in the nation?
29. Looking at the British monarchy and the royal family, how well has this family been conscious of the mission of God? To what extent has it carried out the mission of God?
30. It is true that the monarch today no longer has the authority that kings had in the past. The role of the King or Queen has been reduced to that of the constitutional (or ceremonial) head of government. Do you think this has diminished, in a sense, the spiritual authority of the King or Queen? What of the role that the monarch has in governing and protecting the faith? Is there any reason why this should not be used advantageously to guide the church and spread the gospel? King Charles III

has barely begun his rule; what was said and done during his coronation service that might inspire the hope of a just and righteous rule?
31. What would the world look like if kings, presidents, prime ministers, and all civil authorities ruled in the fear of the Lord, keeping the laws and commandments of God?
32. In ancient Israel, God is presented as the Father, and Jesus as the Son of God. What does this say about the family? What did the family of God include then? Study the diagram presented in Fig. 1 of section 4.10.2.
33. Read Genesis 3:15, Isaiah 11:1; 41:8–9, and John 7:42. How do these passages of Scripture enable you to trace the family line of Christ, the Messiah and Saviour? How are the institutions of marriage and the family important in the history of salvation? See Fig. 2 (section 4:10.4).
34. Regarding the family, the king/kingdom, and the priesthood, state why each was important in the salvation of the world.

Chapter 5: Marriage in the New Testament

1. Jesus came into the world through a family. God could have made His Son, the Messiah, appear suddenly in all His power and mystery, without the instrument of a human being. Why did God choose for the Christ, the Messiah, to be born into a human family? What does this say about marriage and the family? How important is the family in God's mission?
2. In the New Testament, we read about the brothers of Jesus. How many are mentioned in the Bible? Name one or two of them you think were important in the spread of the gospel, and explain why you think they were important. Did Jesus have sisters? Do we know how many they were? Why were they not named? In what way does this indicate how the girl child was viewed in the Jewish culture? Can you give evidence of the fact that Christ changed this culture and gave more value to the girl child and children in general?
3. How did the gospel widen the concept of marriage and the family? Study the diagram in Fig. 6 (section 5.2.3). In light of

the teachings of Paul, explain how Gentiles came to be included in the family of God.
4. In the church or in mission organizations, how can the concept of family change the dynamics?
5. How would life and work in a Christian organization or mission organization be affected if the CEO, department heads and the rest of the staff (or members) saw themselves as brothers and sisters involved in the work of the Lord God, our Father and Master? What needs to happen to create such a perspective?
6. What should the CEO do to improve working relationships and effectiveness in service?
7. What instructions did Paul give to bond servants regarding their attitudes and service to their masters? How were masters to treat their bond servants?
8. In the New Testament, we do not see polygamy in practice. Why is this so?
9. What is the responsibility of the man regarding his family? How should he provide for his family? What is the responsibility of the woman? How should she contribute to the needs of the family? Comparing the woman and her husband in Proverbs 31:13–24, how do you view the woman concerning work? How do you view her husband?
10. In our society today, as it was in ancient Israel and in Africa, people marry several wives. If some of these men come to believe in Jesus, how should we treat such men? What should they do with the several women they are with?
11. Paul says that in a marriage and family situation, those who have become believers in Christ should remain in the state they were in before they became born again (1 Cor 7: 20; 12–16). How do you interpret what he says? Do you agree with him? Should a woman or man remain married if the unbelieving partner is violent and abusive?
12. Paul says that husbands should love their wives as Christ loved the church (Eph 5:25). What is so difficult about loving one's wife as Christ loved the church? How can a husband love his wife as himself (Eph 5:28)?

13. What does it mean for a wife to be submissive to her husband (Eph 5:22; 1 Peter 3:1-4)? Should the husband also submit himself to the woman in some circumstances? See Ephesians 5:21.
14. Why is it important for the wife to be of good character? Read 1 Peter 3:1-3, Proverbs 4:12; 31:23, 28; and 1 Cor 11:7b.
15. How should a godly woman dress?
16. Should women (or men) spend a lot of money on their attire? How do you understand 1 Peter 3:3-5?
17. As regards child rearing, how do you understand "Train up a child in the way he should go; even when he is old he will not depart from it" (Prov 22:6)? If a child who was brought up by Christian parents who did their best in raising him or her up departed from the faith and became wayward, does it mean that the parents did not train the child in the way he or she should go?
18. How should we train our children in the discipline and instruction of the Lord? What role does family worship play in this? Read also Deuteronomy 6:4-8.
19. When Paul says, "Fathers, do not provoke your children to anger" (Eph 6:4), what does he mean?
20. When Joshua said, "But as for me and my house, we will serve the LORD" (Joshua 24:15), what did he mean? What does it really mean to serve the Lord? How does this apply to you and your children? Do all your children follow the Lord? What do you do if some of them refuse to follow the Lord? Why is it that some children raised up by ministers and godly parents revolt against the God that their parents serve?
21. When children who are raised in a Christian home turn away from the Lord, does this mean that the parents have failed? Read 1 Samuel 2:22-29 and 8:1-4. What do we learn from the way the children of Eli and Samuel were brought up? Did these servants of the Lord fail in their parental duties? Should we be guilty or feel ashamed when our children fail to follow the Lord?
22. What does it mean when the Bible talks about disciplining children? Read Hebrews 12:5-11 and Proverbs 13:24. How does the proverb "Spare the rod and spoil the child" align with Hebrews 12:5-11?

23. How do we understand Proverb 23:13–14? Is it bad to punish a child when he misbehaves? What is the best method of punishing a child? Does the Bible approve of corporal punishment? Is beating or spanking a child to discipline him bad? What should determine when a child is punished and how much punishment he should be given?

REFERENCES

Abumbi II, HRM. 2016. *The Customs and Traditions of Bafut. (Àŋwaà'ànə̀ Bînɔ̀ŋsə̀ bi Bifù)*. Limbe: Presbook Plc.

Allender, Dan B., and Tremper Longman III. 1995. *Intimate Allies*. Wheaton, Illinois: Tyndale House Publishers Inc.

Anderson, Margaret. 1975. *Let us Talk about God*. Minneapolis: Bethany Fellowship Inc.

Banks, James. 2022. "Keepers of Light." in *Our Daily Bread*, 2022 Annual Edition. Grand Rapids, MI: Our Daily Bread Ministries. p 284 23 May 2022.

Barton, Ruth Haley. 1960. *Strengthening the Soul of Your Leadership*. Downers Grove, Illinois: InterVarsity Press.

Dowley, Tim. 1999. *Life in Bible Times, Essential Bible Reference*. Abigdon, Oxford: Candle Books.

Edersheim, Alfred. 1971. *The Life and Times of Jesus the Messiah*. Grand Rapids, Michigan: Erdmans Printing Company.

Eldredge, John. 2020. *Get your Life Back*. Nashville, Tennessee: Nelson Books.

ESV Study Bible. 2008. Wheaton, Illinois: Crossway.

Friesen, Garry, and Robin Maxson. 1980. *Decision Making& the Will of God*. Portland, Oregon: Multnomah Press.

Fryling, Alice. 1979. *An Unequal Yoke in Dating and Marriage.* Downers Greove, Illinois: InterVarsity Press.

Gangel, Kenneth. 1979. *The Family First.* Winona Lake, Indiana: BMH Books.

Hiebert, Paul G. 1985. *Anthropological Insights for Missionaries.* Grand Rapids, Michigan: Baker Academic.

Honor Books. 2003. *Glimpses of an Invisible God for Teens.* Tulsa, Oklahoma: Honor Books.

Jane, Mary Jury. 2023. "Queen Elizabeth's last words to Sarah Ferguson?" The Royal Insider. 7 September 2023. https://royalinsider.quora.com/Queen-Elizabeth-s-last-words-to-Sarah-Ferguson.

Johnson, Jan.1996. *Enjoying the Presence of God.* Colorado Springs: NavPress Publishing Group.

King, Philip J., and Lawrence E. Stager. 2001. *Life in Biblical Israel.* London: Westminster John Knox Press.

la Rose, Monica. 2022. "The Way of Love" in Our Daily Bread, 2022 Annual Edition. Grand Rapids, MI: Our Daily Bread Ministries. P 284

Lisé, Romain, and Isabelle Mascaras (eds.). 2013. *Splendors of the Creed.* Paris: Magnificat Inc.

Lizorkin-Eyzenberg, Eli. 2021. "Torah and the Apostle Paul." Israel Bible Center. 17 February 2021. https://weekly.israelbiblecenter.com/not-under-law.

Morgan, Robert. 1997. *On this Day.* Nashville, Tennessee: Thomas Nelson Inco.

Ngwagwendoline. "Getting married to a Bafut lady." Cameroonian Spy. 19 June 2013. https://ngwagwendoline.wordpress.com/2013/06/19/getting-married-to-a-bafut-lady/

Nouwen, Henri J. M. 2011. *A Spirituality of Living.* Nashville, TN: Upper Room Books.

———. 1981. *The Way of the Desert.* New York: *Seabury Press.* Publication

Pollock, John Charles. 1996. *Hudson Taylor & Maria.* Fearn, Tatin, Ross-Shire, Great Britain: Christian Focus Publications Ltd.

O'Reilly-Smith, Ruth. 2021. "Do the next thing" in Our Daily Bread, 2021 Annual Edition. Grand Rapids, MI: Our Daily Bread Ministries. November 5

Schaser, Nicholas. 2021. "Love in Hebrew Thought." Accessed December 4, 2021. https://lp.israelbiblecenter.com/lp-biblical-studies-content-love-in-hebrew-thought-en.html?via=c496cb1.

———. 2023. "Joyful Learning." In *Our Daily Bread.* 2023 Annual Edition, 29 September.

Schuldt, Jennifer Benson. 2021. "Our Guiding Light." In *Our Daily Bread.* 2021 Annual Edition, 9 December.

Sittser, Gerald L. 2000. *The Will of God as a Way of Life.* Grand Rapids, Michigan: Zondervan.

Thomas, Gary L. 2000. *Sacred Marriage.* Grand Rapids, Michigan: Zondervan.

Thompson, Becky, and Mark Pitts. 2021. *Midnight Dad Devotional.* Nashville, Tennessee: Thomas Nelson.

Torrance, David. 2023. *The Coronation of King Charles III*. House of Commons Library. commonslibrary.parliament.uk.

Trobisch, Walter. 1971. *I Married You*. Bolivar, Missouri: Quiet Waters Publications.

ABOUT THE AUTHOR

Dr Joseph N. Mfonyam has been a missionary with SIL Cameroon and Wycliffe Bible Translators, UK, since 1981. He is a Bible translator and a linguistics and translation consultant. He has been involved with teaching and training for more than four decades. He has taught courses in Cameroon, France, England, the USA, and Canada. He is an adjunct faculty member of the Cameroon Baptist Theological Seminary, Ndu. Dr Mfonyam has a passion for souls and has been involved in personal and world evangelism, discipleship, and leadership training for years. He has attended conferences on world evangelism in Africa, Europe, the USA, and Asia. He has published a number of books and technical papers in linguistics, Bible translation, and theology. Joseph Mfonyam is married to Rev. Becky Mfonyam, (pastor of the Presbyterian Church in Cameroon), and together they have five grown-up children.